T0365683

# CONQUERING
## *the*
# PROMISED LAND

## *A True Story*

V I O R E L   B I L A U C A

authorHOUSE®

*AuthorHouse™*
*1663 Liberty Drive*
*Bloomington, IN 47403*
*www.authorhouse.com*
*Phone: 1 (800) 839-8640*

*This book is a work of non-fiction. Unless otherwise noted, the author*
*and the publisher make no explicit guarantees as to the accuracy of*
*the information contained in this book and in some cases, names of*
*people and places have been altered to protect their privacy.*

*Published by AuthorHouse   05/18/2015*

*ISBN: 978-1-5049-1269-3 (sc)*
*ISBN: 978-1-5049-1268-6 (e)*

*Library of Congress Control Number: 2015907890*

*Print information available on the last page.*

*Any people depicted in stock imagery provided by Thinkstock are models,*
*and such images are being used for illustrative purposes only.*
*Certain stock imagery © Thinkstock.*

*This book is printed on acid-free paper.*

*Scripture quotations marked KJV are from the Holy Bible, King James*
*Version (Authorized Version). First published in 1611. Quoted from the KJV*
*Classic Reference Bible, Copyright © 1983 by the Zondervan Corporation.*

I dedicate this book to my children, Estera and Dariu, and to my grandchildren, Kristen, Savanah, Kayla, Adam, Kylee, Desiree, Anabel Marie and those still to come.

I am thankful to my wife, Maria, for supporting me in this venture.

I pray that God will use this book to strengthen the faith of those who are going to read it, so they will reach the goals they have set for their lives and earn the "crown that will never fade away."

# CONTENTS

# FOREWORD

There are so many things that make us different one from another. No two people are alike. God does not love copies. Elohim only makes originals. We differ more one from another because of our own histories. We all have our life stories made of the memories of our travels through time. We differ through our memories.

The memories that form our life stories define us in such a way that we become their sum. Ultimately, what we are is our histories.

Our life stories need to be told. Telling our stories to others is not only a therapy for us, but also shares lessons that others need to learn. Visiting a sick person, you may discover that his greatest need is to find someone ready to listen to his life story. Death, hidden behind every medical diagnosis, stirs up the desire of our souls to open up the door to our memories, to share them with others. There are therapists who consider that healing would come much faster if the sick person had someone to share his life story with.

Viorel Bilauca is a man with a special story, a story of escaping the Communist gulag, of his pilgrimage to "the Promised Land," of all the convulsions of a dramatic change, of the struggle to adapt to a new world, and of the difficulties and beauties of this adventure that most immigrants experienced.

You will meet on Viorel's pages feelings and experiences similar to the adventure of the uprooting of our diaspora. Some of his experiences are so familiar to you because they have contributed to the shaping and molding of your own memories.

Viorel is writing with passion and with vivid memory of the things he experienced. On the one hand, he is writing in order to explain himself in his own eyes, to set himself free from the past, from the story he has been holding in his heart for years. On the other hand, Viorel is writing for his children, for the generation born in this country of promise for which he longed and for which he crossed the sea and the dry sand of the desert. He is writing so he won't forget that, on this transforming journey, God's good hand of provision was upon him. "If the Lord had not been on our side when people attacked us, they would have swallowed us alive when their anger flared against us; the flood would have engulfed us, the torrent would have swept over us, the raging waters would have swept us away"(Psalm 124:2–5).

Without God's help, the stories of our lives are sad ones. With Him, all our memories are converted into life lessons that bring healing and light on our path.

I greet with joy the publication of a book that I warmly recommend to readers.

Petru Lascău
Pastor of Agape Christian Church
Phoenix, Arizona

# PREFACE

Due to the fact that there are not many people who have written a detailed account of their adventures in leaving their home countries to get to clear destinations, and especially due to my children's persistent urging, I finally set about writing what made me determined to leave Romania illegally, as a contemporary pilgrim. This book describes the steps I took crossing the border and stopping at many "stations" until I got into the Promised Land, the first emigrant among my whole family.

The Communist system involved centralized planning. The planning and its implementation were achieved by robotizing the population. Every person had to live and work where the country needed him, irrespective of his personal desires. Those who broke the rule had to pay.

An atheistic ideology was implanted in the minds of children from their early school years. It was a kind of ideological slavery, as the priest Gheorghe Calciu Dumutreasa said. After he said that, he had to spend twenty-one years in a Romanian prison, while his children were educated to become loyal to the Communist Party and to depend on what it offered them.

Here is heaven and there is hell, proclaimed the party, and it all depended on the individual: "As you make your bed, so you must lie upon it." Those who trusted in God considered themselves free. Believers were saying that nothing could frighten them, not even death, because death would only take them home. That is why they were considered "retrograde elements" and were systematically eradicated.

The Communist system created unproductive people who had better lives than those who were working. You only had to be a party member and you were protected.

As an economist, I realized that communism was built on clay feet and would crumble very soon, so I experienced a personal revolution ten years earlier than my compatriots.

A special influence on me was my pastor, Petru Lascău, who, through his repeated exhortations from the pulpit, urged me to do something for God and for His kingdom in this life, before it was too late. We should not present ourselves empty-handed before Him. We need to leave something behind, not only our financial obligations.

I have to be grateful to my Romanian teacher, Antonovici Clement, who encouraged me for eight years to plan my time and read and write in Romanian. I could write nothing now if he had not done that.

# CHAPTER 1

# BETWEEN FEELINGS AND REASON

*April 1978*
*Timişoara, Romania*

IT WAS A usual April day in Timişoara, Romania.
Even though the snow had melted more than a month
before, the Town of Flowers still carried the mark
of winter. I expected the Banat region, and especially
Timişoara, to look very different from other cities in the
country, but this spring, the streets, the buildings, and even
the parks needed more retouching to confirm their places
of honor. It is said that "Banat is the forehead," but for this
year, "habit is second nature" seemed a better description.
This city had the power to capture the imagination of any
visitor, worker, or seeker of adventure. The climate, the
school, the jobs, the housing, and the western border were
chief among the reasons it attracted many people. My first
year in Timişoara was 1978.

The Park of Roses, the Green Forest, the Bega Canal,
the private markets, and the farms in Banat tried to tie
me every day to them with many strings, as well as to the

nation I was raised in. Before that, I left Brasov with great difficulty. It was a town I never expected to leave, blessed with strong industry, a breathtaking mountain setting, and many impressive tourist sites. I would exchange it only for the Western world, where I had dreamed of going one day. Before that, it was difficult for me to leave Suceava, the place where I saw the daylight for the first time. It was home to my parents, grandparents, five brothers, six sisters, nephew, and many friends and colleagues.

Reading my Bible, I realized that when God told Abraham to sacrifice his beloved son, Isaac, God's reason and Abraham's feelings were in conflict. For the time being, like Abraham, I had to follow reason and ignore my feelings in the service of a greater good.

I got to Timişoara carried by a dream and a desire. I was close to the border, very happy in a way. I had dreamed of a life in the West, but at the same time, the thought of not seeing my country again soon, if ever, troubled me deeply. What bothered me most was the thought of leaving my wife and children behind. Try as I might, I couldn't shake the belief that through my inaction, I was assisting at the funeral service for my most wonderful memories and dreams.

I had made the decision to leave Romania many years before. I dreamed of completely changing my destiny and that of my whole family. I had dedicated that year to the great risks and trials of leaving the country. I forced myself to face the reality of choosing between a new life outside the country and accepting the life I had in Romania, with all its needs, discontents, troubles, and compromises.

For most of the families in my home country, money, fairly earned, hardly lasted from one payday to the next.

In Timişoara, as well as in the whole country, we faced crises of all kinds, including food crises. People waited in line to get meat, flour, and oil. We waited in lines at the convenience store, the drug store, and the doctor. We lined up for the bus and even to get a gas cylinder.

Despite all the challenges, Timişoara was a beautiful town, yet many people were still living with the desire to leave the country. We all knew that life in the West was easier. We knew that wages were much better and goods were of better quality. It was nothing new to hear that somebody you had never expected to succeed had done just that after he or she crossed the border illegally.

After I got off the bus from Utvin, I got on the first tram heading downtown. Vasile Tepei got on at the first station, Iosefin Square. When he saw me, he came straight to me. Before he even greeted me, as if we were supposed to meet, he assaulted me with a question. "Do you have the photos with you?" he demanded.

I knew that Vasile had connections with somebody who was making passports in Italy. There was the risk that if you were caught, tried, beaten, and condemned to jail, you would also be marked as a traitor for the rest of your life. When Vasile Tepei first talked about this possibility of leaving the country, it had seemed a dream to me.

"I thought you were joking," I said. "You said nothing about photos!"

Leaving the country was the most important topic in every conversation and meeting we had, so I was surprised by his question. Was it meant to remind me of my plan to leave, or was he simply continuing our ongoing conversation about leaving the country?

"Seriously, don't you have the photos? Today is the last day. I have to give them to our connection; he's leaving soon to go to Italy to make the passports."

"I am very serious," I said without hesitation. "But until now, I haven't heard a thing about passport photos."

Vasile worked at the tram factory with Ionel Ciuruc, my brother-in-law. If Vasile had sent any news to me via Ionel, I never got it—or was he just a bigmouth?

"Have you sent me any word about photos?" I continued. This meeting had been completely unplanned.

Vasile just looked at me with equal parts guilt and gravity. I thought it was better just to drop the issue of messages not reaching me. I had more important concerns.

Now I needed passport photos. I was not sure it was even possible to make passport photos without any legal documents related to an eventual foreign visit. "What can I do in this situation? Is there any possibility of urgently making some photos?" I asked him.

"Yes. You can make some photos downtown, right across the street from the Continental Hotel. They make them in two hours. They have a white shirt and a tie," he said in a hurry. The time was passing quicker than we thought.

"I am going there right away. Where can I find you to give you the photos?"

"I am coming with you and will wait until they are ready. Our man leaves today. If he doesn't have your photos, you'll miss the transport."

"Vasile, what are we going to do with my brother Costică? I told you I have to take him with me. I cannot leave him behind. I brought him from Brasov in order to take him with me. Did you know that?"

"I know; don't worry. He is going to leave with the next group. We are a group of eleven people now. I have arranged that we will leave first, together with Ionel and some other men. Next Saturday, the first four of us will leave. Our man, whom I know and trust, will come from Italy with the passports and the visas already issued. We will get in the car and learn our new names. That way, the border guards won't question us. Unless we look suspicious to them, they won't even realize who we really are. We will wait for you in a concentration camp in Austria. In the meantime, we will set things up so the others will be able to come soon, including Costică for sure."

"Okay," I said, thinking aloud. "I hope it will be so."

Was this the day when I opened a new chapter in my life? I wanted to think so, but I was running out of time. I did not want to lose my clearest and surest opportunity to leave the country. I could not imagine what might have happened if I had not met Vasile on the tram. If everything depended on such an accidental meeting, it was proof that life can offer us something good too. The saying "life is full of surprises" fit the situation perfectly.

I was not sure what to tell Costică. I didn't know if he would understand what was going on. I told myself, "All's well that ends well" and "Luck never comes twice in a man's life." The fact that nobody in our family had left the country before made any legal attempt impossible. If a single family member had left the country, it would have given us all a chance to leave. I was sure that once I got to the West, I could bring any interested family members over.

I entered the photo studio pensively. They took my photos, and I gave them to Vasile. With a worried smile on his face, he accepted them and assured me that everything was all right. "Only God has made us meet," he said to calm me. "Surely this is another sign that our way to the West is open."

We separated quickly. I left to go to work at Electromotorul Factory, where I had been working since the beginning of 1978. I can't say that I didn't enjoy my job and my life in Timişoara. Besides my regular job, I also painted apartments with Ionel and Aurel Ciuriuc, my brothers-in-law. Sometimes I also worked with Vasile.

At the factory, I had no regular working hours or time sheet, and I liked it that way. I was working according to an arrangement with the quality-control guy, who noted when and how much we worked. Nobody was interested in how much money we earned; the earnings were limited. If we worked more on one day than on another, the people who decided the workload would come and readjust everything. As a result, workers were careful when reporting the number of parts we made, so as not to exceed the workload. Otherwise, all workers suffered.

The following Saturday, while I was working the morning shift around ten o'clock, I was called to the main gate of the factory. Somebody was expecting me. I left in a hurry. I knew that Vasile Tepei, Ionel Ciuriuc, my brother-in-law, and the other men were leaving that morning.

I reached the gate of the factory to see my brother-in-law, Ionel, and Vasile. They had come to say good-bye. They were dressed in suits and white shirts. Each had a Bible hidden in a nice pouch under his armpit.

"Hey, dear brother-in-law, we had some time so we stopped to say good-bye. The car that was supposed to come in the morning is late," Ionel explained. "We will go back to Vasile's home because the car could come any minute. We think it was too crowded at the border. I hope we see each other in a week, in the concentration camp."

They left quickly so that the car would not have to wait for them. Vasile Tepei was living in Iosefin Square, the meeting place. I returned to my workplace a little worried.

When I left work that afternoon, I stopped by Vasile's house to see if the four of them had already left. There was silence in the inner yard, where the entrance to Vasile's house was. I approached the door and knocked. The door opened immediately, and Vasile appeared in front of me. I was expecting Lenuţa, Vasile's wife, or one of the children.

"Has the car not arrived yet?" I asked him. "Is there any chance it will come? What do you think?"

"Sure, it has to come," Vasile replied with a smile. "We are still waiting."

My brother-in-law was relaxed. I saw him sitting in a chair, very calm, but tired and anxious. I left in two or three minutes. It was not good for so many people to be in one place, given the circumstances. We hugged and said our good-byes for the morning, and I simply left.

The next day, I found out that the connection person had not come. There was nothing to be done. Helpless, we had to leave everything for the following week.

One evening, not long after these events, all the lights were on at my place when I got home after midnight. I entered the house and met some worried looks. "You are here? Haven't they arrested you?" were the welcoming words of my mother-in-law.

"Who should arrest me and why?

"About eight o'clock, a police car stopped at the gate and asked about you. Coca was not at home," she said. "I told them you were at work. They asked where you worked. I told them. They left a note for you before leaving. They insisted that I give you this note and tell you to go to the county police tomorrow morning at eight, in case they didn't find you at your job."

"They found Ionel at home and took him with them," my wife intervened, her anxiety easing after the emotions she had had in the last hours. "They arrested him," she continued in a scared voice and with tears in her eyes. "The police told us that Vasile Tepei had given your photos to an acquaintance who proved to be from the secret police. Now the police are looking for all of those who gave their photos. What shall we do? What if they arrest you? Would it be better if you go to the police? Will they arrest you? What shall we do?"

"Until now, things have been going well," I replied. "The police did not find me at work because I left about nine. I hope we'll have an idea by morning. Maybe we can find something out about Ionel."

I did not know what else to say. After a very long night, when nobody in the house could sleep except Estera and Dariu, our children, Ionel stopped by at six in the morning. He was free. The police had interrogated him about the passport photos and reprimanded him severely, and then they let him go home. Ionel wasn't worried at all.

Who could assure me that I would get only a reprimand? Vasile Tepei had been arrested too, and was released after he was beaten to make him tell everything. If Vasile, who was our boss, escaped with that, what was I to expect?

After I calculated all the risks, I decided to show up at the county police. I got there long before eight in the morning. I looked around carefully to see some familiar faces, to find some moral support, not that I wanted to see anybody else in my situation. I would rather not see any person I knew going to the police.

My joy soon vanished when I saw Aurel, my brother-in-law from Sanmihaiul Roman, approaching the gate of the police station. I stepped in front of him and asked, "Why are you here? Have you got an invitation?"

"Yes," he answered, calm but concerned. "For you it is a piece of cake, but not for me. I am a recidivist, and I am very afraid that I won't get out of here. That is why I am not in a hurry. It is possible that I won't taste freedom again for a while. I struggled all night wondering where to go: the police or the border."

"I don't know where you were heading, but I know for sure that you are at the police now," I said, trying to make a joke. "We will go to the border once we get out of here."

"I am afraid that it will take a while—if I get out of here!"

"If Vasile, our boss, is out, we will get out too." I was trying to encourage myself once more before Aurel. "Have courage!"

It was eight o'clock when another lady whom Aurel knew came. She had the same "invitation" in her hand. We introduced ourselves and then we headed toward the main entrance of the county police station.

We presented ourselves to the first officer that we met. We showed him our invitations and he took us to the first office. Everything looked in a perfect order. The sculptured furniture, made probably of walnut wood, was arranged in very good taste. Paintings and maps hung on the walls, like in a museum. Cleanliness, discipline, and politeness were at home.

We had to wait a short time—we were not in a hurry—until a middle-aged, serene-faced, and very spiritual officer came. He was slim, of average stature, with hair and mustache longer than I expected for a police officer. He was dressed in civilian clothes.

He introduced himself as Captain So-and-so, and then went straight to the point. He tried to convince us that Romania was a very advanced country. We did not have unemployed people. Every worker had social security provided and free access to higher education. All the civil and religious rights were guaranteed. Every citizen had the right to vote. We could vote for whomever we wanted, and any citizen could stand for election. We didn't have antagonistic social classes; we were all equals.

In capitalistic countries, it was not like that, he continued. He showed us a pile of letters he claimed to have received from people who had left the country and were sorry now for leaving. He spoke very convincingly. I didn't asked him why people in the West did not come and ask for political asylum in Romania or Russia, or how would he explain the fact that we saw those foreigners spending their vacations in Romania and then returning to the "hard lives" they had in their own countries.

There followed four hours of lectures about a theory I knew and that had very little truth to it. Then we were completely left alone. After a few minutes, another officer came. We were taken to separate rooms.

I was taken into a small office. It had nothing imposing: no flag, no picture of the president on the wall, not even the pictures of Lenin, Marx, and Engels that were part of the usual decoration of official offices. No painting, no map, no furniture, no typing machine, no copying machine, no telex, no telephone. (Correspondence was conducted via messengers.) There was only an ordinary desk and a young officer. He must have been around twenty-five, the same age as me, but he was wearing a uniform. He was a lieutenant with three little stars on his shoulders: the police uniform used to intimidate many people. Without any introduction, he gave me some white A4 sheets.

"Write!" he started the conversation, trying not to yell at me. "Write all the reasons that made you determined to leave your country illegally, and why you haven't applied for a passport. Romania issues passports to all *honest* citizens! There are so many Romanians who spend their holidays abroad, not only for job purposes. Of course, they are *honorable and trustworthy citizens!*"

I started writing. I wrote about three pages. In the meantime, he kept asking me all kinds of questions: if I knew people from abroad and how I had met them, if I had been persecuted at my job by my superiors, if I had been arrested unfairly, if my parents or relatives had complained against the Romanian government, and so on.

Evening came. It took me almost three hours to write that statement. I did it extensively. After I finished writing, I signed it indecipherably, as required, and then I was moved immediately to another room.

It seemed to be a small room for meetings. I had to wait for more than an hour. I remembered the detective books that I had read. I was calm. I wanted to look indifferent. I knew that my statement was full of realities. I was searching the whole room very carefully, trying to guess where the spying devices were hidden. I was convinced they were monitoring me, but I was not able to discover anything. In the office where I had written my statement,

I had noticed the young officer doing something under the table at which we were sitting face-to-face. I was convinced that all of our conversation had been recorded.

When I started thinking that I had been forgotten in that meeting room, an officer slammed the door open. "You are free to go home. Think better of your future and the future of your family," he told me while showing me the way out.

I had no time to tell him that my family's future was what really concerned me and was the reason why I was at the police station. As I was leaving, I was thinking, "How is it that they haven't asked me to write a commitment?"

There was a great difference between the dream and the possibility of leaving the country. From the dream or the desire to leave the country and to the belief that this dream might come true was a long way, full of obstacles. I was convinced very soon that only faith could help me. Many people have strong desires in life, but only a few have the faith necessary to succeed.

## CHAPTER 2

# REPRIMAND AND COMMITMENT

SOME DAYS PASSED without any news. I was prepared for anything. I continued to go to work. I was working night shifts at Electromotorul, and during the day I was painting apartments. With the money I earned at Electromotorul, I could not afford many things, which was why any extra income was welcome. I made two painter ladders, I bought some painting rollers, I made some rulers, and I looked for work every day. The money I earned from painting was the best, because it was not taxed.

"Mister, you need to stay later to talk to the office people," said the shift chief one morning. He seemed worried. "For some weeks now, we have found a request written in the registry each day to let the office people know immediately when you arrive for the day shift. But you only do night shifts. Would it be possible for you to come one morning, so we could get rid of this problem? I told them you have two small children, as far I knew, and that you have nobody to leave them with. It seems to be something important. They really want to talk to you. We don't know what it might be about."

"I did not know I was being looked for," I answered, studying him. Maybe they remembered I had requested to be transferred, even though my transfer had not been approved. I could not think of anything else. From among the thousands of workers in this factory, the leadership really needed me here in this miserable section? Why should I go to the offices? Would they transfer me to another section? Ask me to become a party member? Make me leader of a crew? I tried to guess the purpose of the meeting, but I found no reason. My intuition was no help this time.

The following week, I went to work on the day shift. I was very curious to see if somebody would remember me. I did not have to wait long. Around nine o'clock, two men came up behind me as I was working. One of them took my arm. "Are you Viorel Bilauca?" he asked.

"Yes, I am."

"We have been looking for you for a long time, but you managed to avoid us. Stop the lathe and come with us to the section chief's office."

Those two were walking quickly. I had to move quickly too, because one of them was holding my hand.

The other workers had no time to notice that I had disappeared from the section. These people were walking very fast, no joke! That was the way many people used to disappear, and nobody ever saw them again.

"I would like to wash my hands and get rid of the cast-iron dust, at least on the outside, not to mention what I have already swallowed." I was trying to make a joke.

"You don't need to. We do not have time," he told me, pushing me toward the office. I arranged my overall before entering the office. I was about to ask what was happening, when the heavy, soundproofed, leather-coated door opened.

"Here he is. We got him," one of them said.

In the chief's office, where usually there were only a few people, there were now many, most of them unknown to me. There was no empty seat at the meeting table. The desk was bigger than one could imagine, with more chairs than usual. It was packed.

"Sit here on this chair, so everyone can see you." The voice came from my right side—the voice of someone I did not know. I was scrutinizing everyone, looking for the section chief, trying to find a refuge, but even though he was a tall, blond-haired man, I could not see him. Eventually I found him right in front of me, on the other side of the desk.

"Comrades, I am a security lieutenant colonel," said the secure and sarcastic voice from my right side. "We are here to correct the criminal intentions of this good citizen—a very good one, but one who has strange ideas. Together we have to help him get rid of these ideas, and not only him, but also those who have the same ideas. They are not a few in number."

With this introduction, I found answers to the prior week's mystery. According to the bylaws of the RCP (Romanian Communist Party) and the YCU (Youth Communist Union), this was a public reprimand for working people. The bylaws stated that a working person who made a "great" mistake would get a notice and then a reprimand in front of his colleagues. If that person did not change, the next step was constraint.

"This citizen," the lieutenant continued, "tried to betray his country. He considered himself smart. He intended to obtain a counterfeit passport abroad, but we laid our hands on his passport photos. Isn't that bad for him? We know he is a good element, a very good one. We have investigated him, and we received an exceptional report about him. He has nobody abroad, he doesn't know where he is going, he doesn't know how people work there, he doesn't know how people live there, he doesn't know any foreign language, but he tried to break through the border! What a shame! Shame on you!"

"I have many acquaintances in Federal Germany," the head of another section interrupted. "I have talked to many of them, and they are so sorry for moving to Germany. They speak the language better than some of the Germans, and they have relatives there, but they feel like strangers. They would come back to Romania, but their children don't want to. The children have friends and don't want to come back. Jobs are another problem. They work for several months, then comes unemployment; then they work again for several months, then unemployment comes again, and so on. Life is very hard in Germany."

Another person said, "Mister, here in this country, I didn't see or taste chocolate until I was fourteen years old, but my children by the age of three already have bad teeth from chocolate. You must be blind not to see how fast we are progressing."

"We have no idea what tools they have in the West. I have been to Bucharest many times for exhibitions of tools and machines, and what I have seen shocked me," another said. (I think that person worked in the supply department.) "Automatic machines, with screens, sir, and numerical programs—who can learn to work on them? Immigrants don't get a chance to work on that kind of machine; they can hardly fathom them. The thing is that technology is very advanced..."

It was a very long meeting. I think all of those present were accustomed to that kind of meeting. No one left the room. They showed a lot of patience. The phone never rang. It must have been a very important meeting. I imagined an imposing guard securing the door of the office.

For five hours, I thought about what to promise and if I would be asked to make a promise. A commitment had to be the resolution of such a meeting. I did not know what commitment to make. I knew my future depended on this promise. I did not want to tell them the whole truth. What I was thinking was a different issue. On the other hand, I knew that I was already written into their "black book" for the rest of my life, and that could never be erased.

After all kinds of comments, stories, examples, encouragements, and discouragements from most of those present, given with the purpose of convincing me about an imaginary good life in Romania and an awful imperialism that dominated the West, the lieutenant gave me some pages, ordering me to sign them.

"Sign here." He showed me a blank space on a page of the minutes. "This is the confirmation that you were reprimanded in front of your colleagues. Let's end this meeting."

I hurried to sign it, happy that I hadn't been asked to make any promise.

"Let me intervene," said the head of the section. "We have not allowed him to say anything. He has not told us the reason why he wanted to flee. He has made no commitment."

"Okay," the officer said, "what commitment do you make for the future?"

Those present were all eyes and ears.

"I don't know how, legally or illegally, but I will leave this country," I said without hesitation while I was signing the minutes. "I would like to leave legally so that, if I become convinced that everything that was said today is true, I will be able to come back."

All of those present in the office were astounded. Suddenly they seemed to have even stopped breathing. The lieutenant's eyes were stuck on the papers he was arranging. All of them looked at me, and then at the security officer.

Only then did I realize what I had just said. I was expecting an appropriate reaction, but none of them said a word. I gave the signed papers to the officer. To my surprise and that of all the people present, he stood, thanked everybody for their participation and cooperation, and left in a hurry. The office emptied in few minutes.

I found myself alone. It was past two o'clock in the afternoon. I left for home, thinking of the "spirit of duty" toward the policy of the party and how loyal to the party everyone wanted to seem during those meetings—even those who otherwise were my best friends and complained openly every day about the situation. During those meetings, everybody said what they were supposed to say, not what they really thought. It would have been insanity or an extraordinary act of courage for someone to publicly express his complaints about the party.

And you could leave nothing to chance, even if you had such courage. The system changed most people by using force and intimidation. There were very few who confronted the system and survived. Some of them disappeared overnight, for good.

Next day, my supervisor approached me when he saw me and whispered to me, "Didn't those people seize you last night?"

"Not yet. I couldn't just disappear so quickly. It would have been suspicious. They do not make such mistakes. But they won't wait for long, I am sure."

"We have been to meetings like this one, but until now, I hadn't heard and never would have thought someone would have the courage to make such a direct promise. I was simply astonished. We were sure they were about to arrest you. Be careful! Protect your family. If you can leave the country, do it as soon as possible. This is my piece of advice to you."

My supervisor, my foreman, and the chief of the section were all Serbian Romanians. Most of them had passing permits for Yugoslavia and could understand us better than our communist fellow-countrymen.

# Chapter 3
# AUGUST 1978

I HAD TO ESTABLISH new connections if I wanted to leave the country. I was determined to leave in 1978. Many of my acquaintances and friends had been talking about leaving, but had not made any progress for years. Everything was just a dream. Time was passing. The year I had had great hopes for was passing very quickly, and I could see no progress. Costică, my brother, was becoming impatient, so he suggested we try it on our own.

All day long we were doing nothing other than plan for leaving, just the two of us. We had managed to lay our hands on some dinars. The most difficult problem was to get close to the border. It was not easy, given the controls in place for trains and buses.

The month of August offered us some hope. Aurel Ciuriuc, my brother-in-law and brother to Ionel, was working at the Cinematographic Enterprise in Timişoara. With his work badge, he could get close to the border without any problem. Besides that, his wife, Sida, had some relatives living in Beba Veche, the westernmost point in Romania. We decided to act with Aurel and pass through Beba Veche.

"We have to be very careful not to reveal our plans," was Aurel's repeated warning. "Make sure you have your ID cards, work badges, and no luggage with you. On the frontier, every peasant works with the secret police. He would turn you in very quickly. It is said they receive a reward for every person they turn in. Everything is possible."

"We promise," we answered. "We hope nobody will approach us speaking Bulgarian. They speak Bulgarian too in Beba Veche."

"Let me talk to them in that case."

One Saturday in the middle of August, we were on a train going toward Beba Veche. We passed by the control guards on the train with no incidents. From the train station, we walked about one kilometer. On our way to the village, we scrutinized the field on the left side of the road, toward the border: the distance, direction, possible hiding places, and obstacles. The sun was setting so we had no time to lose. We needed a very good sense of our surroundings in order not to find ourselves going in the wrong direction at midnight, when the moon was up. We all were measuring distances, but we could not talk to each other because of the other people around us. From the train station to the village, there was a road leading straight to the West, to the border. We could see the guard booths in the distance. They seemed to be only about two or three miles away.

"I thought of a strategy," Aurel said after we were by ourselves. "We will eat dinner with one family and then I will tell them we going to sleep at another one. On our way, we will head toward the frontier. Nobody will remember us by tomorrow, and we will be on the other side."

"There is no doubt that we are going to be on the other side," said Costică. The plan seemed perfect. We only needed to get rid of our "guard"—that is, the family members.

"I don't want to think of another ending," I added. "Tomorrow we will breathe the air of Yugoslavia, and then the air of Germany."

"If it were darker, we could go to the border right now," said Costică.

"It is too early," Aurel said. "I would not be surprised if one of the people we talked with on the train came looking for us at our relatives' homes. If they don't find us where we said we would be, then they will search for us. Anything is possible in the area! I have even heard that many times people have been turned in by their own children!"

The relatives were very hospitable to us. Shortly after, other relatives from the village came to meet us. Aurel's relatives, the ones we stopped with the first time, insisted that we should sleep there, but another family, good people and also relatives, wanted to give a hand with the guests and insisted that at least one of us should go and sleep at their house. We almost couldn't implement the plan we had for that night.

"I have an idea that will satisfy everyone," Aurel said. "What if we all go and have dinner with you, in the center of the village? And then we will come here to sleep. This way we'll all have our way." We all agreed on that.

It was becoming dark. We left our host without saying good-bye and went to have dinner at their friends'. Those from the household where we were supposed to sleep did not come. At almost midnight, only the three of us were on our way to the house where we were supposed to sleep.

These were the perfect conditions for us to disappear. At the first intersection, we headed West. We all knew what we had to do.

We walked without saying a word, being very careful not to hit something or wake up the dogs in the village. We breathed carefully. It was like we were floating.

We got out of the village on the side toward the border. We expected to get into a wheat field that we had seen that afternoon, but we got onto grazing land, a place where peasants would let their sheep, chickens, pigs, and geese graze and their children play. The wheat field was beyond this grazing land. On the pasture, everybody could see us easily, very easily, so we had to change our route.

We went toward the train station. It was a strategic change of direction. If someone asked us where we were going, we could answer, "To the train station." It wasn't the shortest way to the border, but the safest, because from the train station we could hide in the beet fields that began there.

So we headed to the train station, with the village on our left and the border on our right side. The station was very well lit, so we could not get lost. There was no visible obstacle between the station and the border. We had to cross a road we had seen earlier, a road that led to the cooperative premises and probably to the border. There was a risk in crossing the road, but we had no alternative. The time was passing fast. We were in a hurry, hoping to cross the border before sunrise.

We hadn't crossed the road when we heard dogs barking. People from the cooperative premises started shouting to us. The wheat fields were between us and the cooperative premises, so we could hide in the wheat. We hid and, without saying a word, continued going toward the road.

The dogs continued to bark. People in the cooperative gave the alarm. All the lights went on. An Auto Romania SUV searched the surroundings and the yard of the premises. The dogs would not be quiet. People kept shouting at us. They did not know why the dogs were barking, but they felt it their duty to shout. We gave them no answer. We took courage when we realized that they had not let the dogs out. Our emotions and fears were growing, but we never stopped for a second.

The road was not far. Crossing it, we would find safety. We kept one eye on the road and one eye on the cooperative. Before getting to the road, we faced a stream of water that we had known nothing about. It did not seem deep, but we would have to take off our clothes to wade through it.

Aurel tried to make a little bridge with some plastic pipes that seemed to be specially placed there for us, pipes used for irrigation, but he ended up making a lot of unnecessary noise. Besides the fact that he got completely wet, from his head to his toes, he also lost his wallet.

So we took off our clothes and waded across. In few minutes we were on the other side of the stream. In the meantime, the voices coming from the cooperative had gone quiet, as well as the dogs.

The distance from the stream to the road was short. We crossed the road without any incident. The moon was going down. It was becoming darker and colder. Because we were dressed very lightly and we were wet, we started shaking. The beet field was wet from the dew, and the ground was wet as if it had rained. My shoes were soon soaked through. Our walk was becoming more and more difficult, but none of us was complaining.

We headed to the right. We did not want to follow the road or go too close to the railway station. We had two more kilometers to walk to the guard booths that we had seen.

The moon set and it became very dark. Daylight would come in an hour or two.

"It seems to me we have no chance to cross the border tonight," I said quietly.

"I think so too," Costică answered, "but let's get as close as we can. We will be able to study the guards, so we can cross tomorrow night. It would have been good to have the binoculars with us that I bought at the market in Arad, when I was at Gheniu Ujeniciuc's wedding," Costică continued, thinking aloud. "But how could we?"

"I agree, but the question is, where are we going to spend all day?" Aurel demanded. "What are we going to eat and drink?"

"We have to hide in the beet field all day," I whispered. "We are going to eat beets. They belong to the cooperative, don't they? If we aren't able to lie down, we will start weeding, pretending we are volunteer workers in the field."

We laughed softly. But a short distance in front of us, we found some bushes in the middle of the beet field. They seemed, and they really were, a miracle, our saving oasis. We entered the bushes. Some were quite small, but they were taller than the beets. We could even stand without being seen. We decided to spend all day there.

It became very cold before dawn. I was wearing a thin shirt I had bought in the market in Arad, from some Serbians. It was made in Italy, but in spite of its beauty, it was very thin and cold. Costică and Aurel were also dressed very lightly. We could not take warm clothes with us to avoid suspicion. We were freezing. The cold penetrated to our bones. We could not stop shaking. We eagerly waited for the sun to rise.

When the day came, we looked around and realized that the bushes were smaller than we had thought. It was almost impossible not to be discovered. Some peasants arrived to work in the field. It was very risky. Although they were spread all over the field, not able to communicate with each other, we watched them. There was no toilet in the field, so the bushes we were hiding in were the peasants' sole toilet! We were lucky that only a few visited our den, and then only on the edges.

The sun rose quickly and the weather got warmer. Thirst became a problem. We had nothing to drink. Time passed very slowly. The minutes that had passed so quickly during the night now seemed to have stopped.

By noon our discussions took a new and unexpected turn. "When I think what they are going to do to me if they catch me," Aurel mused, "I know they will dehumanize me. I have had experience with them. It will be the worst for me; these people are going to destroy me. I already spent a year and a half in jail for attempting to cross the border, when they caught me in Constanta. I know what awaits me. You will escape easily. They will consider me your chief. It will be woe to me!"

"You are not intending to go back?" I asked him, panicking.

"Yes, I am. I have decided. I don't want to be caught again. They can destroy me completely, and then my family and my five children ..."

"It is too risky to go back to the village without us. Any peasant or soldier from the railway station will recognize you and turn you in. Then you will have to tell them where have you been, where were you coming from at that hour, and where your brothers-in-law are."

"I thought about this too," he responded immediately, very puzzled. It was obvious he was upset with us for not understanding him. "I will go back with these peasants. I will intermingle with them. I hope nobody will notice me. I will give the impression I am one of them. It will be evening by that time. You don't need to assume that these peasants have nothing better to do than watch those passing by."

"What do you say, Costică?" I turned to my brother, who had become speechless at what he was hearing. "We will go on, won't we?"

"I am not even thinking about changing my plan," Costică answered, very determined. "We are closer to Yugoslavia than ever. We have already passed the last control post and the last village."

We studied for hours all the possible alternatives. How could we resolve the newly created situation? We considered all the pros and cons: What if we did not succeed in crossing? What if we were caught? What if we separated? When and how could we cross without endangering other people?

The discussion continued until evening. We forgot about hunger and thirst. Aurel maintained his decision to return home. Considering the risks, I finally decided to return home with Aurel. I vowed that the next time I would leave only with Costică, on condition that he also give up the idea of crossing the border that night. Costică insisted that he would not return home with us. Finally, we gave him all the dinars we had and wished him success. We assured each other that we would never turn each other in.

The sun was setting, and the moment of our departure approached. The peasants hid their hoes among the beet rows for the next day, and then left slowly for the village. We were ready to separate when Costică told us that he would return with us. He realized that it was better to stick together.

We entered the village like any other villagers. Nobody suspected anything. We stopped at the first water pump and drank. We stopped at the next water pump too. We drank a lot of water. It was not easy to quench our thirst. We had to stop at the next water pump too. After we had had enough water, we realized the risk we had been exposed to. We could have died of thirst.

We stopped at the convenience store in the village and bought a loaf of bread and some mineral water. Then we left on the first train to Timişoara. I arrived at the Electromotorul factory in time for the night shift. Aurel and Costică went home.

## CHAPTER 4

# ON OUR OWN

IT WAS SEPTEMBER 1978. I had nobody to make leaving plans with besides Costică. All the other pretenders had found different reasons to postpone their leaving, especially those planning to do so illegally. Rumors about those who had been caught at the border were circulating among our acquaintances. I spoke only about those who succeeded in crossing, encouraging myself to continue trying.

Costică and I were ready to try again. The heat of the summer had passed. Conditions for crossing were becoming worse by the day. Because of the cold weather, Costică's job at UMT was becoming more difficult. He was anxious to leave as soon as possible.

"I am ready to leave by myself," Costică told me one day. "May I borrow your bicycle?"

"If your departure depends on it, I will give it to you. Maybe this way I will buy myself a new one. I couldn't before, even when I used to work at the airplane factory! This bicycle is made of old parts. You can abandon it."

"I thought it might be easier to get to Uivar by bicycle. It is too risky by bus. If I can make it to Uivar, I can walk from there."

"If you do not have patience to wait for something more secure, you can try," I told him. "I have to set some more money aside for my family. Winter is knocking at the door."

My brother disappeared one afternoon. He did not tell me where he was going, in order not to make me an accomplice. We had decided that long before.

Days passed without any news. I kept quiet. I was waiting. Hope grew in my heart when there was no inquiry from the police, from our parents or from any hospital. Normally, I would have had to report him missing to the police, but in this case I reported nothing.

More days passed before I got a phone call notification from the city of Suceava. (We used a central line; not every home had a telephone, and mobile phones would not come until much later.) When I returned the call, at the other end was Costică.

"It's me … They caught me at the border. I cannot say too many things, other than the fact that I am all right. I will go to Bucharest in November. I have to pick up my diploma from the school in Băneasa. I will try to make a side trip and visit you too." He was short, telegraphic.

"I would be glad if you could call me from somewhere else," I told him. "Why haven't you called me before? I have been anxious about you for days."

"I will explain everything to you if they approve my side trip to the country. I have to hang up."

"We will be waiting for you. Take good care of yourself."

Disappointment and discouragement on one side were assaulting me, but the desire for freedom on the other side was growing day by day. Costică had not succeeded this time. What had happened? I was anxious to find out. I realized once again that it was not easy to illegally cross a very well-guarded border, like the one of Romania. The guards were brutal, but the desire to have my revenge overwhelmed me.

I was working at Electromotorul. I was very punctual. I did my job and tried to protect myself against any suspicion relating to my plan of leaving the country. Toward the end of September, one of the foremen, of Serbian origin, stopped me and told me very carefully, so as not to be overheard by anybody, that it would be good for me to look for a job in another factory, because he was responsible for reporting on me to the police every day. I was under very strict surveillance. Not only was my presence reported, but also my attitude toward my colleagues and my job.

Any discussion with my colleagues was analyzed by the secret police. I was followed to prevent me from corrupting other people. I made some friends, but not from my work. I never knew who the people I was talking to actually were. I had seen some of them at the meeting in my chief's office when I was reprimanded. Most of them were loyal to the secret police.

I was very receptive to what my foreman told me, so I changed my job. At the beginning of November, I moved to ISIM (Welding and Testing Materials Institute) in Timişoara.

I kept my connection with Vasile Tepei. He was the most interested in leaving and seemed to be the most determined to leave. I had lost my confidence in most of his connections after the incident with the passport photos, but I believed he had good intentions. That was why I met Vasile and Mihai Manea in Balcescu Square, at a Lacto.

Lacto was a small restaurant where you could buy cold yogurt and fresh cracknel, specifically Romanian. This Lacto had several tables where you could eat standing. Vasile and I listened very attentively to the unfortunate experience Mihai Manea had had. Mihai was an old friend of Vasile who had been caught at the border and spent one and a half years in prison. Mihai was punctual for our meeting. He was a good man, and at first sight seemed very tired and ravaged, like he had just come out of a sanatorium. He was of medium stature, with dark hair and a warm voice. At his age, around thirty, he gave the impression of having given up his dream of crossing the border.

"Dear Mihai," Vasile started, "we want to try to cross to the other side. I know you have been caught once. Can you tell us what to expect in case we fail? Viorel's brother, Costică, was caught one month ago at the border. Now he is under house arrest in Suceava, and we cannot talk to him."

Mihai looked at me. We had never met before. "I am Viorel Bilauca," I introduced myself. "I am from Suceava. I work at ISIM, and in my free time I also paint apartments with my brothers-in-law, the Ciuriuc brothers, and Vasile. Don't be afraid. I was in the group discovered with the fake passport photos. I think you have heard about it."

"If you are a friend of Vasile, I do not worry at all," Mihai answered. "As for the prison, I won't say too many things. In the jail you are treated like a traitor, like a person selling his country, like a coward, someone his own country should be ashamed of. You won't be able to get rid of this label, not in the prison and not in civilian life."

"First of all, we are interested in the way they caught you and what happened to you there? We are not planning to go to jail, but it is good to know about these things."

"I know," Mihai replied quickly. "I tried to cross the border at Jimbolia. I was caught in a cemetery, waiting for the right time to cross. I was living in Jimbolia, and I thought I knew all the moves of the guards. However, I realize you cannot know everything, and there are risks even in the greatest and most certain promises. The soldier who caught me probably was promoted, if he is not in the West already. Soldiers are like robots. The country rewards them, but when they realize that life can be different, they cross the border. And not alone— they take other people with them too. The biggest human traffickers are former guards!

"Anyway, besides the people you know, you also need a lot of luck to succeed. You can trust nobody for a job like this. There are traitors everywhere. I was condemned for one year and six months, time that I did to the last minute. I repeat, you need a lot of good luck. There are many people who have paid tens of thousands of lei, who have been hidden in the cargo trains and then turned in to the secret police by those who took the money. What can you say? Actually, there is nothing new; you already know many similar cases."

"Do you think you made any mistake that caused them to catch you?" Vasile asked. "What would you do differently if you were to try leaving again?"

"I don't think you can be one hundred percent sure. All the preparations help a lot, but there is always, without exception, a great risk. I have applied for legal immigration with my whole family. I will wait. I will knock at all the doors, and I will leave legally. It is said that those who have been in prison for attempting to cross the border have the highest chances of getting passports."

We could have continued talking forever, but we all felt guilty. We did not want to raise any suspicions and have any more trouble, so we decided to cut our discussions short and separate before we would be arrested.

"I have a dream and a belief," I said at the end of our discussion. "When we meet again in the free world, we will remember today's meeting. Maybe we'll find a Lacto there too. What do you think?"

"Sure, sure," both of them said.

We departed full of hope.

## CHAPTER 5
# NOVEMBER 6

GOOD NEWS! BAD news! "Vasile Tepei crossed the border yesterday afternoon in a Dacia 1300," my brother-in-law, Ionel Ciuriuc, told me.

"In a Dacia? What Dacia?" I answered without being too excited. "Vasile had no car."

"Vasile did it. He did it to us! Last night he did not come to work. So in the morning I stopped by his place, and Lenuţa, his wife, told me that Vasile was already in Austria. He crossed with somebody from Arad, in a Dacia."

"And you knew nothing?" I asked.

"Vasile spoke about different possibilities for leaving, but I never heard this one. The good thing is that one of us has already left. The bad thing is that he did not take us with him. Sooner or later he will get us out of here too, if he doesn't forget about us. I think we helped each other so much that he won't forget us!"

"Let's suppose he doesn't forget about us. Until he is able to send a guarantee for us, a lot of water will run under the bridge," I said.

"Vasile knows some people there. I hope he can ask them to help us, even if he isn't able to do it very soon."

"Well, at least we can encourage ourselves freely. Autosuggestion! We need very close relatives. We don't have them. The shortest way is to cross as he did. I don't have enough patience, and I won't wait until I have relatives on the other side, no way. I hope that my family will be able to say they have somebody out there, and I will be that one."

I was not saying this with pride, but in faith. I was determined to cross the border as soon as possible. I set aside one year for study and preparations, and I would not give up my plan.

Disappointed that Vasile had crossed the border without us, but encouraged that crossing was possible, we returned to our planning for leaving and to our daily lives.

Concerned for my family, concerned for my departure, I forgot that Costică was supposed to visit us from Suceava. With no mobile phones, no phone in the house, no Internet, communication was very difficult. Telegrams were the fastest way of communication in those days. Even in an emergency, like an accident or a funeral, there was no other means of communication. You could make a phone call only with a telephonic notification. In order to do that, you had to go to the post office. There you sent the notification, and in two or three days you got to talk to the person you wanted. Most of the time, you just got guests unexpectedly, in person.

That was the way Costică came. Dressed in a new light-colored suit, with a white shirt and tie, he was unrecognizable.

I found him at my home in Utvin one afternoon when I returned from work. I heard some joyful sounds from the house. Estera wanted Costică to lift her with one hand, as usual. It was an old custom. But Costică avoided doing this thing that previously had brought him so much joy!?

"I am glad to see you in the flesh," I told him very happily.

"Me too," he answered, trying to protect himself from Estera who was holding his hand wanting to be lifted up.

"I cannot lift her for now," he told me quietly. "I have the marks of some dogs that bit me on my hand, and the wounds are not healing very fast …"

"What happened that they let you leave home so quickly?" I asked him.

"I told them I needed to pick up my diploma from the school in Băneasa. They allowed me to leave for this reason. Nobody else can pick up the diploma, and the school will not mail it. The graduate must be there in person to sign the documents. That is when I bought a ticket to Bucharest; I actually got a side trip ticket. They did not realize what I intended to do. This is how I got to Timişoara."

"I hope you were not followed," I told him jokingly. "Tell me what happened when you went toward the border? I hope we have many things to learn from your experience, things not to do. It is good they didn't terminate you. They could have killed you on the spot."

"It is good they didn't terminate me, but I was not far from that. Look what happened: I left from here and I got to Uivar. From there I came to a small bridge, that I found later was called 'at the three bridges.' That seemed to be my last obstacle, and then I only had to be very careful.

"I took heart and walked on the first bridge. After a few steps, I heard a voice summoning me. I stopped. A soldier came from under the bridge and forced me to lie on the ground. I followed the order immediately. It was getting dark, so I could not see the soldier's face, not that that would have made any difference. He was very angry and cursing in the worst way.

"The chief guard came a few minutes afterward, with two other guards. They started kicking me with their feet and hitting me with their rifles. They repeated, 'It's better for your mother to cry than for my mother!' Soon after that a military SUV came with the chief of the post and took me to the post. The curses did not stop for a second.

"They were right in a way. They told me that if I had succeeded in crossing during their time of service, they would have ended up before the court for not catching me.

"At the post, after getting out of the car, all the soldiers came to see who they had caught. I could distinguish among the curses voices threatening my life. All of them were hitting me constantly. Fists, feet, and gun stocks struck me, and as if all of those were not enough, they let the dogs out. The dogs bit my hands and pulled me as if I were a corpse. I could not defend myself.

"The soldiers and their superiors were having fun seeing me fighting for my life. They enjoyed such fun any time they had a chance. It was obvious that in those moments they were making up for all of those who had successfully crossed the border in their area.

"While I was fighting the dogs facing me, the soldiers let loose another dog, much bigger than the others, that came from behind me. It was a German shepherd. It jumped on my back. I had no time to see it, but I felt such a strong blow in my back that I fell to the ground. In the meantime, the other dogs came at me even more wildly.

"I saw myself being torn into pieces. I told myself this was the end for me. I imagined myself dead. The soldiers continued to encourage the dogs, which seemed to get tired after that much fighting. They stopped and waited, probably to be sent to their cages.

"I felt no pain in my hands and feet. Instead, the blow in my back from the German shepherd hurt me. It not only took a piece from my jacket, but also from my skin. I moved until my back was against a wall. I did not expect to survive. It seemed to be a life-and-death fight. I saw no chance of escape. The soldiers and officers encouraged each other to hit me and curse me, as a way of revenge. Those people were worse and more wicked than all the animals that were attacking me.

"After a long time, the dogs got quiet. I could not move. I was convinced that the show was over when a sergeant came with a gun ready to shoot and ordered everybody to withdraw. I stood up. The sergeant approached me and from a distance of few meters shouted, cursing very badly, 'Pull back, everybody. I will shoot this one right now.' He fired the first shot. I saw the fire come from his gun.

"I told myself, 'I am finished. I will die.' I felt the chill of death and gave myself up. I thought for a second of my short life, of my mother who would find out about me. I was expecting to fall any moment. A second of life seemed an eternity to me.

"Some seconds passed, and I was still standing. It was dark. I saw and I heard a series of two or three more shots. I watched the barrel of the rifle and the fire and smoke coming out of it, and I was still standing. All my dealings with life were finished. The other soldiers were making fun. The dogs disappeared after the first shot.

"All the soldiers became quiet when they heard a car coming. When the military EMS stopped, a petty officer got out. The sergeant reported me. He mentioned nothing about the bloody show that ended suddenly. He entered the post for few minutes.

"I had some moments to realize I was not dead. The wounds on my hands and feet started hurting me. My jacket was torn in different places: on the sleeves, on the back. My pants were torn from knee to hem. It was a good thing I could not see my face.

"The petty officer came out from the post after a while, with a piece of paper in his hand. He took me and the sergeant, and we left for Jimbolia. I could not believe they asked me no questions, not even my name. I could not believe I was still alive. The sergeant had been shooting blanks.

"Once we got to Jimbolia, they put me in jail. The following day I was sent to Timişoara, where I spent two more days in jail."

"How did you get home, and how did our parents react when they saw you?" I interrupted to give him some moments to breathe and relax.

"Oh, everything went better than I expected. After two days under arrest by Timişoara's police, I was entrusted to two policemen who came from Suceava especially for me. They put handcuffs on my wrists, pushed me into a police car, and drove me to the railway station. I cannot tell you how I looked. Besides the handcuffs that I could not hide, my clothing was still all torn by the dogs. My clothes hung on me worse than on a beggar. Besides, I was unshaven and dirty.

"We spent two hours in the station until the Suceava train came. The policemen did not allow me to stay in one place. They asked me to walk because of the cold. All the people were staring at me as they would stare at a bear. I did not know many people in Timişoara who could see me in that condition. I met no person I knew. It was so obvious what the other people were thinking of me. I looked like a thief, like a criminal caught by the police, who was facing his punishment. I found a seat in a corner of the train compartment, so I could hide the nightmare reality I was living."

"What did the other people in the compartment have to say?"

"I had two policemen with me. Nobody said a word. The policemen spoke quietly. When other travelers entered the compartment, they did not stay for long. All of them were scared to ask questions. Actually, nobody expected any answer, neither from me nor from the policemen. What they could see was enough for them to understand everything. The other travelers did not feel comfortable in the company of those policemen, especially due to my handcuffs."

"I imagine that these policemen had to accompany you to the toilet."

"I didn't move from my place. I hadn't eaten any good food in days, so I could make it all the way to Suceava without going to the toilet, a twelve-hour trip. A military EMS was waiting for me at the railway station in Suceava."

"What did the policemen in Suceava tell you? How did they behave toward you?"

"They talked among themselves. They checked my pockets and took everything. I thought they would give me back what they had confiscated, but no way. I had money enough to buy new clothes, but they took all my money, my pen, my wallet—everything I had in my pockets. I was in front of my house in a few minutes.

"They took the handcuffs off my hands. I look up and down the street, and I could see nobody. It was afternoon.

I jumped from the EMS directly into the yard. I only walked three steps and I heard the car leaving. I had expected our parents would have to sign for me. They were not home, nor our brothers and sister, except for one of the youngest ones. Full of emotion, she started crying without observing the condition I was in. I was glad that nobody was home. I ran into the attic and changed my clothes. I hid the torn clothes very well. I could not tell our mother what had happened to me."

"I think it is good that you kept those clothes. They can be evidence in front of the court," I told him.

"Evidence to get a worse condemnation," Costică replied. "How can you defend yourself here, under this regime? Nobody interrogated me seriously about my motives. If I had died, who would have condemned my killers? Police have all the power. The guards only do their duty, and when they catch someone like me, they are very glad because they may get a promotion. The one who is caught at the border deserves his punishment. Who knows how many people have died at the border after the savage beatings, being shot, or being eaten by dogs? It is worse than during the time of Nero, with his bloody shows in the Roman arenas."

"After all, it is good that you escaped alive, without losing your mind. You had an unforgettable experience! I hope next time you will be luckier," I told him.

We talked a little bit about Vasile Tepei. He was now in the West, an example that leaving was possible.

Dariu and Estera had no more patience to wait for us to finish our discussion. They wanted to play with Costică. Any time they tried to hang on his hands, he winced. The wounds were almost healed; however, you could easily see the marks of the dogs' fangs.

Costică was a very good athlete. While he was studying to become an airplane mechanic, in Bucharest, he exercised in Băneasa Stadium with professional athletes. He even won some national contests. His physical fitness helped him withstand the tortures he went through, in spite of the fact that he was very young, under the age of twenty.

He left the next day. He returned to Suceava. I stayed with my wife and children. I don't know which one of us was more determined and anxious to get our revenge against such a cruel regime. Another attempt, an unsuccessful one, but we wouldn't give up until we succeeded.

## CHAPTER 6

# A PROVIDENTIAL MEETING

I T WAS THURSDAY evening, one week before Christmas. I was on my way to the church led by Pastor Codreanu. On the way, I caught up with Lenuţa Tepei, Vasile's wife. Vasile had been in Austria for more than one month. Since Vasile left, Lenuţa had become more secretive. In spite of the fact that she was an outgoing person, now she spoke carefully and seldom. She chose her friends very carefully. I was convinced she was protecting herself. She had all the more reason to do that. I would have expected her to be more confident, but, to my surprise, she was more preoccupied.

"What do you know about Vasile?" I asked her directly.

"Viorel, you know I do not know so many things. I only know he is in a refugee camp in Traiskirken, next to Vienna, waiting for someone from the United States to deposit a guarantee. He told me he has everything he needs in the camp, but he has no work, and the winter has come. It will take several months before he can go to America."

Lenuţa walked much slower than other people because she had lost one of her legs in a motorcycle accident before she married Vasile. I looked at her and couldn't see too much joy over Vasile's success, nor the hope of seeing him again. I ventured, "I think you are looking forward to seeing him again on the other side ..."

"I believe God made it possible for us to meet today. I have a big secret. I want to tell it to you on one condition. I want you to promise me something, very seriously. I will put you in contact with somebody who wants to cross the border. That person knows the way because he worked at the border. He was a tractor driver. I will put you in contact with him if you promise me one thing."

"Tell me what it is about. We are approaching the church. I cannot make promises without knowing the facts."

"This is what I want you to promise me: promise you will not let Vasile forget to call me to come to America. Since he crossed the border, I have lived with the fear that he is not going to invite me to join him. I am afraid for our children. I want to know that they will get there. I am what I am, but the children would get a better chance over there. It might happen that Vasile will not invite us to come over ... That's the promise I want you to make."

Her voice and face expressed great concern. Lenuţa used to have great confidence regarding the future, in spite of her wooden leg. She used to be cheerful, full of life. But now, thinking of her husband, she was a different person. Their children were too small to understand what was happening to their family.

"Lenuţa, I promise you that I will do everything I can to convince Vasile to get you out of here. But why are you so afraid? Has he threatened not to invite you? Has something happened that nobody knows of?"

"No. Everything is going well, but I still keep thinking it. I am obsessed with the idea that he might find somebody else there and leave us here."

"Since I have known Vasile, I haven't heard him speak about anything like this. I am sure that he will invite you over. He has always said that he is looking forward to seeing his children free in a free country. I promise you once again I will do everything I can."

"Great. I will count on your promise. The person I was telling you about is my brother. He has decided to cross the border during this holiday. He has vacation to the end of January. He is working in a mine in Maramureş now, but he is staying with us for a few days. You could meet next week at my place to get to know each other. He is a good boy, even though he is not a believer."

"But why haven't you asked him what you are asking me?"

"My brother has never been on good terms with Vasile. I don't think they could get along even for one day."

"What's your brother's name? How old is he? Why does he want to leave?"

"His name is Viorel, like yours. Actually, his real name is Vasile, but we call him Viorel. He is thirty-two years old. He used to work as a tractor driver at the cooperative by the border for several years, but later, after he got married, he moved to Maramureş. He makes better money working in the mine. I don't know why he wants to leave the country. He might not have such a good relationship with his wife. I know that he curses a lot, especially when he drinks. If he had friends who did not drink, he could be a very good person. He might even repent. My mother, my sister, and I, we have repented, but my father and brothers do not even want to hear about it."

"When is Vasile going to come to Timişoara?" I asked her.

"Next week. Come on Thursday afternoon. He will be with us. I told him about you, and he will be expecting you. From what I told him, he is looking forward to meeting you. I did not know how to find you. I prayed to God. Now I see that God answers our prayers."

We were already in the front of the church. There was no better place. I cannot remember a thing from the church service that evening, but I felt there was something mysterious beyond what I could see. Peace and trust flooded my whole being. I had heard promises like these before, and I always ended up disappointed. This accidental meeting with Lenuţa Tepei and the new connection that I got confirmed once again that God was in control. No hair fell without His knowing it. I was convinced that great things were about to happen in my life. Was it possible for my future to change completely, beginning with that evening? I would see if it was so.

On the following Thursday, I went to meet Vasile Magda. I had the maps of Yugoslavia and Italy with me. I thought they might be useful. I had received those maps from Aurel, my brother-in-law.

I rang the doorbell. The door opened immediately, and I was face-to-face with a young man. He had dark hair, combed on the left side, and on the right side the hair fell over his eye. He was thin, newly shaved, wearing a suit and tie. I was about to leave, thinking I had mistaken the door, but then I recognized Lenuţa among the people in the room. She invited me in.

The house was packed with friends and relatives. Lenuţa, in spite of the fact that she had lost one of her legs and walked with difficulty, was a person full of life.

She compensated for her infirmity with great enthusiasm. She enjoyed every day. The two children she had were very happy. She introduced all those present. Some of the adults were playing rummy at the table. The others continued their conversations. The children, who had not stopped playing, were enjoying their winter vacation. It was cold outside. I was invited to play rummy, but I refused politely.

"Mister Viorel is an old friend of my brother," Lenuța intervened, "and I am sure they have a lot of things to talk about, since they haven't seen each other for a long time."

"Please don't bother; continue to play," the one who had opened the door said. "I am not playing anymore. I have something to talk about with my friend." A lady took Vasile's place in the game. The break was short. All those present continued their activity after giving me a short look. I knew nobody and nobody knew me, except Lenuța and her children.

"Let's go to talk in the bathroom. Her one-room apartment is too small for so many people," Vasile said loudly enough to be heard by all of them. Smiling, he went toward the bathroom. I followed him without saying a word and without being surprised. The bathroom's size was half that of the room. He left the door open so the others could see somebody was in there. The children who had been hiding in there had to get out.

"I am Lenuța's brother," Vasile introduced himself.

"Viorel Bilauca, Vasile's friend. We haven't seen each other for a long time."

"Sorry for not introducing myself when I opened the door, but one of the people at the table, playing rummy, is a policeman, a neighbor and friend of my sister's. I did not want him to realize we did not know each other. It is good that you asked no questions in front of them. We would have been caught."

"I am glad to know you! I have to admit that I was surprised to see so many people. I expected there to be only the two of us. And you say he is a policeman? I hope he did not have the idea to search my pockets, because I have maps of Italy and Yugoslavia with me."

"Don't worry. Nobody suspects anything. My sister told me you want to leave the country. Me too. I am ready to leave. I am so upset with the communists, and I want to leave before the end of January when my vacation ends."

"I would like to leave before the end of December. I want to say that I am ready to leave anytime. This is what we used to say as communist pioneers."

"I see," Vasile answered, laughing. "I am also ready to leave anytime, even though I have never been a pioneer." We both laughed.

"What shall we do?" I asked. "Do you want to look over the maps?"

"Open them. I have an uncle who lives near Belgrade. I haven't seen him for a long time, but I know he lives there. I think he can help us after we cross the border." We looked over the map and identified the town where Vasile's uncle lived. We also looked for some minutes over the map of Italy.

"I think we will go to Austria," Vasile said. "I was raised with Germans and I can speak German very well. You should take the map of Yugoslavia so we can find my uncle. From there we will go to Austria or Germany."

"Germany would be very good. When shall we leave?"

"Come to Uivar on January 13. It is a Saturday. I will send Dănuț, my youngest brother, to take you through the border controls to our village. On Sunday, January 14, we will go to Pustiniș, where my wife's family lives. They asked me to help them kill two pigs that stopped growing. They want to send some meat to my family. We have two daughters."

"Will we leave at that time?" I asked him, full of hope.

"I don't think we can leave then, but Pustiniș is very close to the border, so we can see the guard booths. What else do you need?"

"I am anxious to leave, so I will be ready."

"See you in Uivar in two weeks." We shook hands in friendship, and we went out into the yard, almost unnoticed by those who were so preoccupied with their game. It was dark. We separated. I went to take the bus to Utvin, and he went back to take his place in the game.

I got home and told my wife everything that had happened. She encouraged me, but was still fearful that I should not go through the same experience as I had with the passport photos.

## CHAPTER 7
# FROM ISIM TO UIVAR

O N THE FIRST workday of the year 1979, after the New Year's Day holiday, the leadership of the factory summoned us for a compulsory general meeting. The agenda: one of our colleagues had attempted to leave across the border illegally. When I heard the agenda I thought it had to do with me, but then I found out it was Fritz Hantz, a colleague I worked with at the second laboratory. I was working on a lathe and he was working on a milling machine. He had told me that he had a pedigreed dog, especially trained to get the badgers out of ground, and that he had killed seven pigs one year just to feed this dog. He told me he could have made money with the dog by participating in contests, except that the animal had a defect in its tail.

Before the meeting, Fritz approached me and told me he had tried to cross the border on Christmas Eve. Because it was raining, he had fallen into a pit on top of a soldier. He had been unlucky, but he promised to continue trying until he could get to his relatives in Germany. "I told everybody in the workshop what happened to me. I don't know what they are going to do at the meeting."

"Fritz, you've taken a weight off my mind," I answered. "I thought it was about me. I have also tried to leave, without success as you can see. I met somebody recently, and I was ready to jump to the conclusion that it was another trap."

"Viorel, tell me what to expect. Will they put me in jail? I was so scared and upset for not having any luck! To fall on a soldier!" He complained once again that he was most unfortunate for being born in Romania.

"I can assure you they won't arrest you. They could have arrested you on the border if they had wanted to. I have been through this. They will only reprimand you in front of your colleagues. If you repeat the mistake of falling on a soldier and they catch you again … it will be different."

"I think you are perfectly logical," he said and laughed.

The meeting took place. There were the same theories, threats, and allusions to those targeted, but it passed. I was under a strict surveillance. I talked to Fritz at times, but because we worked in the same area, we had reason to talk, so we could also talk about leaving the country. I told him about my unsuccessful attempt and that I had not given up. After I was convinced that this was not a trap, I began to trust him, so I told him that on January 13, I would be in Uivar to study the border line.

"You know what," he told me very excitedly, "the same day I will be in Pustiniş. It so happens that I am enrolled in a hunting club. I was accepted to go with my dog, in spite of the fact that I was recently caught on the border. Viorel, if you can, take me with you, please. I will take you to Germany with me, I promise. Promise you won't leave without me!"

"It would be great to cross the border together," I told him. "I have nobody abroad. Let's promise each other that we will use the first opportunity to cross, and that we won't forget each other. We are the same age, we have the same profession, and we can get along wherever we end up."

Saturday, January 13, 1979, in the morning, it was still dark and cold. It was the middle of winter. The snow was not so thick. It was only about five to ten inches deep. The air was warm enough to melt it during the day, and it was not snowing very much. I and Coca, my wife, prepared to go to work as usual, but I was also preparing to make a visit to Uivar. I took with me two pairs of socks, nothing else. I did not want to draw attention by taking luggage, especially the soldiers' attention.

I looked at my children. They were still sleeping. Dariu was one and a half years old, and Estera was four and a half. We had chosen their names from the Bible, a queen and a king, and Coca and I were the servants. We served them with our love and devotion, and they were very happy. We were happy too because they were healthy, beautiful, and good children. After kissing them on their foreheads, I covered them and then left.

On Saturdays I worked until one o'clock. I finished my shift, but because I still had about two hours until the bus would leave for Uivar, I stopped by the Bega convenience store and bought some cereals and a toy bus for the children. On the way to the bus station, I stopped by the home of Lenuţa Tepei, where I was supposed to meet Dănuţ, another of her brothers. Dănuţ was the youngest in their family.

"Lenuţa, in case I don't come back from Uivar," I told her, "please give these to my wife. She will stop by on her way home. Ask her to give these to the children and to tell them that when we meet again, they will have real cars." Coca was very concerned at the idea of me crossing the border on foot, but Lenuţa tried to encourage her, reassuring her that there was no risk because Vasile, her brother, knew the border very well.

"Okay, I will tell her that, but do not forget what you promised me."

"I promised, so I will keep my promise."

Dănuţ, a seventeen-year-old boy, was thin, of medium stature, brown-haired and cheerful. He was dressed lightly, as all the young people did. He went to the door, ready to leave. "Lenuţa, I am leaving. I kiss you! Don't you have any luggage?" he asked me, seeing me carrying a folder only.

"It is enough. I don't want to raise any suspicions among the soldiers."

"Do you have your ID with you? Where do you live?"

"I live here in Utvin. I have my ID, my service record, and my birth certificate."

"The ID should be enough."

We continued our trip, talking only about generalities. We got to Uivar easily. Dănuţ didn't know who I was, but he never asked. He didn't ask me where I knew his older brother from nor what my business was in Uivar. We didn't talked about a departure plan. I had had no restrictions from Vasile about talking with Dănuţ. This visit was only supposed to be a study visit. Dănuţ knew was that I was a good friend of Vasile and that I was going to Uivar to talk to him; that was it. Dănuţ was not interested in Vasile's friends or business.

I met Vasile in the village, immediately after getting off the bus. He was waiting for us in the bus station.

"Dănuţ!" he shouted when he saw us. "Did he make any trouble?"

"No, dear brother. Don't you know me?" Dănuţ answered. "I can handle everything very well."

We headed toward a house. The weather was cold. It took several hours to get there. Vasile had left Uivar many years before, but he still knew the whole village. He had something to talk about with every person he met. He spoke aloud using all kinds of "Romanian adjectives," without any reserve. He was very confident and bold, behaving like a boss.

It was midnight when we got to his family home. It was cold in the house. The fire had gone out long before. We found their father at home. He was sleeping in a bed in the kitchen, lying on his right side. He was covered all over, so we could just see his face. We did not wake him up. We had not decided yet what to say to family and neighbors about my presence in Uivar.

"Vasile, what are we going to tell those who may be curious? We are so close to the border!"

"I don't think anybody will ask, but those who do ask will be sorry!" he answered, laughing. Vasile was so confident. "My fellow villagers do not usually ask anything."

# CHAPTER 8
## AT PUSTINIŞ

WE SPENT SATURDAY night making plans. We finally went to bed with the intention of continuing the next morning after returning from Pustiniş. Vasile had two sisters-in-law, the sisters of his wife. They were the ones who had the two pigs that had stopped growing. With the excuse of butchering the pigs, we could get to within one mile of the border. Everything was prepared, to the smallest detail, so we could get close to the border without any problems.

Sunday morning, even though it was freezing outside, we left for Pustiniş. The policeman who was patrolling on the railway station platform was looking carefully at everyone. His duty was to identify any unfamiliar person. Vasile started talking to him as we approached, so he asked nothing about me. I was protected by Vasile. The policeman did not seem too aggressive, but he could ask anyone unwelcome questions. He did not ask to check my ID or if I had a border visa or any other frontier document. He was relying on the soldiers who were responsible for checking the trains.

The train going to Pustiniş, coming from Timişoara, was almost empty. The soldiers did not have too much controlling to do that Sunday morning, immediately after the winter holidays. Guests had already gone home, so the only people left were locals who knew each other very well.

We had a friendly conversation with the soldiers. We talked about liberation, about family, about the places they came from, about their professions, and about the plans they had for the time after their military service. I was interested especially to know when they were going to be discharged. I found out they had less than two months left. That meant that the present cycle was about to be discharged having completed almost eight months of their tour. That also meant that the guards currently on the border was less vigilant. Newly enrolled soldiers were more dangerous and more alert. With the passing of time, soldiers became more accustomed to their duty of guarding the border, so they became less vigilant.

Another important fact I found out was that the watch dogs were sent every year for two months of training. During January and February, there were no dogs on the border. These details gave me a lot of courage.

"I hope the same soldiers will be on the train tomorrow. We will not have to worry about them," I thought aloud after getting off the train. The soldiers who patrolled the train were changed often so as not to make friends.

"Tomorrow? What is going to happen tomorrow?" Vasile asked after a while.

"Tomorrow is going to be Monday. If everything goes well, we could go to Pustiniş for the last time tomorrow, and from there continue to—"

"I cannot say anything because I have not made plans to leave so early," Vasile interrupted. "Anyway, today we have to look very carefully toward the border to see where the guard posts are and establish a route to avoid any guard posts on our way. We can see the border very well from behind the house of my brother-in-law, so we will have to study it whenever we have the opportunity."

"I cannot wait to see those guard posts. Tomorrow night we can cross the border for sure."

"It seems to me that you are in a hurry, more than me," Vasile chastised me. "We will have to be careful not to raise any suspicions among my relatives."

We left the railway station and walked quickly due to the cold. We had to cross the whole village to get to Vasile's relatives. Pustiniş was a typical Romanian village, with a wide main street and houses covered by a fresh layer of snow. It looked like something from a fairytale. You could not see the older snow, but it was obvious that the road had previously been cleared. The tractors had made a channel that, with a new layer of snow, looked very beautiful.

We were in the middle of the village when, unexpectedly, I heard somebody calling my name. "How are you, Viorel? Have you been hunting anything?" It was my colleague with the pedigreed dog.

"Hantz! What a small world! Are you following me?" I shouted.

"This is my cousin. I was telling you about him. He does not want to cross, but he came hunting with me. We are going to meet the hunters. Have you had any chance to see the border line?"

"Not yet. Today I will have the chance to see it closely. If you don't see me tomorrow afternoon at work, you will know that I have left!" I told him that only to upset him.

"If I don't come to work tomorrow, you should know that I have left," he replied. All four of us laughed at this good joke. "It is set then. Anyway, whoever has the chance to cross first should not forget the other one."

"Don't talk too much in the middle of the village," Vasile warned us. "It might raise suspicions. We are strangers to this village. You can trust nobody."

We left in a hurry. We walked even slower, not only because of the snow, but because we thought to establish a route for the next time we crossed the village to go to the border. Vasile knew the village very well, but I wanted to see how to get to the West.

The streets of the village were not complicated, but we had to be very well oriented. We had to know what to do in case one of us had to turn back home. The heavy clouds could become an obstacle. A clean sky would help a lot. The weather was changing. The wind was blowing slowly, but strongly enough to move the clouds. We could not predict the weather for the next day.

"Don't worry," Vasile said after a break. "My sister-in-law lives on the last street, which backs onto the border. We can get to her without any problem. From there to the border, there are no more streets and no other houses. You will see."

"The village and the villagers are the first obstacles that we need to avoid," I told him. "There will be other people on the nine o'clock train. We will have to rid ourselves of them without letting them know where we are going, where we are spending the night, and whom we are visiting so late. I hope there won't be unwanted people on the train. I am thinking of other relatives who might want us to talk to them or visit them."

"Tomorrow is going to be Monday. People are going to be busy. I do not think we will have any unpleasant surprises."

As we got closer to the end of the village, the risk of being seen by somebody the night before leaving decreased. We entered the yard of Vasile's sister-in-law. We met more relatives there. Among them was another sister-in-law and her husband. The house and the yard seemed crowded, even though there were only seven people. We started killing and cutting up the pigs at noon. We dealt with two pigs. It warmed up outside when the sun came out from behind the clouds and the snow began to melt a little bit.

When evening came, all the work was done. We hurried to catch the five o'clock train, but we had to promise to come back next day because they wanted to thank us for the help and to send something to Vasile's daughters, their nieces.

We went to the railway station. On our way, I could not stop thinking of the plans we had already made and of the things that were going to happen.

The same evening, we visited a family whose husband had left the country illegally. We hoped to get some information. The one who had recently crossed the border used to be called "the soldier." (Everybody knew he had been in the army.) The soldier's wife, two little children, and her parents were at home, but the wife was scared by our presence there. When she saw us at the door, talking about crossing the border, she panicked. We could not find out anything from her. She hid immediately with her children in the other room.

Her mother, who was a believer, talked to us, but not before we convinced her we were not from the secret police. I told her I was a believer too. I also told her about the people I knew and about some of my relatives. She opened up only later. She showed us the radio he had sent from Austria, as proof that he had arrived in that country, but gave us no other information about crossing.

Before we left, after we told them that we also planned to cross the border next day, the soldier's wife came out of the other room. She had heard all our conversation. She felt better when we took the great risk of telling them our plans to leave the country. She could turn us in to the police, but we trusted her. We would have loved to meet her husband in the refugee camp and bring him good news about his family.

She told us she did not know the exact place where her husband had crossed the border. She only knew that he was caught by the Serbians and then allowed to go on to Austria. This was all we could find out.

It was becoming very cold outside. It snowed several times throughout Sunday, with big and unusual snowflakes. The snowflakes turned into ice and the wind started to blow. The snow slowly covered everything. The weather was changing due to the wind. The heavy, dark clouds moved fast, letting the moon and some stars appear from time to time. It was not bad, because we needed both dark and light. Our problem was that we needed that weather for the following day.

"Is there anybody who could give us more information tonight?" I asked Vasile after we left the soldier's family.

"The soldier is the only person who has left recently without returning," Vasile answered. He showed concern and some dissatisfaction over the fact that we could not find out more useful details. "I don't know how, but he succeeded. I thought his family was going to tell us more, but she doesn't know or is afraid to tell."

"It wasn't a great day," I continued. "We could not see the guard booths because of the snow."

When we got home, we found Dănuţ talking to Lucian, a friend of his. Dănuţ looked at us and asked, "Hey, do you want to cross the border?" (As if he weren't aware of that.)

"Yes," Vasile answered.

"When? How can we help? We can help you!"

"Do you want to come with us?" Vasile asked, mostly from curiosity.

"No, but we know many things around here ..."

"We want to leave tomorrow night, on the nine o'clock train to Pustiniş, if you don't mind," I intervened.

"Okay. You will need food for two or three days and some white sheets for camouflage. Everything will be prepared tomorrow afternoon."

"Great, boys. We owe you," we answered and then left.

"Vasile, what is your opinion about these boys? How old are they?" I asked.

"Dănuţ is seventeen. His friend, Lucian is ... nineteen, I think. They are very good friends. I hardly know Dănuţ. He has grown a lot. He is independent now. I see they get along very well. They do everything together. They love adventure. They don't like to work. I don't know how they manage, but they do. They do not have jobs, they are not sick, and they haven't been in jail. I thought perhaps they were planning on coming with us, but it seems they haven't decided yet. Less for us to worry about, isn't it?"

"It is so," I answered. "I have tried before with my brother and my brother-in-law, but I have learned the lesson. If we are fewer in number, there are fewer opinions, so there are greater chances of success."

"This kid, with his friend, if he determines to do something, there is nothing that will change his plans.

They seek adventure. If something gets into their heads, they won't give up until they do it."

We left the next day on the eleven o'clock train to Pustiniş. There were very few people in the village and in the railway stations. We felt exposed. It was obvious we still had vacation. The train was almost empty. We could go to Vasile's relatives without incident. We were already familiar with the village.

It was snowing from time to time, so there were about ten inches of fresh snow. The weather was not so cold. We ate the food we were supposed to have eaten the day before. It was tasty. Because we wanted to catch the three o'clock train to Uivar, we said good-bye early. Vasile got a little package for his wife and daughters: some meat, some pork rind, a sausage, and two liters of raspberry wine for his wife. I also got some pork rind and a fresh sausage for my wife and children. We wished each other happy New Year and then left. It was Monday afternoon.

The train to Uivar was almost empty. The same soldiers looked at us, asked the same questions, and received the same answers. I assured them that we still had two more weeks of holiday, so we would meet again. They needed to know this because we had to return to Pustiniş the same evening, for the last time.

## CHAPTER 9

# THE SHEETS WITH ANOTHER PURPOSE

ONCE WE GOT home, Dănuț and Lucian were waiting for us with food for the trip and some big white sheets.

"Are you not coming?" Vasile asked once more.

"We will come later," Dănuț answered. "You leave first, and if they catch you and do something to you, they will not have to deal with us. Then we will leave too. Nobody can catch us. We have prepared all you need. You have very little luggage, so as not to arouse suspicions."

"What are we going to tell the soldiers on the train if they ask us what we are looking for in Pustiniş this time?" I asked more for myself.

"We will say that we are going to buy some raspberry wine," Vasile answered, looking at the bottle in front of him. "Boys, do we have some food from our relatives? Prepare everything and put it in my suitcase."

"Good idea," Dănuț said. "But what are you doing with a full bottle in Pustiniş if you are wanting to buy more wine?"

"This bottle has only two liters. We want to buy more."

We had to wait three more hours. The time passed slowly. We had nothing to do. We were ready to leave. Dănuţ and Lucian disappeared. In the meantime, I tried to remember the moment when Vasile decided to leave the country. I didn't know exactly, but now he was fully dedicated to it. Maybe he just did not want to disappoint me or look like a coward.

The last hour was the most difficult. We could not stay outside because it was cold, we could not stay in the railway station because of the unwelcome questions, and sleeping was out of the question.

After only a few minutes, Dănuţ and Lucian came in, very excited and anxious to leave. The meat was boiled, put in the jars, and then placed in Vasile's suitcase. The suitcase seemed empty except for the food and the sheets.

"Are you ready?" Dănuţ asked.

"We are. We have been waiting for an hour and a half," Vasile answered.

"We are coming with you. We have two more sheets. What do you say? Will you take us with you?"

"Are you kidding?"

"Seriously! We decided in haste, but it is better to be together. Our plan was not to leave before getting our revenge on these people, but this afternoon we changed our minds. Let's share the luggage and go."

I looked at Vasile inquiringly, but I asked no question. I arranged the food, the sheets, and some other stuff in Vasile's bag. That bag was heavier, so Dănuţ and Lucian took it, holding one handle each. I put some sheets and socks in my folder, and Vasile took the bottle. We made sure we had all our documents with us. The father of Vasile and Dănuţ wasn't home and their mother had gone to Timişoara before the holidays, so we could not say good-bye to them.

It was quiet, cold, and dark outside, and the neighbors were in their houses. Nobody would have supposed that an empty-handed group of people like us would dare to leave the country in weather like that. We walked slowly. We spoke loudly and laughed just to get warm. There was nothing special at the railway station: the same soldiers, the same bored policeman, and the same people. Nobody had any new questions.

When we got to Pustiniş, we got off the train together with a handful of people. Everyone hurried to get home except us. We were leaving home. Nobody cared about us. We walked slower than the others in order to let them get home. Small clouds danced in the clear sky with a full moon. It was snowing from time to time. The moon appeared and disappeared behind the clouds. It would have been better if it had been colder because the ice wasn't thick enough to hold us. Not everything can be perfect.

When we arrived in front of the house of Vasile's sister-in-law, we looked around very carefully. Everything was silent. The whole village seemed to have fallen asleep.

"It is okay here," Vasile said. "I saw yesterday that there is a step in the fence between my brother-in-law's house and his left neighbor. We can cross the fence using it, so let's look for it. This way we can jump over the fence without waking up all the dogs in the neighborhood."

"And if somebody sees us, what are we going to say?" Dănuţ asked.

"We'll say we got the wrong house. But let's not think of that."

"I think I found the step you were talking about," I told them.

Because the fence was tall, the neighbors had decided to leave passages for those wanted to go behind their houses. Those who had to work the land behind the houses had to cross their yards—something not so pleasant. A wooden board was put into the fence, supported by two pillars half the height of the fence, to make the crossing easy. The method had been used for a long time.

In a few moments, the four of us were on the other side of the fence. The neighbors were sleeping. There was no light, no dogs barking. We headed toward the border in single file. We felt like we were floating. We could not hear our steps, nor even our breaths. In a few seconds, we were behind the houses.

After several hundred feet, we heard voices. They were speaking loudly about tractors. We realized we were getting close to the SMT (mechanized section of tractors). Our path was leading directly to it. We might have been walking for half an hour. We could see nothing because of a dark cloud that covered the moon completely.

"Are you sure there is an SMT?" Vasile asked quietly.

"Why couldn't we see it yesterday?" I asked.

"You can hardly see it from behind my brother-in-law's house. An SMT is not so big, and with this fresh snow, it is more difficult to see. I did not see it, but I know it is there. It has been there since the cooperative was established."

"If this is the SMT, I think I saw it," I interrupted him. "But it was more to the right, and I know there is a guard post in that direction."

"That's it. We have to go more to the left. This path leads to the SMT."

We made a correction to the left, approximately forty-five degrees, and continued our journey. The wind that brought waves of snow that blew even the largest clouds across the sky. For some minutes everything became clear around us. Our eyes scanned the darkness that we had gotten used to already. We stopped.

"I think it is time to put on the sheets," Dănuț said. "It seems to me that we are very close to the border."

"Sure, sure," we all agreed.

I was the only one who had a light-colored coat and a brown hat with white fur inside. The back side of the hat was worn rolled up, but when the weather was very cold it could be unrolled to cover the ears and neck. I had it rolled up, and I rolled up the peak too, so my head was white all around. Vasile and Lucian had black jackets with hoods. Dănuț had a long coat and a green hat with a small peak, like Robin Hood. It was fashionable, but would not keep him warm. We put the bed sheets on our head and after we tied them in the front we continued our journey.

We leaned forward. We were sure nobody could see us; we were one with the ground. We stopped often just to look through the night. The dark was very deceptive, especially after the snow. The dim light coming from the snow created an optical illusion, similar to a mirage in the desert on a hot day. Everything seemed to move. We stepped very carefully.

We were ready to give up several times in front of some small trees. We had the impression that there were many soldiers watching us. It was very risky. According to the military's "Regulations," a guard had to hail anybody who got close to the watch post, ask for the password, and then shoot if he did not get the correct password. But most of the time, especially on the border during winter and at midnight, a guard would shoot first and then ask who it was. "It is better for his mother to cry than for my mother!" was the saying, and the thought of a court martial terrorized the poor soldiers.

"Guys, we have to keep our eyes open," I told them. "Each of us should look in one direction and, if you see something, pull us all down. We are so close to the border. We will communicate through signs, not words."

"Agreed," Vasile whispered.

We had been sitting for a minute and looking at a bush.

"It looks like a soldier with a dog," Dănuţ said, hardly breathing. The words stopped on his lips.

"There are no dogs on the border," I told him. "They would have already been on us. It is only an illusion."

"I think you are right," the others said.

It was almost midnight when the moon came out from behind heavy clouds. It was a miracle. I looked at the moon and realized we were heading south. We had to go west. When we had turned left before the SMT, we had turned too much to the south. A compass would have been very useful. Compasses and infrared binoculars were illegal in Romania.

We followed the moon. We thanked God for that miracle. But a few minutes later, we were again in the dark. After that moment of light, the darkness seemed more intense. We could hardly see what we had previously seen before the coming of the light. We walked slowly and quietly.

Vasile, who was first, stopped. "We've reached a channel. It is full of water and not too frozen," he said. "Let's follow it. Maybe we can find a bridge." We followed without saying a word.

After a few minutes I suggested, "If I am not wrong, we are going parallel to the channel. We have to cross it; otherwise we will get to Jimbolia or Giurgiu. These channels go parallel to the border line. Most of them have alarm wires. Be very careful not to touch one."

We looked at each other for a few moments. We were already very tired. In spite of that, none of us showed any sign of discouragement. Dănuţ, the youngest, who was not even eighteen, carried the bag with the food. Lucian, his friend, was very courageous. He didn't talk too much with us, but he talked all the time with Dănuţ. He was very cooperative. I think he trusted Vasile, who was the oldest among us.

Vasile was five years older than me. He carried the two-liter bottle of raspberry wine. He shook it from time to time to make sure it wasn't frozen. At the age of twenty-seven, I was still in good shape. We all walked resolutely.

I was the last one in the formation. Besides my mission to cover the back of the group, I was also determined to help any who might fall due to the severe weather conditions. I prayed that none of us would break a leg. It would have been a disaster. Walking on a plowed field was difficult in normal weather conditions, but in the current conditions it was hard to even imagine. Vasile was in the front. He pretended to know the area better than us.

After we were convinced that we had to cross the channel, we jumped over the cold water. It was impossible not to get wet. The ice was too shallow to hold us, so our feet broke through and we got wet up to the knees. We quickly got on the other side and continued our journey. The furrows from the plowing were even deeper here.

No regrets, no discontent. Nobody said a word. We were saving energy.

We walked like four robots. Our feet went in all directions. After we corrected our direction once again, we got to another channel about a thousand feet away, similar to the first one. This one was almost full of water. We looked very carefully to see if there was any wire, but we saw none. We jumped on the other side, as in the case of the first channel. We got wet once again, but we were not complaining.

It must have been past midnight. We could not see a watch face. At one moment, we heard voices in the distance, from both sides. We stopped. We even held our breaths. We could not understand what they were saying, but we supposed they were soldiers from the guard posts.

"Who understands what they are saying?" Vasile asked. "Have they noticed us?"

"I don't think so," I said. "Normally they would keep quiet to let us get closer. If they are making so much noise in the night, they are either changing the guard or have caught somebody and are celebrating."

We kept quiet for some minutes, trying to decipher the voices that paralyzed us. We could hear our hearts beating.

After ten minutes, the voices ended. It was again silent. We realized that the noise had come from the change of guards. We waited some more, and when we were convinced that they were nothing to do with us, we continued our walk.

The white sheets proved to be very useful, in spite of the fact that they could not cover us completely. They hid us more than we had imagined. On that deeply plowed field, we also looked like snowed-over furrows. We advanced very slowly, the ground increasingly inclined. In spite of that, we could not walk without any noise. Our feet slid uncontrollably. The furrows became deeper as we got closer to the border, which was understandable. Such ground would slow down any fugitive. If you got caught, you had no chance to run; you had to give up.

After another thousand feet, we got to another channel. At first we thought there was only some water at the bottom. We were ready to jump. Vasile, who was in front, signaled us that there was something in our way.

"Careful, fellows! Alarm wire," whispered Vasile nervously. "Make sure you don't pull it!"

We were very tired. It was more and more difficult to control our movements. The sheets that had been so useful were hanging now like icicles and could catch on any alarm wire.

On the left in the channel, a few feet away, an anchor made of rail track was holding the wire taut. A thin layer of snow, blown by the wind that had started an hour before, made both the anchor and the wire visible.

This kind of wire was stretched about three feet above the ground along the border line. They were installed on the way down into the channel, so the person who wanted to jump over the channel would catch it. The water level was maintained in such a way that a person who wanted to jump over without getting wet would have to run. In the summer it was very hard to see the alarm wire. The wires were connected at one end to a post and at the other to a firing pin, so the moment you pulled on the wire, the pin launched a signal rocket. The guards would notice and there would be nothing you could do. There were also false alarms triggered by wild animals.

We crossed the wire by leaning on the post that was holding it. Without saying a word, but with our hearts beating very fast, we looked once again at the moon that appeared from behind the clouds. The wind got stronger, blowing the clouds faster. When the sky was covered with clouds, the night was so dark that you could hardly see. We stopped several times, wondering where to go. We bypassed anything that seemed to move. We corrected our direction several times, following the moon like ghosts in the night. We continued swimming desperately among the deep furrows.

We avoided useless talk. We had two reasons not to talk: first, not to be heard, and second, to save energy. We lost our sense of distance and direction. We walked through the dark and the wind without any marks to follow. When the moon came out, we could correct our direction. We always found we were going in a wrong direction. We thought we had to be close to the border, but with all the corrections, we did not know where we actually were. I had heard of many cases in which those who wanted to cross the border ended up going alongside it until morning … when they were caught.

The furrows in front of us seemed endless. We stopped more often to recover our strength. The weariness was taking its toll. Dănuţ stopped talking to Lucian for a while. They had been murmuring to one another all the time.

"Boys," Vasile said, "who wants to drink from this raspberry juice? I want to leave this bottle behind. I think it is almost frozen."

We each drank a sip, but everyone complained it was too cold, so Vasile left the bottle on the field. The cold weather did not allow us to stay in one place, so we continued our journey to the West.

After a few minutes, we saw on the horizon something that looked like a forest. Without leaves, the trees were almost invisible that season, but I thought we were close enough. The forest had its advantages and disadvantages. We could hide very easily, but the guards could also hide very easily. Then, walking through a forest was impossible without making noise. The broken tree branches would crack under our feet in the winter when snow covered any path. Even during the summer, it would not have been good to follow trodden paths. You could meet the wrong person.

We continued our journey in the same formation, each of us supervising his sector. We faced false alarms at every step. When one of us seemed to see something moving, he lowered himself, and we all did the same without saying a word. We all had good sight; none of us were wearing glasses.

We got closer to the forest. We analyzed very carefully any noise. We could only hear our breaths and the muffled noises of our feet sliding on the snowy furrows. The snow muffled our chaotic steps and our frequent slips and falls.

When we got close to the forest, we realized it was only a curtain of tall, rare trees, with lots of bushes between the trees. When the moon came out, we saw a village beyond the trees. Nobody asked any questions. We continued our journey, following the moon and the person in front of us, except Vasile, who followed his instincts.

After a few minutes, Vasile stopped. "We have to cross another channel," he whispered. "It seems full of water. It is wide; we cannot jump over it. Let's hope the ice can hold us. Otherwise we will take a cold bath. We will have to cross it one by one."

"Don't yield if the ice breaks," Dănuţ added.

Trying to see if the ice was thick enough, we stepped carefully to get to it.

"This is not ice!" I exclaimed. "It is the border line!"

"You are right; it truly is the border line," the other three confirmed before I could finish my sentence.

We looked around. We saw nobody. We could hear nothing, as if we were the only survivors on the face of the earth. We searched behind the shallow snow in several places to convince ourselves that we were on the border. It was thirty to fifty feet wide. It looked like a vegetable garden, carefully raked. The joy, the tiredness, and the emotion of the moment made us forget our walking order. Dănuţ went ahead.

"The wire! The wire!" I shouted. "Dănuţ, wait! Don't move! There is a wire on the middle of the border! You touched it." We all froze.

When I saw the stretched wire, my heart stopped beating. One more step and the rocket could have been launched, revealing us. Dănuţ had touched the wire with the frozen corner of the sheet that he was pulling through the snow. I don't know how I saw it, but I ran with lightning speed and caught it before it could be released. With all the cold, I felt my spine wet with sweat.

I carefully held the wire until Vasile and Lucian passed it. Then I put it very, very slowly back into its normal position. We all stopped and waited a couple of seconds. There was no rocket released.

We searched under the snow to convince ourselves that we had just crossed the border and that we were on the other side. We stopped again. We looked at each other. We were bent over with frozen sheets on our backs. Awakened from a nightmare, with serene faces, eyes full of tears of joy and an indescribable satisfaction, we looked at each other as people do after an unexpected victory. We were ready to burst with joy.

We did not celebrate. It wasn't the time yet, nor the place. We had to leave the border behind quickly. There could have been Serbian guards nearby.

"Keep quiet," Vasile warned us. "There are fake border lines in some places. When I was a tractor driver, we plowed and harrowed them. Some people, after crossing them, thought they were in Yugoslavia, but they were still in Romania. They rejoiced in vain, because after that they were not careful anymore, so they were discovered and caught. Let's postpone celebrating the victory."

We went fifty more feet and then crossed a channel without water, three feet wide and another three feet deep. We passed through the curtain of trees we had seen earlier and stopped in front of a bridge that crossed a river. I had had no time to study a strategic map of Romania. I did not have one at home because that kind of map was kept under lock and key.

"What river is this?" I asked.

"I think it is Bega Veche," Vasile answered, unsure.

"What does it matter?" Dănuț said full of satisfaction and contempt toward the regime. "We are not interested!"

We approached the bridge with the same caution we had shown when we approached the border. What if the border we had crossed was a fake one? The bridge was much longer than it should have been. The water was shallow, or seemed so to us. The riverbed appeared narrow. The long bridge made us wonder. It could have been guarded. My brother Costică had been caught while crossing a bridge.

We decided to cross on the bridge. The water under the bridge wasn't frozen. We could hear it rippling. We realized it must be deep; otherwise it would have been frozen. We saw no footprints or car tracks in the snow. It meant that no patrol had passed by there for a long time. We gathered our courage and crossed.

"Why does this bridge have no railing?" Dănuţ asked. "It is long and dangerous."

No answer. Who cared about that?

After we crossed the bridge, we arrived behind some gardens. There was no fence and no other obstacle. We saw a row of houses at the other end of the field, about three hundred feet away.

"What village is this?" Dănuţ asked. "A Romanian or a Serbian village?"

"It is hard to tell by listening to the dogs barking," I told him jokingly, "but wait here until I come back." I had studied Russian in school for eight years, and I hoped it would help me. "I see a plow. I will try and read what make it is. I hope it is Serbian ..."

I approached the plow abandoned in the snow. After finding the rusty tag, I read something that was not Romanian. I could not understand what was written there. I couldn't even read all of it, but I was glad for the first time that I could not understand. We were in Yugoslavia!

I could not shout for joy because I did not want to wake up the dogs, but I felt for the second time a warmth on my back. This time it was not fear, but satisfaction.

Finally I got back to my friends, who were waiting for some good news, I was living one of the greatest victories in life. The dream I had had for more than seven years was coming true. It happens often that what you dream during the night comes true during the day, but now it happened vice versa: what I had dreamed during the day came true on the night of January 15, 1979, around two o'clock in the morning.

"We are in Yugoslavia," I told them, full of joy. "It is Serbian writing on the plow. We did it!"

"The border that we crossed was the real one," Vasile confirmed, "and that small channel after the tree curtain was the Serbian border line. The land between the two lines was the neutral territory. There is nothing that the Romanians can do to us!"

"We are free! We are free!" we murmured without ceasing. Our hearts changed their beat. If our hearts had beaten fast due to the risk we were exposed to, now they beat fast due to the joy of victory. Courage had won, despite the fear and the risks.

To have courage means to see the risks and overcome them. In our case, courage and the desire for freedom gave us the manhood to overcome all obstacles. Everything had happened in three days. For Dănuţ and Lucian, everything had happened in a few hours. It was unexpected for Vasile too, who had planned to leave the country, but not so soon.

"I cannot stand this sheet anymore," Dănuţ said. "It bothers me; I will leave it here." Without any permission, he took it off his head and put it down. We did the same. We got rid of the sheets and, guiding ourselves by looking at the houses, we headed toward the center of the village. Backs straight, walking on smooth land, we felt like giants in comparison to the way we had walked for the last few hours.

Some dogs started barking, but nobody woke up. At that time and on that cold night, who would have imagined that somebody would risk crossing the border illegally? In other weather conditions, anything was possible. On a summer night, a Serbian peasant might have come out of his house, hoping to find a Romanian to turn in to the police. It was said that the Serbians were very patriotic and turned in anybody, without expecting any reward from the Serbian government.

We reached the front fence without incident and jumped over it without making any noise. We were on the main street of the village. Lights hung on wooden pillars, as in our own country, lighting the center of the village. On our right, about six hundred feet away, was the end of the bus line. We could see the tracks of the last bus that left the village. We looked at the placard of the store; it was written in Serbian.

"Can we shout now?" Lucian asked. We had hardly heard him before. He had been talking to Dănuţ all the time, but not to us. Probably he was studying now.

"We can," I answered, "but not too loud and not in Romanian. The guards might hear us. They would gladly come and send us back to our own country."

"I have heard of many situations," Vasile said, "in which Romanian soldiers crossed into Yugoslavia and took fugitives back home, dead or alive."

"In the meantime, let's eat something," Dănuţ said. "This bag is hurting my back."

"Let's see what food you packed for me. I will see now how much you care for me," Vasile replied.

"I am lucky I like to cook. You will be convinced I am a great cook!"

"I hope it is warm; otherwise we will disqualify you." I helped Vasile.

"Lucian and I are champions in the kitchen, regardless of your opinion," Dănuţ said. He got the food out of the bag that he could hardly take off his shoulders. "Oven-cooked fresh meat from your sister-in-law, but it has frozen a little bit. We should have eaten it last night, but nobody was hungry then. The fresh sausages that your

wife and daughters should have eaten are as frozen as the
meat. We put some pickles in this jar, first-class. They are
not frozen."

We each took a piece of meat and a piece of sausage
and tried to chew what we could unfreeze. Everything
was frozen. We had no water to drink. Instead, we ate
some snow. We could not tell the taste of the meat, but it
was good considering the situation we were in.

I looked at my watch. It was two thirty-five in the
morning. We sat for several minutes, even lying down in
the middle of the road, on the fresh snow. We could finally
stretch our bones. But we jumped back on our feet so as
not to fall asleep in the snow.

While I was lying down, I imagined my whole family
being in the West. I remembered Joseph from the Bible.
Time did not matter anymore. My desire was to get all my
family out of Romania. Besides my wife and children, I
had five brothers, six sisters, my parents, and all my in-
laws. Dreams for the future … I knew they were possible.
The first step toward a new future was almost complete.

After a few minutes of relaxation, we realized how
tired we were. We stood up and continued our journey,
walking with the energy we had left exactly down the
middle of the road. We knew we had to get as far as
possible from the border. We did not trust the Yugoslavian
villagers who lived close to it.

We had been walking for about an hour when Dănuţ
began to show signs of exhaustion. He was almost sleeping
while standing. Vasile and Lucian held him and dragged
him as if he were injured. We were walking like robots.
The cold wind was getting stronger, and it started sleeting.

I wondered how far we would be able to go, where we
were going to stop and get warm. We had no more food.

We had abandoned the bag. It had become a hindrance, so the boys just left it on the roadside. It would have been nice to go through a larger town with open stores. We could have found shelter. But this was an impossible dream in the small villages where people know each other very well.

We walked without any direction. We made some jokes and laughed. Actually, we were laughing in order to get warm. We imagined what the guards would say when they realized that someone had crossed the border. We had made more trails than we intended because we wanted to make sure that we crossed the true border. It must have seemed that a whole troop had crossed. What reports would the guards write? What lies would they invent? Was the guard responsible for that sector going to suffer?

"Look, a hut," Vasile said.

We had left the village behind, and after few miles, in the middle of a field, on the left side of the road, we could see a wooden hut.

"Let's go in to rest a little bit," Vasile suggested. "This kid is exhausted. We cannot carry him anymore. He is wearying us."

"Let me help." I took Lucian's place. He was ready to fall down.

"Who is going to help me?" Lucian asked, joking. "I am freezing now. I was better when we were close to each other."

As we headed toward the abandoned hut, which must have belonged to a peasant who had some beehives, I saw a river in the distance. "What river is that?" I asked. I was trying to keep them talking and laughing. Only the jokes had kept us warm all the way.

"If I am not wrong, that must be the Timiş," Vasile answered.

Dănuţ did not hear a thing. Lucian, still joking, said, "Gentlemen, I have never been here before. I don't know this place, and I know nobody here. Don't ask such silly questions. What I will remember forever is this terrible cold. I cannot feel anything. It seems that my legs are not mine. I feel them as if they were sticks. I think they are frozen due to that water."

We entered the abandoned hut. We had hoped to be warmer inside, but there was not such a big difference. The only improvement was that the wind was not blowing as much. Somebody had stolen what he could from the little hut—the door, the windows—so what had seemed to be a shelter proved to be little more than a wooden floor. The floorboards had some cracks, so we could feel the wind blowing even through them.

Dănuţ, who woke up glad that we had found a shelter, tried to make some fire with Lucian. They made kindling from a stick that had been left by the thieves and tried hard. They gave up after a few minutes when they had used up all the matches. They lay down in the corner of the hut and fell asleep. They snored. Vasile looked for another corner in which to rest. Without saying another word, all three of them were snoring. The corner that was left for me was the worst. It was next to the door, and the wind seemed to turn right over there. I was polite and stayed awake to watch.

I considered letting them sleep, but the minutes became longer and harder as the tiredness that had accumulated lately asked for its tribute. Sandman was visiting me. I imagined in those moments what people would say about us if they found us dead, frozen to death. What bad news would that be for our families? Our children would have nightmares anytime they remembered us. Terrible!

I could not let that happen. I stood and pulled Vasile up. I urged him to wake his brother and leave; otherwise people would find us frozen to death.

Vasile stood up with some difficulty, but after he realized the risk of freezing to death, he helped me wake the boys. They began to move only after we threatened to leave them there to die and be eaten by wolves.

We got to the main road. We could see a village in the distance, about one mile away. Morning was near; the moon had already set. We could not see the sky anymore. A cold sleet wet us to the bones. We were indifferent to the cold wind. We were glad morning was here. Light would not keep us warm, but at least it gave the impression of warmth.

In the station situated at the center of the village, there was a bus, probably the six o'clock one that was taking people to work. We gazed at that new and nice bus, very well illuminated, the windows frozen and covered in snow on the outside. They turned on the engine that promised heat and comfort.

"I wonder where this bus is going?" I asked, seeing that the others were saying nothing. No answer. "I haven't seen any mileage poles on the roadside, as we have in Romania. That would tell us the name of the town and how far it is to the next one, but here we have nothing."

"I also realized that there is no sign around," Vasile confirmed after a while, "but we have needed none so far. The moon, the wind, the sleet, and the dogs have accompanied us."

"We could get on this, but we might go directly to Jimbolia," Lucian said. "It is said that for every Romanian given back, the Serbians receive a wagon of salt. This is the ransom Romania pays! Living or dead, the same ransom."

"And after they get you, they send you to the salt mine, for you to pay your own debt," I responded. "And for sure you have to pay it for those who haven't been caught too."

We laughed and continued our journey. We left the bus with its engine running, facing in the opposite direction. We headed on foot toward the west, with what strength we had left. The desire to sleep passed off. We felt as if we had slept all night. We crossed the village slowly by the main road. The road looked like a channel because of the frozen snow on each side, making it hard for two cars to pass by at the same time. The bus we had seen in the village passed us without stopping. It had changed its direction somewhere, probably in the first village we had been through. It was going slowly due to the difficult weather conditions. The tires followed the same tracks the bus must have made on its way into the village.

The day had come. I looked at my watch, which showed Romanian time, to see that it was past eight o'clock. Looking on the right, I saw a cornfield. The wind continued to blow, and the sleet had turned into real ice bullets that whitened our left sides from head to foot. We looked like trees, bent from the waist in order to withstand the wind, whitewashed on the left side, the direction the wind was blowing from. Our shoes were frozen. Our pants were frozen too, at least up to the coat. The cold got to our skins, if not to the bones. We had to move in order not to freeze. I shivered at the thought that we might die.

"Shall we change direction and make a bed in that corn?" Dănuţ asked. "Don't you think we could get warm under a pile of cornstalks?"

"How are we going to cut so much corn?" I asked. "We could have lit a fire much earlier, but we do not have matches."

"A fire would make a lot of smoke that could give us away," Dănuţ retorted, more lively now.

"I see no village around. There is no hope for us to get warm soon. Let's see if we can break some cornstalks," I said. We agreed unanimously to try.

We approached the corn with great hopes, but without a sickle on that freezing cold morning, we were too tired to do anything. After trying for a while, we realized it was a waste of time. The corn was much harder to break than we imagined.

Before returning to the main road and continuing our journey, we lay down on a concrete slab next to an electric pole to rest a little. The morning sun was trying to come out from behind the clouds, and from time to time the stronger light gave us a false impression of warmth. But the concrete seemed to be much colder. My friends lay down on the cold concrete and fell asleep. Sleep had become our worst enemy. We forgot about hunger, we got used to the cold, and we simply could not stay awake.

I looked toward the road, and I hardly noticed the first car. I realized we were far from the town. One car in three hours! After fighting sleep for about fifteen minutes, and in fear of freezing to death, I woke my friends. With all the complaints in the world, I convinced them to continue our journey to the next village.

"We should have gotten on that bus," Vasile complained.

"And gotten some sleep on the way to the jail in Jimbolia," I said. "We should get to the main road and pray that God will bring a car our way and a good man to help us, especially these kids."

"You are no more alert than we are," Dănuţ said.

"I am more alert than you. That is how we got here. If I had not awakened you, we would still be in the hut, dead by now."

"Dănuţ!" Vasile intervened. "We are tired, but it is very clear that if we fall asleep in this cold, only a priest can wake us up. Let's go to the next village. There we will go to the police, in the worst case, and it will be what it will be."

Lucian said nothing. He was too busy to give an opinion. Commenting, complaining, and pulling each other, we finally reached the road. We could not control our feet. We were sliding in all directions, but we did not stop. We continued to walk slowly, but at least we were walking.

"I have the impression that we were traveling faster in the furrows," I commented. "We are on a smooth and straight road, in the daylight, without hiding from the guards. We are already in Yugoslavia. We have passed the greatest obstacles. Let's think positively."

"We will stop the first car and ask for help," Vasile declared.

"Agreed," we all said.

When we talked, we got tired more quickly. I remembered the history of the Roman Empire, when the Roman soldiers had to communicate with signs in order to save energy. I also remembered the marches we had to do in the army, when we had to sing. It was the heaviest punishment. None of us said a word.

After a few minutes, I felt like something pushed me into a pile of snow on my right. I heard nothing. It was like I had just woken up. My friends, one step behind me, were also in the snow. I pushed myself up, and when I looked to see what had happened, I saw a small vehicle had stopped right in front of us, in the snow. We were hemmed in between the snow and a car that seemed to have fallen from the sky.

The next moment, I saw a policeman get out of the car with a rifle pointed toward us. He was shouting something in Serbian. My Russian language skills were good for nothing. Vasile, who could speak some German, could not understand a word, but said in Romanian, "We are immigrants! We crossed the border last night."

I was glad that at least one of us could find a few words to say. We other three froze when we saw the rifle pointed toward us. I was the first in the group. If he had shot, I would have been the first one to fall.

"Do you have any guns?" the policeman asked in Romanian. He spoke so well, I would have thought he was from Romania if he had not had an accent.

"We have no guns," I quickly answered, very scared. I was three feet away from the gun, so I assumed the question was addressed to me.

"Any knives, dynamite, explosives, or stuff like that?" he continued, as if I had said nothing.

"No," I answered. "I have a little knife that I use to open cans," I explained as I searched my pockets. When I finally found it, he grabbed it from my frozen hands, even though I was not resisting at all. When I raised my eyes, I saw the driver pointing a pistol at us. He was also a policeman. I looked quickly behind to see what my friends were doing.

After the policeman took my knife, he put the rifle in the car and, while the other policeman still pointed his gun at us, searched us to see if we had any other arms. He found nothing. We had no other luggage. We had abandoned everything we had on the way. We only had our IDs in our pockets.

"Get into the car," the policeman ordered.

He did not have to tell us twice. We sat in the backseat of the police Lada, a car of Russian make. It was comfortable and clean. The seats were soft, and it smelled like new. There was enough room for four skinny people like us. There were no mobile phones at that time, so we did not wait for other instructions.

The policeman drove very slowly because of the icy road and because the car was overloaded. The engine was ran smoothly, so we could not hear it. It was quiet. Dănuţ and Lucian fell asleep in less than a minute.

"What are you going to do with us?" I asked. "Are you taking us back to Romania?"

"Not for now," the policeman in the passenger seat answered.

"It is said that all of those who cross the border and are caught by the Serbian police are extradited. Is that true?" I desperately tried to get some idea about what lay ahead of us.

"We send some back, but not all. I think most of the people get to go where they want. It depends on the Serbian government."

Vasile was awake. We looked at each other. We were not afraid or nervous; on the contrary, we were calm and totally indifferent. What could we do?

I was completely awake and thankful not to be frozen to death. There were many things I could still do as long as I remained alive. I did not lose courage; I got new and greater hope. The boys were sleeping. But I was making new departure plans in case I was sent back to Romania.

I thought of Papillon, the French prisoner who never gave up until he succeeded in leaving the island to which he had been exiled to serve his life sentence. I was convinced the Serbians would send us back. All of those who had been sent back had said they were caught by Serbians. Those who got to Austria or Italy had not been caught by the Serbian police, or at least they said nothing about it. "This policeman is protecting himself from trouble," I thought. It would not have been good to tell us we would be extradited. They knew what they could tell us, so they did not tell us more than necessary.

"How did you find us?" Vasile asked. "Were you looking for us, or did you just find us by chance?"

"We were looking for you," the same policeman answered very openly. He was talking to us as a good friend. In Romania, on occasions like this, the policemen became very quiet. These policemen answered questions in a friendly tone. They did not seem desperate, as though they were hiding something.

The driver either could only speak Serbian or did not want to tell us he could also speak Romanian.

"The bus driver told us he saw you walking," the policeman continued. "He realized you were Romanian immigrants by looking at your frozen clothes. We left immediately to look for you, but we could not find you. You had disappeared in less than five minutes. We could not explain how. The driver was not joking. We circled around until we found you. We thought that you had seen us and had hidden from us. But where? In this cold weather, you would have died. We had to find you."

"We did not see you," Vasile explained. "We crossed a ditch and tried to gather some cornstalks to build a shelter and get warm, but we couldn't. That must have been when you passed us the first time, and you could not see us."

The wind was still blowing, snow limiting the visibility. I looked at all the road signs and indicators on the side of the road, but I realized once again that the Serbians had no signs giving the names of places at the entrance of a town. That made me more anxious. I had the impression they were taking us back to the border. My heart was beating very fast. I felt my blood pulsing in my veins.

After half an hour, we entered a town. The road was clearer, so we gained speed. A few minutes later, we stopped in front of an old building. We climbed wooden stairs and arrived on a large porch, such as would be found in a summer garden. We crossed it to get into a room. It was the police headquarters.

There were four policemen in that poorly furnished room, all of them young and very cheerful. It was hard to say if they were happy for us or for themselves. I got the impression that we were in Jimbolia, due to the fact that two of them were speaking Romanian.

"Do you want a tea?" one of them asked us. "You need to warm up."

"Are we in Jimbolia?" Vasile asked straightforwardly. He sounded very confused.

"You are in Zrenjanin. Jimbolia is far away."

The policemen were very kind to us. They spoke calmly. That convinced me we were not in Romania. Romanian policemen would have sworn and threatened us immediately. Here we were treated in a civilized way.

"Take off your shoes and dry them and your socks," the same officer continued. "You can drink the tea; it is for you."

It was hard to listen to him. Distrust!

We took off our heavy clothes and then we took off our shoes. Our clothes were wetter than they had felt before. Last night's wind had penetrated our bones. Then I saw that my pants were wet to the knee. The skin on my feet was wrinkled from the water. We drank the hot tea with lumps in our throats. What was to follow?

"What do you do with people like us?" Vasile asked, regaining his courage. "Are you going to send us back?"

"You will go through a trial, and after all the legal investigations, a decision will be made. Did you have any incident on the border with our soldiers?"

"No. We think we crossed without seeing anybody and without anybody seeing us."

"Then you have no reason to worry. You just tell the truth. Most of the immigrants like you, we help get to relatives they have abroad."

Because we were so tired, we acted mechanically. We stayed for a few minutes in front of a diesel stove. After we had had our tea and gotten warm a little bit, we were asked to go into the neighboring room, which was a prison room. It was a tall, large, and cold room, without any furniture but a grill. The small, bare window had its glass broken. It was cold, but not like outside.

We had had no chance to exchange a word among ourselves before the door opened again and a voice said, "The oldest among you, follow me!" Looking at his clothes and stripes, we realized he must be a superior officer. His Romanian was broken. Vasile followed him without any comment.

"Where are they taking him so quickly?" Dănuț asked.

"They must begin their investigation before we get a chance to agree on the story we will tell," I said.

"What do we have to hide?"

"We have nothing to hide, but they do not know that. You can imagine that many spies, thieves, and criminals cross the border, besides the good people like us!"

Suddenly we were not sleepy anymore. We were walking around, thinking. Ten minutes passed. The time went by so slowly. We became more anxious as Vasile's return was delayed.

"You, come with me." I heard another voice through the door that had just opened. The officer looked straight at me.

I followed him. He led me through the backyard of the building, an interior yard that looked more like a park with winding alleys, flower beds, and old trees. It was covered now in a very white snow, as in fairy tales. We headed toward one of the many entrances of a U-shaped building that surrounded the beautiful park. I climbed eight stairs that led via a large corridor to the office where I was going. I met Vasile, who had just finished his interview and was leaving the secretary's office. I could not exchange a word with him, and I could not read anything on his face.

I was invited to sit in a chair at one end of a meeting table. An officer was at the other end, ready to fill out a long form. Another officer, the translator, was sitting on the right side of the table. There were two other bureaucrats in the same office, busy filling out all kinds of documents.

"Name and surname," the translator asked before the guy at the typing machine said anything.

"Viorel Bilauca," I answered.

This was followed by all the usual questions related to birthplace, family, profession, job, religion, political affiliation, the reasons why I left Romania, the place I wanted to go, and the person who was going to help me get there. Who were my three friends? How had I met them and for how long had I known them?

I answered all the questions without hesitation. I knew that any hesitation would raise questions about my honesty.

"Where did you cross the border?" I was asked toward the end.

"I don't know exactly because I haven't been living around there. I know that after we crossed the border, we crossed a long bridge over a river. The bridge had no balustrade. After walking through some garden, we reached a Serbian village, but I cannot remember its name. I read a name on the wall of the village store, but I cannot remember it."

"Okay, okay, we know where," the person typing said in Romanian. "Did you encounter any Romanian or Serbian soldiers?"

"No. We saw nobody. We had no incident with any soldier or civilian."

After half an hour, I was back in the cell. Vasile and Dănuț were speaking quietly about the examination. "What did they ask you?" both of them asked me at once.

"Usual questions. I had to introduce myself," I replied.

"And what did you tell them?" Vasile continued, worrying a little bit.

"I told them the truth. Besides my name, they were interested to know if we had any conflict with soldiers or civilians on the border, if somebody had seen us, if they had summoned us or fired any shots at us. I think it is normal to examine us, even if they decide to send us back to Romania, in the worst case. They need to send us with some documents if they want to get their salt. We cannot tell them anything but the truth. I am sure they will compare our statements, and it does us no good for them to find out we have hidden something from them. Besides your sister, Lenuța, who introduced us, nobody can be accused of any complicity."

"Lenuța is going to get rid of anything incriminating. She will go to her husband soon." Vasile was thinking aloud.

Very efficiently, the Serbian officers finished the first interviews. After Dănuț came back, we were all put into a police van, similar to those in Romania, and without any explanation driven from the police headquarters. We went toward the center of town, or at least so it seemed to us, because we could see nothing from the van. None of us said anything. We were more than sure they were taking us back to Jimbolia. I tried to encourage myself by saying that everything was going to be all right. They had not put us in handcuffs, which made me think they did not consider us dangerous. The fact that the policemen had seemed to change their attitude after the interviews, become more reserved, made us ponder. Actually, these were different policemen.

"What did you declare?" Vasile opened the discussion while we were fighting to guess the direction we were going. We could not see anything outside the van. Through the little ventilation windows, we could only see the ground.

"The truth," the boys answered together.

After only a few minutes, with many sudden brakings, swerves, horn-blowings, and bumps, the van finally stopped and we got off. They led us into another inner yard surrounded by some old buildings. It seemed to be a museum. The thick walls were covered with moss, lianas, and frozen, bare windows. In the yard were old trees clothed in snow and icicles, and a large entrance paved with stone. Everything made it resemble a secular prison. The presence of civilians going in and out of the offices, instead of the military, gave me some hope. In a prison, most of the people were supposed to be policemen and soldiers.

We entered and approached the door to a room. One of the two guards who had come with us entered the office. After a minute or two, a civilian with gray hair, tall and dressed in a suit and tie, invited Vasile in. The guard who remained outside with us did not speak. We assumed he could speak Romanian, but he did not say a word.

I took advantage of a short conversation between the guard and a passerby and told the boys to watch what they said because I was almost sure that the guard could speak Romanian. If the boys were tempted to say something bad about the Serbians, that would make our situation more complicated.

Our clothes were still half-wet and cold. We moved around the entryway. We were the only ones waiting in front of the door. It was not unusual for us to have to wait at a door. In Romania, whenever we had to go to a doctor or to an office to get a signature, we had to waste whole days at different doors. Being with a policeman made all the passersby stare at us, even though we were not handcuffed. The cold, the hunger, and the standing kept us awake.

I switched places with Vasile after a time of waiting that seemed like an eternity. We wanted to know the plans they had for us. That anxiety was consuming our energy.

The office was a luxurious, first-class one. I felt the warmth and the comfort. The translator asked me to sit down on a wood-and-leather armchair at the end of the desk. At the opposite end, the typist was preparing her paper. On the right and the left side of this office were two armchairs like the one I was sitting on. On the right were the translator and the policeman I already knew, who had accompanied us at the first interview.

"Do you have any complaints related to the way you have been treated so far?" the translator asked me after they had had a long conversation in Serbian.

"I have no complaints," I replied after a short pause, surprised by such a question. I thought he was asking the policeman.

The secretary moved her eyes back and forth, looking from me to the translator, typing all the time. The boss, the man in the suit, stepped into the discussion from time to time. Next to the wall, behind the desk, was another desk with some people sitting at it. They were talking all the time but also listening to us. One of them would stand and go out from time to time, but then come back to continue the discussion and our examination. I focused only on the translator's questions.

"Name and surname?" I heard in Romanian. The question was for me.

"Viorel Bilauca."

"Date and place of birth?"

"March 30, 1951, Mitocul Dragomirnei, Suceava County, Romania."

"Parents, brothers, and sisters?"

"My parents are Aurel and Aurelia Bilauca. I have five brothers and six sisters."

"All of them alive?"

"Yes."

"You are the oldest*"

"I am the second oldest. I have a sister older than me."

"Where have you been working and what position?"

"My last job was at ISIM, Timişoara, where I worked as a turner and miller. I also worked in the same capacity at Electromotorul, Timişoara, and at ICA (an airplane factory), Ghimbav, Braşov. Before that I worked as an accountant in the financial department of URA (an auto repair factory), Suceava."

"Suceava, Braşov, Timişoara, Yugoslavia," the typist concluded with a smile that the other bureaucrats shared.

"Have you ever been fined or been in prison for breaking the law in Romania?"

"No, never."

"Have you tried to leave the country before?"

"Yes. I have tried it twice, illegally, but with no success. I could not apply legally because they would not have accepted my request without me having somebody from my family in the West …"

The typist typed everything we said, but in the short breaks between the questions, my eyes and my mind were falling asleep. Despite my determination, they would not cooperate.

"Who helped you cross the border, and how much did you pay?" the translator brought me back to reality.

"I am a very good friend of Vasile Magda. Another friend, Vasile Tepei, left the country at the beginning of November, last year. Before the New Year, with the help of Tepei's wife, I got to know Vasile Magda, the person you interrogated before me. Magda claimed to know the area very well. I counted on him, and without any other knowledge and without paying anybody, I got here. I went to work on Saturday. After work, I went to Uivar, where I met Magda. It was the second time we had met. On Monday night we tried and succeeded to cross the border—"

"Do you need to pay Vasile later?"

"No."

"Have you paid any guide?"

"No. Vasile worked by the border years ago as a tractor driver. He and Dănuț, his brother, and Lucian are from Uivar. All three of them claimed to know this area very well."

"Do you have any idea if one of them has tried to cross the border before?

"None of them. Thinking how we wandered last night, I am sure this was the first time they tried."

"Did anyone see you at the border?"

"No."

"Were you summoned?"

"No."

"Were any signaling rockets launched?"

"No."

"Did anyone shoot at you?"

"No."

"Do you have relatives abroad? Who is going to welcome you? Do you know anybody, any address, any phone number?"

"I have no family, just friends. I hope one of them will help me, somewhere. I am convinced I can manage by myself too. If I could get to the labor camp in Austria, everything would be all right."

I was answering every question mechanically. I continued, "Nobody has returned to Romania from the camp in Austria, even if they had no relatives abroad."

"Do you speak any foreign languages?"

"No. I understand a little bit of Russian, but that won't help me in the West. We decided to go together to Germany because Vasile Magda speaks German."

The examination came to an end. Those present looked at each other and asked if they had any more questions. No more questions. I was invited to stand and leave. Lucian entered in my place. They were interviewing us according to age.

Vasile and Dănuț were walking in circles in the antique corridor just to get warm. I was invigorated by the cold air and came back to reality. Being so tired, I became more indifferent to what was happening around me. Our senses were telling us that we would be extradited. We were anxious to hear our sentence, whatever it was.

After Lucian, it was Dănuț's turn. We were exhausted. I remembered the detective novels in which the spies and criminals were interrogated for hours, and because they were so tired they confessed everything, even to things they hadn't done, just to escape the torture.

Before the end of Dănuț's interrogation we heard our names. "You all, come," the voice of the translator called through the open door of the office.

"Come in, all three of you," the officer confirmed.

We entered the office. We remained standing while Dănuț finished answering the questions. It was not easy for Dănuț to gather his thoughts because he was tired. He paused after each answer, while the translation was done and typed. The pauses gave him enough time to fall asleep. We looked at Dănuţ fighting sleep between his answers.

At one point he dropped his hat. In that moment he woke up and reached to get it from under the desk, where it had rolled. The secretary shouted surprisingly loudly and stood up. The translator and other clerks followed her. Dănuţ recovered his hat and sat back on the chair. He would not have realized what had just happened if the secretary had not screamed. The policemen had their guns pointed toward Dănuţ, who calmly and indifferently continued playing with his hat.

It lasted only a few seconds, first terror and then laughter; everything was only a false alarm.

After they interrogated Dănuţ, we were invited into a neighboring office. Another officer offered his company. The office was as luxurious as the first one. The large leather armchairs were tempting, but the policeman asked us to stand. We were almost falling down from fatigue. We found things to do: study the physical and economic maps hanging on the wall of the office, and look through the window that led to the yard. More than once, we hit the walls with our heads because of falling asleep, almost falling down. The officer was having fun watching us. The minutes seemed longer than ever.

After a while, when I thought time had stopped, the door opened. We dashed, confused, into the same office where we had been interrogated. We were not interested in their decision anymore; we only needed rest. We were ready to give up our dreams for a few hours of sleep.

The clerks and the officers were not furious. We understood nothing from what they said. A taller clerk, wearing a suit and with his hair nicely combed, approached us and told us with the help of the translator,

"I am the mayor and the judge of Zrenjanin. Because you have crossed the Yugoslavian border illegally, Yugoslavia is going to host you for a few days."

None of us understood what "Yugoslavia is going to host you for a few days" meant. Maybe the translator had not said it right. None of us knew what our fate would be. We were confused about a decision that told us nothing.

They saw us out. We were led to the police van we had originally come in to the city hall of Zrenjanin. Very tired and confused, we looked at each other without saying a word. We all thought we were on our way to Romania, but the phrase "Yugoslavia is going to host you for a few days" stayed in my mind.

None of us tried to read the route through the small ventilation holes of the van. We sat in the corner, trying to gather our thoughts. I looked at my friends, and then I looked at me. Our clothes were ravaged: our shoes had white stripes from the snow, and our pants had stains up to the knees where they had been wet. We did not speak as much as we had the day before. I think none of us had any thoughts. We abandoned ourselves in fate's hands.

# CHAPTER 10
# THE PRISON

IN A FINAL effort to start a short conversation, I began to encourage myself and my friends. "Guys, I think we are on the right road. They haven't handcuffed us!"

"We are safe without handcuffs. Weariness," Vasile replied, pointing to the two boys who were sleeping bent over each other. "Hunger, thirst, cold, and fear are more secure than any handcuffs." He had to make an effort to concentrate before speaking. He was exhausted.

Vasile was right.

We struggled for balance in the police car because we had nothing to hold on to and no seat belts to use. After many stops and starts and many horn honkings, we stopped for some minutes. It was quiet. We could see nothing. Dănuț and Lucian woke up too. The noise of the street could hardly be heard.

We looked at each other, puzzled. Had we reached the Romanian border so soon? Anything was possible. We had no idea how far were we from the border. They could turn us in to the Romanian consulate or who knew what other institution in Yugoslavia. We said not a word. We were waiting.

The officers came back to the van, which moved backward. We stopped in a few seconds. The back door of the van opened immediately. We got out in front of a big building with a massive metal gate. We only saw three officers on the right side of the van. They were watching us and speaking Serbian. On the other side there was a wall, so no guards were necessary.

We entered a long and high corridor in front of us. Five or six feet from the gate, we had to climb some stairs and. We heard the big metal gate close and the sound of the bars that secured it falling into place. In front of us were the cells of a prison, with bars. There was a large desk and a table on the left, with an officer behind it. On the right were some chairs and two benches by the wall, for visitors probably.

The officer at the desk pulled out some forms and scrupulously inserted two indigo papers between them. He called us one by one and asked us to empty our pockets on the table. He took our IDs first and began filling in the form. He made an inventory for each of us of everything we had: money, down to the last coin; bus and tram tickets; pencils; pens; glasses; letters; wallets; and any important or unimportant documents. At the end he took our watches, belts, and shoe laces. He put everything in a personal bag, with a copy of the inventory on the top. He put the bags on the desk.

Everything was done in silence. We only communicated with signs. It was four o'clock by now. We realized we were in prison. It was our "hotel" because we had crossed the Yugoslavian border illegally. We understood.

There was silence in the prison too. We could hear no voices, no chains, and no bars. It was unusual. The prison was, in my imagination, a place for forced rehabilitation.

We saw real cells with metal doors, but nothing made a sound.

We were led along some corridors, up stairs with bars on both sides, and then into a small cell. The door was locked with the same peculiar, echoing noise our footsteps had made in the corridors. The steps of the officers who had led us departed.

We looked at each other and looked around. We thought we were dreaming. We had gone through many things in less than twenty hours.

The door visor opened very noisily. Some food appeared on an inner metal shelf. There were four opened fish cans and four triangles of black bread. We heard something spoken behind the door, maybe a polite invitation to eat, and then the visor closed with the same noise. That noise was awful, at least at the beginning.

I hadn't been in a prison before, and neither had my friends. We knew many things about prisons from books, but now we were living that experience. We were scared, from the top of our heads to the soles of our feet. We were in a prison. Every one of us knew that this wasn't just a dream or a nightmare that we could escape from the moment we woke up. It was reality!

The opened cans had a very strong fish smell, but we started eating anyway. The cell was narrow, with a twelve-foot-tall ceiling that made it seem even narrower. A small window was placed high up, almost to the ceiling. The light showed a one-person bed and a night bowl instead of a toilet, and that was all. While we struggled to eat because we had no water, we got used to the dim light of the cell.

"How are we all going to sleep in one bed?" Dănuţ asked.

"You thought they would take us to a hotel?" Vasile answered. "This is a prison! We sleep in turns or we draw lots."

We were not able to make jokes or laugh. Lucian and Dǎnuţ hurried to jump on the iron bed. Vasile lay down next to the bed. I was still standing next to the door. I was preparing to lay down when I heard steps in the corridor. The bars moved as loudly as they had when they were locked. The door opened, and two officers with badges on their arms asked us to follow them. We were taken to the opposite part of the building, where they put us in a bigger cell with sixteen beds: eight pairs of bunk beds.

"This is a hotel!" I cried after the door was locked. "'You don't know the sweet until you have already tasted the bitter,' the proverb says. This accommodation is great, two beds for each of us!"

Nobody laughed at my joke. Everyone chose a lower bunk and lay on the blankets. Then the visor of the door opened and an authoritarian voice told us we were not allowed to lie on the beds! The officer, though he was not speaking Romanian, made himself understood; especially as he was speaking using his rubber baton and his watch.

We gave up and sat around the wooden table, which had long benches attached to it. The table and benches were built in one piece and bolted to the cell floor. There was a bottle of water and a chess box on the table.

The bucket for everyone's toilet needs was large, with a conic form, a small opening on the top, and some nails on its edge so you could not sit on it as on a toilet. The bucket was always left uncovered and with some water on the bottom.

It was hard to convince the officer that we understood that we were not allowed to go to bed before the sleeping hours. We were not sleepy after that discussion anymore. He showed us some other signs, pointing to his watch and the bucket, but we could not understand what he meant. He just left, satisfied that he had told us what he was supposed to tell us. It was not his problem if we did not understand him. We would figure it out later.

Left alone, we sat at the table, put our heads on our arms, and tried to nap. We couldn't.

After about two hours we heard doors open and shut and many voices and steps go up and down the stairs. We approached the visor and tried to peek through a crack between it and the door. The noise was being made by detainees who were coming back from work. They were wearing prison clothes, but we could not hear any chains. We realized they were not the most dangerous prisoners.

Without words, the evening meal appeared on our shelf: four bowls of borscht … fish borscht. All the prison was filled with the smell of fish. We had eaten fish three hours before. We had had enough. We tasted the food and left it there. After a while somebody came and picked up the bowls. We began to study the bucket, but could not find any positive solution, so we waited. We had not been to a toilet all day.

At ten o'clock, all the lights were turned off. We heard all kinds of orders spoken in the corridor, but we could not understand a word. When it was dark, we each chose a bed and went to sleep. Nothing else could happen till morning.

We fell asleep immediately. For the first time in our lives, we were sleeping in a foreign country.

## CHAPTER 11

# WEDNESDAY, JANUARY 17, 1979

I WOKE UP AT the noise of the bars being pulled back roughly. In the corridor, all the lights were on. Our door opened too. Two officers asked us to take the bucket outside the cell. Vasile and I took it, since we were stronger. We followed the guards and turned left to a big lavatory at the end of the corridor. We met many prisoners there who were doing the same thing. We emptied the bucket, washed it with clean water, and put fresh water in it. After we quickly washed our faces, we were taken back to our cell. The whole process lasted not more than ten minutes.

Our door was again locked, even though we were good people. We waited anxiously for somebody to come and tell us news, but time passed without any. We were more and more anxious to know what was going to happen to us. Would they send us back to Romania? Were they waiting for somebody from Romania to pick us up? No answer, despite all our signs of impatience.

We decided to use the bucket, hoping we could empty it again after breakfast. Breakfast was very small: a triangle of bread and another kind of borscht. At least it wasn't fish. We ate everything very fast, in two or three minutes, and were still hungry afterward. We drank all the water that was on the table. Dănuţ was so hungry that he could not keep from shouting for more food. Nobody answered. He calmed down after few minutes. The guards came, took the empty plates, and left another big jug of water, but not an extra piece of bread.

Soon the prison became quiet. All the prisoners left to go to work. The silence was unbearable to us, as was the waiting. We stayed quietly at the table, waiting for the door to open, but it didn't. We could hear steps coming and going from time to time, but they never stopped in front of our door. We were not allowed to lie on the beds during the day. The big cell allowed us to walk in circles for some exercise. We had no papers, no watches, no radio, no TV, no games other than chess. None of my friends knew how to play chess.

Our former weariness and cold were resolved. Physical hunger and concern for the future, with thoughts that they might send us back to Romania, kept us from talking. We said a word from time to time, always repeating: Why? Why? Why do they not tell us what they are going to do with us?

We thought of our personal problems. Each one of us had a different list of priorities, but the first problem on all our lists was: What are they going to do with us, and when are they going to tell us?

The small windows in the cell did not allow much light to enter, but during the afternoon the sun came out, so we had more light. We discovered then that the table and benches had many names carved on them, presumably of the people who had been "hosted" in that cell. Curiosity made us read systematically the multitude of names in the hope of finding familiar ones, whether of people sent back to Romania or people who succeeded in getting to the West. That would have given us courage and hope.

Walking around the cell helped us make another discovery. We realized that many names had been scratched on the walls. Some were so old that, although they had been covered with paint, we could still read them. Thousands of names had been written through the years. There were names of people of other nationalities too.

At about noon (we could only assume it was noon because we had no clock in the cell), we got lunch: a plate of warm food. It looked good; it smelled good. It was a good stew, but we got no bread. There was only a little, but at least we were encouraged, knowing we had not been forgotten as we thought. A long and silent break followed lunch.

One of the top beds was close to the window. We could see the town from there. It was an important discovery. We would have spent all day there, but we were afraid of the guards who were spying on us through the visor of the door. We discovered the spying very quickly, because anytime Lucian and Dănuț lay on the beds, the guards invaded the cell and threatened them with a baton. We could understand that repeated sign

The morning had been long. It was followed by a long afternoon. After analysis, we included in our daily schedule a rational use of the bucket. We had to take very seriously into consideration every element of the program; otherwise we had to suffer the consequences.

We finished with the normal commentaries about the uncertain situation and about the food that would not correspond with our taste and desired quantity. Because we had nothing else to do, we had a closer look at each other. "Let's get to know each other better," I suggested.

"I agree," Vasile said. "Who knows for how long we are going to stay here? And who knows what is going to happen in the future? It would be nice to know each other better. It is going to do us good."

"Who's first?" Dănuţ asked.

"Let's start with you," I told him. "You are the youngest. I hope you will finish your presentation quickly so we won't be late for dinner! We have just finished lunch and are already hungrier than before!" We all laughed.

"You are wrong, I think," Dănuţ said, "because my story is the longest, for two reasons. First, I have a lot of adventures to share, and second, my story is connected to Lucian's."

"That's true," Lucian confirmed. "We are more like brothers. We think the same, live the same, and dream the same way. We do not like school nor work—only adventures!"

"Don't tell them everything," Dănuţ intervened. "It is my turn to share. I will leave you some time to tell them everything I miss."

"Okay," Vasile said, "you've made me curious. Look, I have already forgotten that I am hungry!"

After a short break, during which Dănuţ put his thoughts in order, he began. "The last two years of our lives we have lived as in fairy tales. Dad, because he was elderly and less interested in my fate, and because I was supposed to remain in my parents' house, did not watch me very carefully. Mother in Timişoara almost all the time, at Lenuţa's home. She was at peace because she didn't hear the truth about me. That opened the door to all kinds of adventures.

"I made friends with Lucian, 'a good boy,' who had escaped his parents' control as well. He was an only child and, like myself, was supposed to inherit his parents' house. Even though Lucian was two years older than me and seemed more reserved, we got along excellently. We did everything we wanted—"

"I hope you haven't been stealing!?" Vasile interrupted him, a little bit scared and hoping it was a joke.

"Of course we have," Dănuț confirmed without any hesitation. "Where else would we get money for travel and food? We haven't stolen from our neighbors, nor from anybody in Uivar, though we were always held up as bad examples of things that other young people should not do."

"It is true," Lucian said. "We have never stolen anything in our village. We have stolen in the neighboring villages. We did not want our parents to hear and make them worry about us. We cared about our parents the most. We cared about our neighbors, about our relatives, and even about the people in our village."

Dănuț continued, laughing, "Now it is time for Lucian to find out how I earned my prestige at one of the competitions we had: 'Who can bring the bigger rooster for our supper?' We had a group of friends, and every night one of us had to catch a rooster to prepare and eat. So, all day, while we were walking through the village, we were looking into people's yards for roosters. In the evening, we would steal the biggest one we saw and cook it at one of our homes, when the parents were away. You can understand that it did not take very long before all the roosters in our neighboring villages had disappeared. People began to complain that their roosters, and not only their roosters, were endangered. Every housekeeper protected his rooster. They put serious locks on the cottages and bought watch dogs. We got to such a deadlock that I had to steal and cook my own rooster in order to defend my prestige."

"You are not sane," Vasile said angrily. "How could you eat our rooster? Were you not choking on it?"

Lucian and I were shocked to see them fighting. Lucian had no idea where Dănuţ had stolen that rooster from. We thought it was a joke, but that was the real story!

"I remember," Lucian confirmed, "that you brought the biggest rooster and it was the last one we ate, but I never asked where you got it. We did not want to embarrass ourselves in front of you. You were the youngest, and you managed better than all of us. We preferred to say nothing and to try to take our revenge!"

"Lucian, dear friend, we were already suspected by many people and even by the police. Everybody was following us. It seemed to me that some friends' parents had found traces of the roasted roosters after our banquets. It was not worth the risk. I told myself that we needed to find something else to do. So, before getting sent to jail, I sacrificed my own rooster. I experienced strong emotions at the time. It was so difficult for me to eat it with strangers, but it would have been more difficult not to eat it, knowing that it was mine and I had no other chance to eat it. I ate it with lumps in my throat, and believe me, I swallowed it in tears. How stupid! Even now I feel like hurting myself!"

"Leave him. He will confess everything," Vasile said.

"It is sad," I said. "What did your parents say when they discovered that their rooster was missing?"

"Nothing. Father thought Mother took it to Lenuţa in Timişoara. He was surprised she did not take one of the many chickens we had. Mother thought that Father might have been drunk and had just killed the rooster. I felt and still am feeling guilty for what I did. I don't think I will ever be able to forgive myself."

"The Communist Party is to blame for counting not only the roosters, but everything people have around the house," I said to distract Dănuţ from his guilt. At the beginning of the New Year, officials with the census did an inventory of everything you had or could have that year. They calculated the taxes on everything you had to declare to the state. This is why people, especially the poor, were not interested in raising animals—not even chickens, let alone cattle, pigs, or sheep. "We can talk about the 'Ottoman tribute.' History tells us that the Ottomans put taxes on every tree in the garden, on any smoke coming from Romanian houses, and even on the toilets at the backs of the houses. Now it is the same and even worse. You have to declare all your goods. If it happens that you no longer have those goods, due to reasons such as rain or epidemics, then you have to buy them again to honor your declaration!"

"That only happened in villages," Vasile said.

"Generally, yes. My father works on the side as a carpenter. He builds houses. He learned the trade from his uncle when he was fourteen or fifteen years old. When I grew older, I used to hear him negotiating every January for the fees he had to pay for his work permit. They calculated that a carpenter could earn five or even ten times more than my father actually did, so they based his tax on that calculated income."

"Did your father not know how much he was going to earn from the beginning of the year?" Lucian asked.

"Sometimes he did, vaguely, when he had promised people he would build their houses. Most of the time the weather, his health, the client's money, and the lack of materials were serious obstacles. But according to the authorities, these were not good enough excuses to recalculate the taxes.

"Once taxes were calculated, the authorities issued the work permit. It happened many times that my father had to borrow money to pay his taxes on time, so he would not have to pay interest. Usually my mother was good at negotiating, and with tears succeeded in reducing the initial calculation. If they had caught him working without a permit, he would have gotten some unbelievable fines."

"What was it to them what your father was doing?" Dănuţ asked, totally resentful of what he heard.

"Dănuţ, my first job was as an accountant. I know the laws in Romania that have to do with finances. Among the notes we got at the office I worked in was one related to income taxes. For example, some Gypsies in Galaţi sold iron to the value of 150,000 lei. That money had to be taxed. I don't know if the Gypsies ever paid taxes, but we were considered responsible if we knew somebody was making money and did not report that person to the authorities. Any income is taxable!"

"In other words," Dănuţ responded, "they were not interested where the Gypsies got the junk. They were only interested in their share of the proceeds."

"Exactly. Junk was junk. For sure it was not bought. The money from selling the junk was real, and they had to be taxed according to the law."

"Is your father still working in construction?" Dănuţ asked.

"Of course he is. He had twelve children. On his salary and our allowance alone, we would have starved. Even adding the money he earned on the side, we could hardly manage. He still renews his authorization in spite of the annual tax."

"But can't he work without an authorization?" Vasile persisted. "Why does he have to report everything?

"You do not know the people working at the financial department in town! Once they have you in their database, they won't let you alone, not even when you are dead. They used to come to our home and ask us, the children, if we knew whose house the boards were for, or if people were asking our father to work for them. What a tactic!

"Inspectors went through the villages. If they saw a new building or a mended roof or new windows, they asked who did the work and then visited that person. It was a big problem if the worker had no authorization. He would get fine after fine and be forced to apply for authorization.

"Unfortunately, there were villagers who would inform on these workers, and not only a few! There were good people too. One of them was our neighbor who taught us, the children, how to speak to inspectors who were trying to catch my father and fine him."

"Could your father give something to those inspectors to leave him alone?" Vasile asked. Bribes always functioned everywhere.

"He bribed them, but that did not mean he did not have to obtain an authorization. Another inspector might come. Once the fines were given, you had to pay them! He could bribe this one and that one, but would have ended up paying more than the cost of an authorization.

"Let us come back to your roosters. What else have you stolen? I hope you won't acknowledge too many petty thefts and send us to jail as accomplices!"

Dănuţ said, "The roosters were recent, but before that Lucian and I visited the Danube delta. We like fishing. We used to fish for anything. Seriously! We fished in the Danube River, and also on its banks."

"You have stolen fish that should have been caught by those poor Lipovans," Vasile said. "They hardly make their living, poor people."

"That's true, but, apropos of what Viorel said, they do not pay any taxes on the fish they sell. Anyway, we used to help them catch the fish, because they needed help. After that, if they were not paying us enough, we stopped by their tents before leaving to take our share. We did not stay too long in one place. We did not want them to know us very well. We gave them plenty of warning when we left. There was enough fish for them too."

Lucian was listening very happily, with a smile on his face. I wasn't thinking of the risk I was exposing myself to in case these two told the whole truth.

"Do you have a criminal record? Have you ever been arrested? Maybe Interpol will find you and send all of us to the Danube Canal. At least you have an idea how to catch fish, but Vasile and I, what are we going to do? We will have to pay too for what you have stolen from the Lipovans," I said, more seriously than joking.

"Don't be afraid," Dănuţ said after a short time of silence. "We have not been arrested, and we have no criminal records. We have been suspected, but we escaped without leaving any traces. We haven't beaten anybody; we haven't killed anybody. We have stolen because it was not worth working. The salary would not have been enough for a decent living! Think of Viorel's father. He works, works, works and cannot do anything but survive. We have strolled throughout the whole country for about two years. Everywhere is the same. Those who have something, they have because they steal. Through honest work, you can hardly make your living. We did not want to reach old age just to realize that we had lived a life not worth living. We planned to leave Romania next summer, but when we saw you were ready to leave, we decided to go with you immediately. We almost changed our minds because we could not find knives with mercury."

"Knives with mercury?" I demanded. "What are those, and what use would they be to you? I have never heard of something like that."

Vasile replied, "Knives with mercury have mercury embedded in the blade and stab however you throw them. Guaranteed!"

"Can you find them commercially?" I asked curiously.

"You can find them, but not commercially. They are used in circuses. When you see somebody throwing knives that always stick to the boards, you can be sure those are knives with mercury. Mercury is a heavy liquid. It slides to the top of the knife, making it heavier. Anyone can do that trick if they have mercury knives."

"Did someone in Uivar have those kind of knives?"

"Yes, but not now. They would have been useful at the crossing, but if someone had found them on us, we would have been handcuffed. They almost caught us with these—"

"With what?" I stood up urgently. "Do you have weapons on you?"

"Calm down," Vasile said. "I sent these two to find mercury knives, but they could not find any. However, each of us had a good knife, just in case, you know, in case of an attack with dogs on the border, or, who knows, a can, a door, a lock … We had to be prepared. But we did not need them. If you had not kept those officers busy with your fish-can knife, we could have been back in Romania yesterday."

"What?" I jumped again.

"Lucian and I threw our knives away when they caught us. While you were searching your pockets to get that little can knife, we discreetly let our knives fall, thanking God for that fluffy snow. I was glad at that moment we had no mercury knives. We would have had to throw them away, and they are so expensive—apart from the fact that we could have been caught and sent immediately back to Romania! And Dănuț forgot his hunting knife in that hut after he tried to prepare some firewood. Lenuța was right. We needed special protection from God."

We stopped for a moment with the confessions.

"Look, I found it!" Vasile screamed. "Here it says *Militaru*. Yes!"

We had still been trying to decipher the names written and scratched all over our cell. Time passed faster that way. Vasile had deciphered the name Militaru. It was a great discovery. We approached it, looked at it, and read it. It was easy to read, having been written recently.

We were so glad because Militaru could have been a man from Uivar. We knew someone by that name who was in a labor camp in Austria. We forgot our worries at once. Our hope that we would not be sent back to Romania rose again. Suddenly, our faces lit up and our voices changed. We were back to life!

"If that man was also caught by the Serbians and got to Austria, it means there is a chance for us too," Vasile continued with enthusiasm.

"The person who said 'He who died yesterday regrets it today' was right," I exclaimed.

We all laughed and then suddenly became silent. Since being arrested, we had not made any plans other than how to get to the border again after being deported to a Romanian prison. Now the room was filled with silence again. It was a pleasant silence, full of new thoughts and plans. We were seeing ourselves free. We experienced an indescribable courage to live.

"Brothers, let's not cross the line to false joy," Vasile mumbled, almost to himself.

"What do you mean?" Dănuț demanded.

"Well, the man from Uivar was not actually named Militaru. That was his nickname. I cannot remember his real name. Would he write his nickname, not his real name? It is possible. I hope it is!"

Darkness had fallen some time before. The lights had been on for several hours. There was a better visibility in the cell in the evening because of the artificial lights. We sat at the table again and talked quietly. We were convinced that nothing would happen until the following day.

Food was served on the door shelf. The visor made less noise; we preferred that to the awful noise the iron door made. The metal bars slammed without mercy and the sound of the key reminded us that we were being punished for serious violations of the law. The food was not bad. At least it did not seem so, because it was so little. "Hunger is the best cook" was the proverb we repeated often.

"They divided one portion into four!" Dănuț burst out after we finished eating. "Do they want to kill us? What do they want from us? They should let us leave; we have nothing to do with them."

None of us commented. We did not want to encourage him. After a while, he calmed down. Unfortunately, we

VIOREL BILAUCA

used the bucket according to a program: only in the morning when we woke up. We all knew the program. We focused on the names scratched on the table and benches, trying to decipher them in our quest for a familiar name. We had been on the road for a few days, unshaved, unwashed, unchanged. We slept in our day clothes. It was good we had no mirrors!

"Let's return to our business," I said, to change the subject from the food. "You say you got hunting knives and never said anything to me? Were you fair toward me?"

Silence covered us. My friends looked at me with guilt on their faces. Vasile tried to explain. "Dear Viorel, we only met three weeks ago, or even less than that. Lenuța, when she heard I was going to cross the border, asked who would go with me. I told her I would go by myself. She looked straight into my eyes and, after she was convinced I was not joking, told me about you. She told me not to go without you.

"She told me some things about your relationship with her husband and that her future was uncertain. She had confidence in your friendship with him and in the fact that you could convince him to invite her to America after he got there. Lenuța was thinking of the children. She wanted them to be free, in America. After complaining about her unhappy life, she asked me to promise her I wouldn't leave the country without you.

"I am not very emotional, not even with my wife, let alone with Lenuța, whose husband I even hit once. I don't know why I promised her that I would not leave the country without you. She asked when I was going to leave. As soon as possible, I told her, before my vacation ended. The following day she told me she met you on her way to the church, and that you told her you were planning to leave any moment.

"I still had one month of vacation. I had different plans. I don't know how, but that day I decided to leave the country. I told myself: 'I will leave in January!' I never thought seriously of leaving before Christmas, except when the money did not last from one payday to another. When she told me you were ready to leave, in spite of the fact that we had never met, I decided to leave too. I think I only needed a push. Suddenly I got courage, and I canceled all my other plans."

"Didn't you think I might denounce you?"

"No. I thought of nothing at that moment. I could not see any risk. I told Lenuţa to invite you to meet me and set the departure day."

"What else did she tell you about me?"

"That you had moved from Braşov with the intention of leaving the country, that you worked with her husband painting apartments, and that you had been investigated by the police, together with eleven other people involved in a false passport picture case. She also told me you are a believer and assured me that God would protect me too when crossing the border if a believer was with me. She counted on your help for me and for her family."

"But you know nothing about repentance?"

"I know, but I cannot repent. My flesh is evil. I want to live my life freely first, without fearing future judgment. I don't like religions nor the laws. I don't like any kind of restrictions. Repentance is not for me, at least not at this moment. I cannot keep it. My mother is a believer. Lenuţa too. Women can go to church. My father and we two, the boys, could not go. We didn't try. We have lived our lives as most of the people do. We respect the church. We go to church at Easter, at weddings, and at family funerals. We respect the priest. But to go to church every Sunday? That is not for me now. Maybe when I am elderly! Prayers, songs, no drinking, no music, and no dancing—boring!"

"What is your opinion about repentant people?"

"Great people! Great people! Beginning with my mother, with Lenuţa and her husband Vasile, great people. I consider all repentant people to be saints. Vasile has forgiven me for what I did when I beat him. I would not have forgiven such a person for my whole life. I know God cares for the repentant."

"God cares for every person in an equal measure, not only for believers," I responded after a pause. Dănuţ and Lucian were equally captivated by Vasile's philosophical statements. "God has given His Son, Jesus Christ, to die for every human born under the sun. I think you have heard this before. Whoever believes in the Lord Jesus Christ will have eternal life. Guaranteed! This is the golden verse or golden promise of the Bible.

"It depends on our own will. We have to recognize God as the only true God and His Son, Jesus Christ, whom He sent. Salvation is God's gift for us humans. A gift is always a gift. It costs nothing. You only have to receive it."

Dănuţ interrupted me. "What you say is interesting, but let's leave it for tomorrow. I want to go to bed and forget about food."

It was becoming late. The light had been turned off for a long time, but we could not fall asleep. We moved from one side of our cots to another—not because of the military bed, or because we had no pajamas, or because we hadn't washed our faces and cleaned our teeth for almost a week, but because of the uncertain situation we were in.

"Sleep heals!" I whispered. "Sick people cannot sleep, but we can. This is a proof of the fact that we are healthy. Let's enjoy what we have. What is to be will be ..."

After a while I heard Dănuț and Lucian snoring. They slept deeply. Vasile was still moving, not able to find a position. I wasn't a good friend of sleep either. I could not be careless of the situation I was in.

I was extremely happy with what I was experiencing. My dream for years had become reality, and I was truly living it. What I had accomplished would not let me sleep. The little hope that we would not be extradited robbed me of the moments of rest my body needed so much. I was more and more preoccupied with future plans. Time was never enough make plans for the free world I was about to live in.

## CHAPTER 12
# THURSDAY, JANUARY 18, 1979

NOBODY KNOWS HOW people fall asleep. I don't know how long I looked at the ceiling of the cell until I fell asleep, but I remember that suddenly the lights were turned on, accompanied by the usual sound of the bars being drawn back. It woke us up brutally. In a second we were on our feet, as in the case of an alert.

It had been very quiet during the night: no screams, no "commentaries," no alerts. Such a silence was quite unusual in a prison. I was expecting to hear all kinds of screams, complaints, banging, guards trying to calm the people—but nothing.

It was quiet during the day too because all the detainees left for work. We could hear guards walk in the corridors. The echo was perfect. We could hear any locks being turned and any words. But during the night, the detainees and the guards were sleeping. It was the silence of the grave.

The usual schedule started immediately. The locks opened noisily and two guards showed up in the wide-open door. We quickly understood their signs. We grabbed the bucket and went to the busy washroom. The water was running rapidly, making a terrible noise, so people had to speak loudly in order to hear each other. (This might have been a tactic to hinder the detainees from talking quietly among themselves.) We competed to see who could wash better. It was our only opportunity during a span of twenty-four hours. Toothpaste and toothbrushes would have been helpful, but we had none. I hadn't seen any soap.

It was Thursday. Silence followed the usual morning bustle and breakfast. Only Dănuț and Lucian could not keep quiet. They were hungry. Vasile gave Dănuț his share of bread and I gave Lucian mine. Their hunger would abate in time, but eating only aroused an appetite that made them cry. Their stomachs hurt.

We received in the morning our bread ration for the whole day. We were supposed to divide one triangle of bread into three and keep some for lunch and dinner. This was impossible. Even if we had eaten the whole piece of bread at once, we would not have been satisfied.

Vasile and I could get used to that situation. We had fulfilled our military service and knew that in a few days we would adapt to the program. But the young boys thought they would never survive, so hungry were they.

As far as I was concerned, for better or worse, we had three meals a day, we had water to drink, we had heat, and we had beds to sleep on. We had nothing to complain of. We were still in Yugoslavia and nobody had mistreated us. We only had to wait.

We could not anticipate the authorities' decision. We asked ourselves, "Why don't they send us back? Why don't they tell us their decision? How much time do they need? Surely we are not the first people to have been caught." Satisfied or unsatisfied, satiated or hungry, the time was passing. Somebody had to be working on our case.

The door visor opened every hour or two. We were being checked on. We were not allowed to lie down. When they saw we needed more water, they brought some. What could we do?

There was nobody I could play chess with. I was the only one who could play. I had tried to play alone. When I learned to play gammon, I used to play by myself, but chess is not the same. In order to pass the time more easily, we climbed on the top bed, the one near the window, and looked at the town. I supposed this was forbidden to the detainees too. We could see cars passing slowly from time to time, and, very seldom, a person walking on the street. It was something different, and that made us very happy.

We heard steps in the corridor before lunch. They stopped in front of our door, and the door opened noisily. Two officers asked us to come out of the cell. After a short hesitation, we lined up and followed them. One officer led us; the other officer followed us.

We went down some stairs, crossed a large corridor, and got into the yard. It was large and nice, a square guarded by tall walls. The officers told us to walk, using signs. We obeyed. We had to go "na spatsira" walking. It was our sun shower. The weather was cold but pleasant. We relaxed, but still had not found anything out about our mysterious destiny.

The others, especially Vasile, started to vociferate in "Romanian style," saying whatever came to them. I don't think anybody heard them except me. They stopped doing it on my insistence. I reminded them that the guards might understand Romanian, and such talk would aggravate our situation. We were very anxious, considering the uncertain future, but we had to realize that everything takes time.

"What do people in Romania say about us?" Vasile asked with his hair in his eyes. Poor Vasile. He had not had a drink or cigarettes for three days, and he thought he could not make it without them. This made him lose his temper.

"Dear friends," I told them, "people cannot live without air, without food, without water, but they can live without cigarettes. You'll see."

"I would give anything for a pack of cigarettes," Vasile said. "Even one thousand lei."

I asked, "How much money do you have with you, or how much do we have altogether?"

"Two hundred or two hundred and fifty."

"So you do not have enough money for one pack of cigarettes. What can I say about the boys? They would have bought bread with that money two hours ago. You can make it without cigarettes. Calm down! If the boys can forget about hunger, you too will forget about the desire to smoke."

They all looked at me, unsatisfied with my logic and rebellious in their hearts.

They gave up and calmed down suddenly. They were ravaged and disappointed. Hair unwashed, uncombed, unshaven, they looked awful. I did not look any better. Vasile kept arranging his black, long, straight, but not too thick hair, which was always covering his right eye. He looked tormented.

I tried to keep my light-colored hair parted on the left and combed toward the back. An aunt used to tell me that I looked like King Michael of Romania with that hairstyle. Dănuţ looked more like me than Vasile, because he was blond. Lucian, somewhat luckier than the rest of us, had black, curly hair, which was easier to maintain. We all had short hair, and that was because we had just passed Christmas. Every Romanian goes to get a haircut before Christmas. The fact that none of us had long hair was, I think, a positive thing in the eyes of the Serbian authorities as well.

"Back to your question, Vasile—what do people say about us in Romania? Who knows?"

"I was thinking last night of what they will say when they find out we crossed the border in these conditions. How many calculated and uncalculated risks we took and faced them victoriously. Why didn't we simply turned back home in that freezing cold? I felt the shivers of death just thinking of crossing the border again in such wintry weather!"

"We were not far from going back home," Lucian said. "I talked to Dănuț several times about leaving you and going home, but Viorel watched us and walked so close to us that he could even hear our breathing. We were about to ruin our reputation! When I think of the risks I have taken, I realize that I wasn't thinking when I decided to go with you. I had no intention of leaving the country. I have nobody waiting for me abroad, and I don't like foreign languages. Vasile can speak German, and Dănuț is going with him. Viorel will find some believing friends. But me? Anyway, now I play the great hero, but that's only for me. It is going to take a long time for somebody to notice I am missing."

"Yes, we were about to become 'great heroes killed by a bull,' as people say," Dănuț added. "If I had been in Romania during that freezing weather on Monday, I would have entered the first house I saw and asked for food and a place to sleep. I was so exhausted that I would rather have died than continued to follow you. All my adventurous dreams would have died in a few hours! How many times did I tell you to leave me behind to die? There has been no other moment in my life when I wished I were dead, with all the courage of a crazy boy. In that freezing weather and as tired as I was, sleep seemed sweeter than any time before. If you had let me sleep in that hut, I would still have been asleep today."

"'The one who died yesterday, today regrets it!' Today, nobody knows what we are going through but us. The people back in Romania will think and say whatever we used to say when we heard about somebody crossing the border. 'They have escaped everything,' they say! For them, we are like those who walk upon air, as a member of the Communist Party said during a meeting."

"We don't know what tomorrow has in store for us," Vasile said. "We won't be doing well if these people send us back. It is going to be woe to us and our futures. This will follow us all our lives. Criminal records! I hope these Serbians don't send us back! For the moment, we are away from the Romanian authorities. The only people missing and worrying about Dănuţ and I are Lenuţa and my mother. They do not know I have taken Dănuţ with me. I hope they will hear only good things about us! My wife had no idea that I was intending to leave the country and she won't come after me. I don't worry about her because she is not worrying about me. The girls will remain in the country with her."

I said, "If they send us back, we will have to pay an awful lot for this adventure. But I don't think we will give up. At least, I will never give up until I get to the West. You know the saying: dead or alive!

"Today is Thursday. I was supposed to be at work on Monday afternoon. Fritz, the one we met on Sunday in Pustiniş, will be anxious to find out something about me—whether I have crossed the border or have been caught.

"More scared will be my chief. She asked permission before Christmas, during a special meeting in front of the Working People's Committee, to visit China. She was a technology professor at the polytechnic and also worked at ISIM as chief of the laboratory. She hired me last year, on the first of November. The first of November is All Souls Day. Significant, isn't it? I brought her good luck. I helped the laboratory a lot during the two months I worked there. All her life she wanted to visit China. Her visit was approved, but with my leaving the country, I am sure her permission was canceled.

"What makes me anxious is my family. They all knew I was supposed to meet Lenuţa Tepei's brother. I am sure all of them are eager to hear something about me or about us. I am sure that my wife, Coca, is walking all day around Iosefin Square. I think she will visit Lenuţa one hundred times a day until they hear something about us. After that, they will be either very glad or very upset. How can we let them know something about us? It will be enough for them to know that we have successfully crossed the border and that we haven't frozen to death or been shot! Nothing else matters ... but it is impossible to communicate with them in these conditions."

"Of course," Vasile confirmed, "of course. We do not know what is going to happen with us either, but we have a fifty percent chance to be free or to stay here behind bars for some time."

"Another Romanian proverb comes to my mind," I said. "The one that says, 'A job begun is a job half done.' As I understood from Mihai Manea, who has been in jail for crossing the border, the Romanian government approves visas for all of those who have been to jail for illegal crossing. He was convinced about that."

Night fell. It was dark in the cell. The corridor smelled of food. Supper was coming.

We had spent all afternoon talking about ourselves, the opinions of those in Romania, and our situation. The food was late, so, with the same appetites as on the first day, we cleaned our plates immediately. The food was tasty but again very little. Between supper and bedtime, we became hungry again. It was a Calvary to wait until morning. We drank water before going to bed. That was all. Our intestines made desperate noises until we fell asleep.

## CHAPTER 13

# BORN AGAIN

Very truly I tell you, no one can enter the kingdom
of God unless they are born of water and the Spirit.
—John 3:5

"TELL US SOMETHING about you." Dănuţ
expressed his curiosity about how I knew
Vasile Tepei, his brother-in-law who had
crossed the border before us.

"I was expecting this request," I told him, "but it is
going to take the whole night to answer."

"Just start." Lucian wanted to hear something new.
There was nothing new to hear about the others. They
knew each other well from home. Besides their pilfering,
besides the adventures Dănuţ had had with Vasile, and
the drinking and regular amusements, they had nothing
else to share.

"Okay," I said. "Be prepared for a long story. I will
stop when you fall asleep, but I will continue tomorrow
and the day after tomorrow until I finish it.

"I was born in a village near Suceava called Mitocul-
Dragomirnei. My father was a very good carpenter,
appreciated in our village and in the surrounding area.

My mother was a dressmaker for the whole village. My grandparents, who raised me until I was eleven, were village people. They raised cattle and worked the land.

"In the year 1962, when collectivization was completed in Romania and all the land was registered into cooperatives, my father bought a piece of land in Iţcani, in the Suceava neighborhood, and built a house there. We were six children at that time. I am the second one. I have a sister two years older than me. Her name is Ileana. The next after me, Silvia, came four years later.

"Before my sister Lenuţa went to school, my grandfather Costache, from my father's side, who lived with us, took care of her, teaching her to read, write, and count. There was no kindergarten in our village at that time. Lenuţa was very diligent. She was a fast learner. I was not even five years old. Because I had nothing to else to do, I also started learning to write, read, and count.

"I often read the Bible. At five years old, I was a kind of wonder in my village. We had two Bibles at home, the only books in the whole house. Grandfather read the Bible when the weather was bad, especially in the winter. I think he also read it every morning before going to work, but I could not hear him because I was sleeping at that hour. However, I often found the Bible opened at a different page, which told me somebody had been reading it without my knowing when. I could remember whole passages from the Bible. Some have been and still are very useful to me.

"With this start in life, we had an easy time in school. Those who knew me said that my parents should have enrolled me directly in fourth grade, something that was impossible in Romania at that time. The system! I was still in the first grade when my teacher, Mrs. Zamfirescu, told my mother that I would become a philosopher. My mother did not even know what a philosopher was, but she imagined it must be something good.

"All of us children were good at school. That is why Father moved us to town. There were rumors that the children of peasants would be forced to remain in the villages to work the land. Office jobs were reserved for town children. I became an accountant. My father's dream was fulfilled. Lenuţa worked in the standardization department of the Zimbrul factory in Suceava. I was allocated to the auto repair factory. I worked in the financial department. I did the payroll for two sections of the factory."

"Sorry for interrupting you," Dănuţ said, "but how has the Bible or different passages of the Bible helped you get to Timişoara, and from there to here? Is there any connection?"

There was a moment of silence. All three of them were listening very carefully to my life story. I would never have believed my life could raise such a sense of curiosity. I had had the impression I was living a normal life!

"Dănuţ, I would like to tell you one Scripture that I believed when I read it for the first time. It was and still is true in my life. I don't want to bore you with Bible passages, although I believe that absolutely everything in the Bible is true. I have read in the Bible many times that God keeps a record not only of people's lives, but also of all the animals and birds. The Lord Jesus assured His disciples that God the Father keeps record of every bird, saying that no bird would fall without the will of the heavenly Father. Then He continued with an even greater statement: 'And even the very hairs of your head are all numbered.' It is hard to imagine such a strict and accurate record. I am an accountant, and I know what it means to keep a record. Even if that statement seems to be figurative and exaggerated, the Bible never exaggerates. The Bible says the truth! God does not exaggerate and He does not want to intimidate people with what the Bible says. Everything is as written."

"This is hard to believe," Vasile said, unconsciously rearranging his hair, which had fallen over his right eye.

"If we could understand God's relationship with man as a father-son relationship, then all the theological complications would become simple," I answered.

"The complication is, to continue your idea, that not even believers are protected by 'their Father,'" Vasile replied very confidently.

"Vasile!" I exclaimed. "The Bible speaks to all people, not only to believers. God observes and keeps a record of each person's life. He has created us for a very clear destiny: to acknowledge Him and to do His will, so that, after the resurrection of the dead and the future judgment, we will inherit eternal life with God the Father, Son, and Holy Spirit, with all the angels and the saints who have believed in the Lord Jesus and in His sacrifice for us at Calvary."

"How do we know His will?" Dănuț asked.

"We can find God's will in the Bible. The Bible tells us where we come from, where we are, and what the final destination of humanity is. The Bible tells us that God has predestined all people so we will live forever. In God's original plan, He wished all people to be saved. No child in this world comes by accident. Every individual is in God's strict record, from his birth to his death. God is a parent who knows His children very well. We find all this in the Bible.

"The Bible is also called the Book of Life. Every car, every device comes with a little book called a manual, in which we find all the instructions needed to operate the device, beginning with the name of the company that made it, its purpose, how to obtain the best results from it, and how to fix it. Man has come to earth with all the necessary instructions, and the book that contains them is the Bible.

"Many people despise and underestimate the Bible. Many people are ashamed of it. Others say the priests wrote it only to get money from people who attend church! Others have found or made up contradictions in it. They have not believed it nor learned what they were suppose to learn from it. They have not repented of their evil deeds, words, or thoughts.

"That is why God sent His Son to tell us one more time what our purpose is on this earth. All the things Jesus taught His disciples and the people of His time have been recorded in the Bible, so that when we read the Bible, we find out everything God asks from us."

"Then why are there different churches?" Dănuţ asked. "Don't they all have the same Bible?"

"All of them have the same Bible, it is true, but every church explains the Bible in a different way. Not long ago, the Bible was read and explained only by priests. People had no direct access to it. They could not read, so even if they wanted to do God's will, they were limited to what they heard. Some priests transformed ministry into a profession and a source of income.

"The most important thing is to have a personal relationship with God. Parents, for example, have a personal relationship with their children, but they do not have the same relationship with the neighbors' children. They may claim to know them, but they do not have the same relationship as with their own children. We all need to seek God. We need to understand what He wants to do through us and what our final destination is. We need to accept the fact that we are His children. We will resemble His Son, the Lord Jesus. Then we will have the same destination as the Lord Jesus, who ascended to heaven and lives with God the Father. You know all these things, don't you?"

"I have heard some of it, but I haven't understood much," Vasile said. "The priest reads and sings from the Bible, people go to church, and our church, as they say, takes care of our souls. If we have been baptized in the church when we were children, then we go to church at Easter, confess our sins, and take Holy Communion. The priest buries us and keeps all the requiems established by the church. That's all."

Lucian asked, "How do you know if you are or are not a child of God? And if you are not, how can you become His child? How can you have Him recognize you? How can you enter into a relationship with Him, so He would protect you as His child?"

"A child is one's child by birth. The Lord Jesus taught us that we have to be born again," I replied.

"Well," Vasile said, "I have heard about this new birth. Is it something serious or just a way of speaking?"

"One could call it a complete change of someone's lifestyle, in common language. It is in this sense that God asks us to be born again. I have a better explanation. We are living it out right now, the four of us.

"Listen carefully! After our first birth, through our parents, we all began our fight for survival, for the life we live in this world. We grew up, went to school, and prepared for a future. We worked and sacrificed for a better life. Our human nature forces us, instinctively, to care for our lives and then for our families. That is what everybody does, or at least what most people do. That is what I have done.

"I heard at a certain point that life in the West was better, easier; that people earned more money than in our country; that goods are better and more abundant; that people are free to say whatever they want without fearing the police; and that they are more respectful and help each other more. I heard that you can live a better life, so I started asking around about how it is to live in Western countries. All the information I could get from different sources convinced me that this was the truth.

"After I was convinced about the reality of the things I heard, I made plans to leave Romania. I had to think about where I wanted to go, what language people spoke there, what society was like, what professions were needed, what the religion of the majority of the population was, if people discriminated against each other, if there were natural risks like earthquakes and thunderstorms.

"From the day I started thinking of another country, I ended all my dreams of a future in Romania. I was still living in Romania, but I was 'born again' for life in another country. I thought day and night of my future life in Germany or the United States. I had to think of Romania only up to the moment of leaving. After leaving, I would not be interested at all in what happened there. I was 'dead' for Romania.

"It is the same with being born again for God. Once again, you can find all the necessary information in the Bible. We learn from it the conditions we need to meet in order to be accepted in God's country. We learn how people live there, whom shall we meet, what relationships will be there, what we will have to do, and all the other things we need to know about our future in the Promised Land. If God wrote our names in heaven before the creation of this world, then the same God will find each person born, irrespective of where, how, and when that person died. God will raise him or her from the dead and bring him or her to the judgment. People will be judged for the good or evil they did while living.

"You remember that God gave Adam and Eve responsibilities. He gave us some too. The Bible says that all people will be resurrected, and then separated by God before the judgment seat. He will send some of them to hell with the Devil, but those whose names have been written in the Book of Life are His children, He will take them to be with Him forever in heaven. We learn all this from the Bible.

"When you hear all these new things about your destination as a man created for eternity and believe in Jesus Christ, you are saved. You completely change your purpose in life. If you have lived until now for life on earth, and from today onward you live for the future life, that proves you have been born again. It is not enough to know all the promises and possibilities. If you do not act, you are not born again! There are many people who know a lot about the new birth, but who are never born again.

"God has prepared for us a new heaven and a new earth, where He wants to live with us, His children. He wants us to be like a family forever, together with those who have been born again for Him. Do you want to be born again?"

I stopped. The others took some time to understand the things they had just heard. Sleep had left us. I kept quiet for a few minutes, thinking, and then continued the story of my life.

"Preparing for the West made me set aside my office job as an accountant and go to work as a porter in a harbor, with the hope of escaping on a ship.

"After a few months, I realized it was hard to leave illegally on a ship. I left the harbor and went to learn construction. The Mining Montage and Construction Trust (TCMM) was hoping to send a team of highly qualified bricklayers abroad. The chief of the team was Pavel Păduraru, a cousin of Teofil Maga, the husband of my older sister, Lenuţa.

"I worked for a year on the TCMM construction site, mixing mortar and giving bricks to the bricklayers. Nobody said a word about leaving the country! I thought I could do better working in construction than as an accountant once I got to another country. But construction work was very hard, during cold weather and warm weather alike.

"Later, I thought a job practiced indoors would be better, both for working conditions and for the fact that it could be practiced all year around, regardless of the weather conditions. So I got a qualification in cutting metals. I worked for five years at the Aeronautic Construction Factory (ICA) in Braşov. I hoped to be sent abroad as a specialist.

"By then, I had been living for more than seven years with all my attention focused on getting to the West. I was committed to leaving Romania under any circumstances. I often think of, and hardly believe myself, how many stupid things I was able to do! To give up everything for a dream? I was convinced that I would succeed in changing my future, and I bet everything on that. Soon I convinced myself that it was the right thing to do.

"Likewise, I had decided as a child to do God's will all my life, because I believe that the promises God made are real. During the last seven years or more, I have made many fundamental changes in my life, dreaming of a better one.

"The Lord Jesus asks us to make a fundamental change concerning our purpose for living. We have the possibility, during this short life we live, to choose why we are living. Every one of us have received from God the freedom to choose: to live for this life here on earth or for the eternal life in heaven that God promised. God asks us not to think any more of this short life, but to think of eternal life and the things that characterize it.

"In conclusion, every man who chooses to lose this life for eternal life is born again for God. So listen first to the promises of God and be convinced that they are true; then do what you can to own them."

"From what I know," Vasile said, "those who go to church to pray and cry are generally women and elderly people. You have to give up every good thing in life and renounce any sin: drinking, smoking, lying, swearing, stealing, and cheating. Then you have to keep the black fast, give your hard-earned money to families with many children who do not want to work, dress poorly, and give up your amusements. These are conditions that most of us cannot meet."

I responded, "The fundamental condition is to believe that Jesus Christ is the Son of God, who came to earth, grew among people, did good to those in need, and reaffirmed what the majority of the prophets said about the plan of God.

"He assured us that heaven is a real place and hell likewise. He said He was the Son of God who came from heaven, from the Father, and who would go back to heaven after finishing His mission among the people. He finished His mission as a teacher and then paid on the cross for the sins of humanity.

"God made, from the beginning of the beginning, an eternal law, a cosmic one, valid for the whole universe, which said that the soul of the man who sins will die. Men, beginning with Adam and Eve, have sinned, so we were all condemned to die and go to hell for eternity. God could not change that law and will never change it. To keep His law valid and for us not to die, He chose a substitute, someone to die in the place of sinners.

"Until the coming of our Lord Jesus, people had offered sacrifices for their sins. God wanted to make man responsible for his sin. For thousands of years, God accepted a substitution: the death of an innocent animal in the place of a sinner's death. For thousands of years, the blood of innocent lambs and pigeons was shed in order to wash away the sins of irresponsible people. Humankind got used to this bloody ritual and continued to live irresponsibly.

"God had one more solution for the salvation of humanity: the death of an innocent man for the whole world of guilty people. That man could not be found among earthlings. The Lord Jesus was incarnated and lived as a man, kept himself free from sin, and died in the place of every sinful man.

"That was the perfect solution for the salvation of humanity from hell. The only one who could save the world from eternal damnation was the Lord Jesus Himself, who was and is the only and beloved Son of the Father.

"That is why God the Father, because He loves men more than we can imagine and wants them with Him in eternity, set up a condition for the salvation of sinners: whoever believes in the Lord Jesus shall not perish, but have eternal life. The salvation of souls from eternal damnation is guaranteed through faith in the Lord Jesus and in His death on the cross for our sins.

"We are sinners, and according to the universal law given by God, we had to be sentenced to death. But we are saved by accepting Jesus into our lives by faith. This favor—which God the Father gave us freely, saving us by faith without costing us anything—is God's grace or God's gift for those who believe. It is simple and at the same time complicated, as complicated as possible."

"I take the simple part," Lucian interrupted, looking at Dănuţ. "I believe in Him, but what shall I do? I love life. If all people repented, it would be simple for me, but here, where all people hate each other, how shall I stay back and make a fool of myself? I will not live as a hermit. No way! Shall I let all the people mock me? You need to be a better thief than the other thieves to live a good life. What should I expect at the future judgment?"

We were speaking quietly, but we could hear each other very well in the silence of the night.

I said, "I believe you know that the Lord Jesus was crucified between two thieves. The Bible tells us that one of them asked Jesus to demonstrate His divine power, come down from the cross, and save Himself and them.

"The other thief rebuked the first one and told him that they deserved their fate, because they had been evil, but the Lord Jesus was being punished unjustly. Jesus had no guilt. Then the second thief spoke to the Lord Jesus and said, 'Jesus, remember me when you come into your kingdom.'

"The Lord Jesus promised him, 'Truly I tell you, today you will be with me in paradise.'

"That second thief was a criminal, a sinner. He had to end up in hell. But in the moment of his death, he saw in the one dying next to him the Son of God. He believed Jesus was the Son of God and believed in the promises He made—that He would have a kingdom, the kingdom of God. That faith in the Lord Jesus saved his soul from hell. He had been all his life a wrongdoer, a thief to his death! He was to go to paradise with God on the same day.

"Let me tell you a joke. It is said that this thief was the biggest thief on the face of the earth because he even stole eternal life! This reminds me of the poem 'The Thief,' written by Costache Ioanid, a great Romanian Christian poet. The last stanza reads like this:

> All people should know: where the thief went
> No one can believe and not receive the grace
> No sin too great for His promise
> Only one without forgiveness: unbelief.

"If God saved the thief in the last moment, why would He not save us in our last minute of life?" Dănuț asked, still awake. All of them were connected to this topic. We had forgotten completely where we were; we had lost the notion of time.

"He can," I replied after a pause. "If you believe in the Lord Jesus as the thief believed, and if you confess with your mouth what you believe, you can be saved. But who can guarantee you that you will have that last minute to take advantage of it, as the thief on the cross did? Death often comes unexpectedly. A heart attack, an accident, a sudden death, and you are lost forever. It would be wise to take advantage of your chance to save your soul when you hear about salvation. Think what a change would have taken place in the life of the thief if he had not died. He would have been a born-again person for sure! This thief has become a great example of a changed life."

Abraham believed God, and it was credited to him as righteousness. (Romans 4:3)

Was not our father Abraham considered righteous for what he did when he offered his son Isaac on the altar? (James 2:21)

"Then why do you need to go to church?" Dănuţ asked.

"You always ask me the same question," I reproached him. "Why do we need to go to church? I would like to make a parallel between a church and a factory. The Lord Jesus, while He was on earth, talked to His disciples and the people of His time about the kingdom of heaven. He used examples from their daily lives—fishermen, peasants, business people, rich people, family, military— according to the people He was talking to, so they would understand better what He was speaking about. I will try to explain something about the role of the church.

"The church that I am talking about is not the building, of course, but the believers who meet in it. I will give you a logical explanation concerning the life of a believer. It is the point of view of an economist, my personal point of view.

"I worked for a while at the auto repair factory in Suceava, in the financial department. Now, please pay attention! You need to know some things about a factory before you apply to work there. You want to find out what it produces, what the work schedule is, what wages it pays for your qualifications, what vacation time it offers, what pension you'll get, and so on—everything of interest to you. Then you decide if you want to work there or not.

"If you decide to apply for a job, you submit an application, and after its approval, you provide all the necessary documents. Isn't that so?"

"It is so," all three of them replied.

"Before you start work, the factory trains you concerning labor protection and internal regulations. Even if all these seem boring, they are important for you as a new employee. You need to know how to behave in the factory and how to protect the factory in relation to the insurance companies. Only after you have signed all the papers will you get an entry permit. The permit needs to be stamped in order to be valid. In some factories, they even give you a uniform.

"Then you can begin your first day of work. Every part needs to be checked by the quality control department. Usually, after two weeks or a month, the first paycheck comes. You get a salary according to your profession, level, number of good parts, and number of working hours. The salary differs for every employee. The porter gets a salary according to his work, an engineer gets the salary of an engineer, a mechanic gets the salary of a mechanic, the director gets the salary of a director, and so on. Each employee will have her or his name written on the payroll. On payday, everyone looks for their names on the payroll, checks them off and then signs for their money.

"It might happen that names are missing from the payroll at the end of the month. Some are missing because they moved to another factory, others because they retired, others because they were fired, and others because they have not come to work. Do you follow me so far?"

"It is good so far. Continue, please," Lucian said, smiling.

"Likewise with the kingdom of God, which we can compare to a cosmic factory. In that factory are shaped characters of the God type. The disciples, who later became the holy apostles, have transmitted to us through the New Testament the character and purpose of the church or the kingdom of God.

"Among those who showed interest in this church, some liked it and got hired. Others did not and went home. Those who went home have the chance to change their opinion as long as they live. Those who are hired will go through the process of hiring—finding out about what is allowed, what you have to do, and what you are not allowed to do, or the list of sins.

"Sins come from two sources: omitting to fulfill an obligation and committing what the Bible considers a sinful act. Those who do not do their jobs and those who commit crimes might be in the same cell! Everything comes down to responsibility: refraining and acting, doing what you have to do in life. You need to be responsible to God, yourself, your family, your church, and every person you meet in life. These rules are usually taught in church.

"The entry permit to the kingdom of God is *faith*, without which it is impossible to please God. After you are hired, you start working: you sing praises to God, you read and study the Bible, you pray, you fast, you visit and help people, and you do all kinds of things that make us better people and contribute to others' conversion. We all produce something and work together at spreading the good news of salvation through faith in the Lord Jesus and in God. We have as a permanent project the salvation of those around us. The reward will be greater as we succeed in bringing more people to God.

"Since we have decided to get hired to work for the kingdom of God, we can remain employed for the rest of our lives. The Book of Life will be opened on the great Judgment Day, exactly as a payroll. God will pay all of those that worked for His church. All of those found written in the Book of Life will get an unimaginable salary! The Bible speaks about a reward that is more than a payment.

"God asks us to be faithful here on earth. He entrusts us with a few things here, which I mentioned before. But there, He will give us many more responsibilities. It is possible that we will be in charge of planets and galaxies!

"Woe to those who have not wanted to hear about God and His Son and who refused to believe in Him. They won't be on the payroll. Woe also to those who believed and then, after a while, gave up work, took the money, and never came back. The Bible gives us as an example of a former believer Demas, who deserted God because he loved this world. People like him won't be on the payroll.

"The Lord Jesus tells us the same thing about people who have preached the Bible on the streets, who have done miracles casting out demons and healing the sick in the name of our Lord Jesus. Some of these won't be on the payroll in spite of the pretence of being faithful in life. This category may include those who were initially faithful and serious in the church, who succeeded in converting many people to faith, but who, for whatever reasons, trusted in themselves or in their knowledge, or who started earning money and became backsliders, or who became atheists and died as unbelievers. None of these will be on the payroll!

"Anybody can learn a profession in a factory and practice that profession outside of the factory. You can always make parts in another place, even good ones, if you follow good blueprints. It is one thing to be employed and benefit from all the guarantees and protection offered by a large factory, and another thing to be independent. An independent may earn more in the short term, but he will have to pay for his own medical insurance, vacations, and retirement. He is not protected by anybody.

"It is a known fact that Marx had been a priest. But he believed that God did not heal his daughter of headaches, and she died. Thus Marx, the priest, became an enemy of God. He became an atheist and died as one.

"If God rewards those who teach many to walk on the path of righteousness, making them shine as stars in the sky, we can imagine the harsh punishment that atheists and all promoters of atheism will get. If there is going to be a difference in rewards, for sure there will be a big difference in punishment!

"The Bible emphasizes with many examples the fate of those who lose their reward. We can read about those who have abandoned their faith in Hebrews chapter 6:

> It is impossible for those who have once been enlightened, who have tasted the heavenly gift, who have shared in the Holy Spirit, who have tasted the goodness of the word of God and the powers of the coming age and who have fallen away, to be brought back to repentance. To their

loss they are crucifying the Son of God all over again and subjecting him to public disgrace. Land that drinks in the rain often falling on it and that produces a crop useful to those for whom it is farmed receives the blessing of God. But land that produces thorns and thistles is worthless and is in danger of being cursed. In the end it will be burned. (Hebrews 6:4–8)"

"I have a question," Vasile said. "If the atheist does no harm to anybody, but does good to those around him, does he not have any chance to be saved?"

"The Bible talks about people who have been enlightened by God, who have 'tasted' God, who have had personal and indisputable experiences with God, but who have fallen away and become atheists. The Bible says that it is impossible for them to be renewed or saved. Atheists, if they won't accept faith in God, won't see God and won't be saved from eternal hell.

"In the same context, the Bible compares those who have fallen away with a dry land. It could produce something if watered properly. They are saved as one escaping through the flames, exactly as the thief on the cross. Saved, but without any reward! Those who die as atheists won't be on God's payroll.

"We have many atheists in Romania. In addition to them, throughout the world, there are all kinds of religions and worldviews. The Bible says clearly that salvation is offered only through faith in the Lord Jesus.

"The Lord Jesus came to forgive the sins of the world. Beginning with Adam, all people have fallen and still fall into sin: lying, stealing, hatred, deception, fornication, drinking, pride, immorality, murder and many others. All can be forgiven through faith in our Lord Jesus! He gave His life for these sins. He forgives them if we repent of them and do them no more.

"One who falls into sin can be saved, but one who falls away from faith cannot be saved! The list of those whose names won't be in the Book of Life includes many categories of sinners: the cowardly, the unbelieving, the vile, the murderers, the sexually immoral, those who practice magic arts, the idolaters, and the liars. I believe the biggest mistake is not to believe in the existence of God.

"Among the many examples of people who have been deceived, there is a special story in the Bible about a couple that made intentional rejects in God's cosmic factory. Their names are Ananias and Sapphira. They sold a piece of land and decided to donate the money to the church. Ananias told the apostles that he would donate all the money. In reality, he kept a portion of it.

"The apostle Peter, through the Holy Spirit, knew Ananias was lying, so he asked him if that was the whole amount they got for the piece of land. Ananias said it was the whole amount. It is sad, but Peter declared the death sentence for lying, and Ananias died there on the spot.

"A few minutes later came Sapphira, not knowing what had happened. Peter asked her what price they had gotten for the piece of land. She said the same amount; she agreed with her husband, Ananias. Hearing that lie, the apostle declared the same death sentence, so Sapphira died immediately after being rebuked for lying. They could have kept all the money, but because they agreed to lie, they died.

"The lies of Ananias and Sapphira can be described as 'intentional scrap,' or deliberate ruin of the intended product of God's cosmic factory. If it happens that we make mistakes at our jobs, we can apologize, ask forgiveness, and promise to be more careful next time. We are forgiven and we can continue our work. But if we continue to make scraps and then try to convince everybody that the parts are good, we will lose our jobs.

"That was Ananias and Sapphira's situation. They and all of those who do what they did are not on the payroll.

"There is another story, this one with a happy ending: the story of the prodigal son. He was a child who got all his inheritance, left home (the church), and spent the money on amusements. His friends forsook him. Nobody would give him a job. He got so desperate that he was ready to take his life. He remembered his father's house and the good life he had had there—and not only he, but all the servants.

"Despite the shame he had brought on his father by leaving home, and the shame of his current condition, he decided to return to his father and ask to become a servant. When he got home, he had a great surprise, and his father likewise. His father rejoiced very much at seeing his son, and the son got to enjoy all the attention of the house. He was received as a son. There were no reproaches about the past. Nobody asked him where his money was. Nobody calculated how much he had lost or how much he would have earned if he had worked all that time.

"This son and all the prodigal sons who come to their senses and return to work, bringing a benefit to the kingdom, will be on the payroll for sure. Different from the thief on the cross, who had no reward, these sons will have a reward according to what they have earned. If they had been working, however, the reward would have been bigger!

"I return to the thief on the cross, saved by the Lord Jesus. What do you think is going to be his reward? The thief, by his faith in the Lord Jesus, was hired to work for the kingdom, but died immediately. What a waste! He is an employee, his name will be on the payroll, but because he produced nothing—nobody accepted Christ through him—he will not get any reward.

"However, he and those like him will be saved as one escaping through the flames, and will be included in the retirement plan of the kingdom of God, which is eternal life. It is also possible that the thief will get a reward because, through his example of faith, many will get converted later—but only God knows that!

"This is how I see the Christian life. As for me, I am convinced that it is good to invest everything in the future life, in all the rewards God has prepared for us. I live every day with joy and excitement!

"I almost cry anytime I watch the medal ceremony of the Olympics. The majority of the champions cry when they get their prizes and are honored with the anthem of the country they represent. I make a parallel in my mind with the extremely high prize I will receive when I get to heaven after a life lived here on earth and after winning the fights. Even if sometimes I kneel, I will receive the crown of life. I will hear the choir of angels sing in my honor.

"I would like to see on the podium of champions, next to me, all of those in my family and those I have known: grandparents, parents, wife, children, grandchildren, great-grandchildren, the children of their children, all my friends, and the people I have met in life, along with the patriarchs, the martyrs and the brave characters of the Holy Scripture. I dream of that time when those heavenly prizes will be handed out and I see myself victorious, by faith! I will receive the crown of life. So I will never give up this dream for anything in this world.

"God gave us the right and the power to choose. Now, since salvation is free and guaranteed by faith in God the Father and in the Lord Jesus Christ, it depends on every person's choice. All the people whose names are not in the Book of Life will be thrown into the pit of fire, into hell, forever separated from God."

"I understand now why my sister Lenuţa wanted me to leave with a believer," Vasile said. "God has been with us, I am sure. He was with you, and because we were with you, God has protected us too."

"Don't flatter me," I replied. "God loves you too in the same measure. He has cared for you too since you were in your mother's womb. He has watched over you from the first second, the first day you came into this world. Not even the mother who gave birth to you could watch and protect you twenty-four hours a day, unceasingly. Every breath, every heartbeat, every function of your organs, your growth, your development, your protection against accidents since childhood when you were small and helpless, all demonstrate His unconditional love for you. Think of the fact that all our hairs are numbered. These words have remained in my mind since I was five years old and read them in the Bible.

"I have made that statement of the Lord Jesus a way of life, based on the fact that He protects me. He knows me inside and outside, if I can say that. More than this, I am convinced that the same God knows not only what I do, but also what I think, what I contemplate, and what I plan. This is why the Bible says that God will judge not only our deeds, but even our words and thoughts!

"Meditating on His care for us, His people, we notice that it would be enough, if only one element from the multitude of elements that make our life possible were not right, for us to disappear in one moment. God has created the environment for life—the appropriate temperature, atmospheric pressure, light, noises, food, water, work power, bodily recuperation through sleep, communication with words—to demonstrate God's love for every one of us. Vasile, we as parents do what we can for our children every day to make them happy, don't we? God has the same intentions for all of us, those who choose to be His."

"I have never thought of this," Lucian said. "I understand we are very selfish. We think that we are the masters, that we can take care of ourselves. I remembered while you were speaking the conditions our lives depend on. Just this past Tuesday, we were close to dying, and that only due to cold and fatigue. This is something!"

I said, "I think we should never forget how God provided for us in recent days, even if it was not He who told us to leave the country during winter season."

"You are perfectly right," Lucian said, and all the others agreed with him. "We have behaved like mindless children, but still He was with us."

## CHAPTER 14
# FRIDAY, JANUARY 19, 1979

RIDAY WAS LIKE the preceding day. We were taken for a walk outside. The gloomy and foggy winter weather that had persisted for the last few days closed us in on ourselves.

We heard the director of the prison talking in German to somebody on the phone. Vasile's face lit up. We had a chance to find out from the director what our fate would be. Since Tuesday, we had had no conversation with the officials in Romanian. We communicated only through signs with the prison guards. But now, hearing German, we felt like the sun was rising after a heavy storm.

The director had a voice that inspired trust. He had a pleasant voice as an orator. He spoke loudly but not tediously.

"Herr Director!" Vasile shouted toward the office. "Herr Director!" he shouted again, to our surprise and the surprise of the guards.

"Yes?" someone answered after few seconds.

The director showed himself at the top of the stairs and continued to talk to Vasile in German. They talked for a few minutes, long minutes. We waited anxiously for some new information.

Vasile, after a long conversation, told us that he had asked the director if he knew about us and if he could tell us what they wanted to do with us. The director told him that he was sorry, but he had no orders concerning us. He also told us, very politely, that he was likewise waiting for orders.

The morning sunbath time passed faster, even if we could not see the sun. The small yard, guarded by a tall wall and wire netting on the top, gave us the impression that everybody in Yugoslavia lived in a prison. Because of the cold, even the guards walked around the yard with us. Anyway, time passed faster, maybe because we were more rested or because we were anxious to hear the final answer to our destiny.

Afternoons were much longer. We tried to solve the same equations with the same unknown terms and got the same results. We could not find any formula that would help us go one step further.

Food was served through the noisy visor of the metal door. We ate everything. In three days we had adapted to the daily schedule. Getting used to the schedule gave us a certain trust. At least we were not treated brutally. We were not abused in any way. We behaved ourselves too. Vasile was bursting from time to time, but we calmed him quickly. We needed no more trouble.

When we finished eating, the guards opened the visor and took the plates. We listened to their steps going away. The noise of their steps was the only music we had to listen to. We could hear any step from a distance, and we always listened carefully to hear if they were approaching our cell. We expected to get our sentence at any moment! We also listened carefully when the steps were going away, to seize the opportunity to climb on the bed situated next to the window.

After they cleared our plates, their steps went away as usual, but we soon heard them approaching our door again. We stood up. We were sure we would find out something new; otherwise we would not have heard the steps until much later. There was nobody on that floor during the day except us. The guards had nothing to do usually, but today it was different.

We were standing when the door opened and one of two guards asked me to follow him. I did so without saying anything. The second guard followed me. My friends were locked back in the cell.

We went down the stairs to the ground floor and then entered a small meeting room. There were four plastic tables with three chairs each, aligned two by two. The room looked like a school classroom. There was somebody waiting for me.

"Have a seat at that table, Mr. Bilauca," the man said. He was older, thin, tall, and had a short gray mustache. He wore a suit and tie, a little bit worn out, giving the impression of a bored bureaucrat. You could not see anything special at first sight. Smooth-faced, he looked like a veteran of that office, but his yellow teeth spoke of the many worries or responsibilities he had.

I noticed an accent when he spoke Romanian, but that was not proof he could not be Romanian. I was afraid he had come to take me "home."

I sat at the table, which had some documents on it. I suddenly thought of the police taking Costică from the prison in Timişoara to Suceava. I could not react at all. The phrase "Mr. Bilauca" would not have given me a good impression from a Romanian official, but his tone, instead of worrying me, gave me a certain confidence.

"Thank you," I answered politely and calmly, sitting on the first chair. He stood in front of the same table.

"I am security major—" and he said his Serbian name. "I was sent by our government to investigate your situation."

"I am at your disposal," I replied, watching his eyes.

"What made you leave Romania? Any serious reasons?" He was speaking Romanian, and his accent was more obvious now. I was used to his Ukrainian accent. We had many Ukrainians in Suceava.

"Human rights" was the first reason that came through my mind. I had a long list of motives, a list that I often referred to, but when asked about serious reasons, only one answer came to my mind—one that I had never before thought of. You could not say anything like that in front of the Romanian police. It would have been suicidal!

"Something more concrete? Have you been mistreated at your work? Have they not paid you a salary or the allowance for children? Have you been detained unjustly?"

"My first complaint, if I can say that, is that we do not have the right to leave the country. We do not have the right to a passport so we can travel around the world. We do not have religious freedom, in spite of the fact that our churches are open. We do not have the freedom to choose our way of thinking and our life philosophy. We are forced to accept atheistic ideology. We cannot find, with all the central, scientific, and rational planning, sufficient goods in the stores. I refer especially to food. Our grocery stores are empty. I am thinking of our children and their children."

"We," my interrogator interrupted me, "have an even worse situation, speaking about food. We go to Romania and buy your salami and meat. We are even poorer."

"I have to admit that the stores in Timișoara are better provided, but if I were to speak about prices, then you are right: only foreigners can afford to buy. Come during the week, not on Saturday, and you will see the same stores empty, completely empty. Saturday is the only day when we can find something to buy, if we have money."

"What was your rank in the Romanian army?"

"Sergeant major."

"A superior officer, isn't that so?" He looked me straight in the eye.

"No! The lowest rank of noncommissioned officer," I explained when I realized he did not know the ranks in the Romanian army. With that, I relaxed a little bit. He was not a Romanian, so my chances were different.

"Here on your service record, it says, 'Discharged with the rank of sergeant major.'"

"Oh, I understand the confusion," I said immediately. "In our language, the word *major* does not refer to a high-ranking officer in the army. We have another word for that, spelled *maior*."

He had not taken any notes until that moment. That was his first note.

We talked about the way my friends and I had crossed the border. I think he was checking something because he was always looking into a file.

"What planes do Romanians build in cooperation with us, the Serbians?" he asked. "You had been working at the aircraft factory. What do you know?"

"I do not know anything official. It is true that I have worked at ICA in Brașov, but they told us nothing about those projects, especially the international ones. We heard, unofficially, that Romania was working with Yugoslavia to build a high-performance warplane. I think they were speaking about R93. That's all I know."

"What parts were you making at Braşov? Could you read the prints? Were they in Romanian or in Serbian? Can you remember?"

"I worked on helicopters. I can tell you that we built helicopters for the French—or at least they were built according to a French patent. I worked using French prints. I have never seen any Serbian prints."

"Are there any other plane factories in Romania, and what kind of planes do they make there?"

"People spoke about planes that were made in Bacău and Craiova, but I don't know what kind. They were only rumors. I heard of nobody coming from there to work in our factory. All I know, from what I heard, was that we received parts from Craiova for some thermic treatment or a special surface coating. We had French baths and equipment. I think they were unique in the whole country. All these were only rumors. People sometimes brag with their imaginations."

"It is true that we build warplanes with you, but I had to find out what people know in Romania about this."

I told him, "We have been raised with fear. Everything is secret. Every factory has its secrets. We are not allowed to talk at all about the factory where we work. Professional secrecy! We watched our shadows too. We felt very insecure. This is another serious reason why I left the country illegally.

"Let me give you an example. One day, somebody wrote some ugly words about the party and the government on the wall of the toilet. Instead of painting the wall in a few minutes, the secret police worked for days and even weeks to take spelling samples from all the workers. Thousands of people! Whether they found the guy or not, I don't know. But you can imagine how much time was wasted! You could not know who was watching you and turning you in. We lost confidence in friends, colleagues, and sometimes even family. There are many who want to impress the secret police and turn in anybody!"

"Have you had any problems due to religion? Have you been treated unjustly as a repentant believer?"

"Yes. An injustice I had to endure occurred when I applied for an apartment while working in Brașov. I applied after I got married and we were expecting our first baby. I knew it would take time, so I waited patiently. Years passed and my turn did not come. There were others who applied much later than me and had already moved into their apartments months or years before. I went several times to talk to the administrative director, but with all the promises, I got nothing. I was always first on the waiting list.

"One very cold February, a colleague from work pulled me aside and whispered in my ear that he wanted to talk to me. We went into a corner, and he told me he had the key from the apartment that had been allotted to me in December. Because he had needed an urban ID, he had arranged with his boss to get my apartment 'on paper.' Now that he had resolved his problems, he was giving me the key and the address of the apartment.

"I could not turn the clock back to change the situation, so I simply took the key and the address and went to the department chief, Mr. Casagranda. He knew me, and he also knew about the 'little detour' the apartment, assignment had taken. After some congratulations, I went out of the office with official approval. The directors were abroad on some business.

"The same day, together with my wife, my best friend Paulin, and his wife Lidia, we went to see the apartment, which was situated in the Red Flag neighborhood. We decided to move into it with Paulin and Lidia, who was also waiting for an approval.

"Next day, I think it was Friday, we moved with our families into that apartment. Estera, my daughter, was six months old, and Lili, Paulin's daughter, was four months old. We were happy!

"Monday evening, three days after we moved in, Paulin and I were at work. We were working from seven in the evening to seven in the morning. Somebody knocked at the door. It was the union leader, accompanied by the chief of the welding section and his daughter. Our wives recognized the two of them and opened the door. After some questions, and after inspecting the apartment, the daughter of the section chief said she liked it.

"When we got home, we heard about the 'inspection.' We thought it was something normal and official, representing the factory. The phrase 'I like it' that the young lady had used did not raise our suspicions.

"Tuesday evening, when we got to work, Ilie the engineer, with a red face, warned us to stay in the factory until eight in the morning to see the director, because the director wanted to talk to us about the apartment. At eight o'clock we were in front of the office door. He was inside. The foremen, the section chief, the administrative director, the chief of the administrative service, and the chief of the porters also went in. We had to wait a few minutes before the heavy, soundproof door was opened and the secretary let us in.

"When the door was opened, we heard the director cursing and swearing, worse than in the army. We could never have imagined such a welcome. We were even more disappointed when we realized all that was concerning us. Paulin, who was a half step in front of me, changed expression. I don't how I looked, but I was speechless. The director, who was wearing the military uniform of a colonel, with three big stars on his shoulders, was raging like a lunatic. He honored us with all the attributes and adjectives from the zoo. All those present stood at attention, aligned to the wall, in front of the director's desk. They were quiet.

"After the director poured out his rage, he turned to the chief of the administrative service and ordered him not to let us enter the factory until we emptied the apartment.

"'Comrade director, we have not broken into the apartment,' I shouted, in order to change the course of the discussion. 'Comrades Casagranda, Râşnoveanu, and Ianoş all knew and approved for us to move into the apartment. The apartment was approved by the Committee of the Working People, as I understood. We have not stolen the key. In addition, we both have infants of a few months old. Where should we go?'

"'You should have waited for me to return to the country, give you the key, and congratulate you. You should not have entered by yourselves, like some vagabonds!'

"'We are both here. You can congratulate us now and let us stay in the apartment. That will solve the problem until the next lot of apartments becomes available,' Paulin intervened, thinking he could convince the director to come to his senses. Paulin and I had both been told we were the first on some lists for receiving an apartment.

"'No!' the director shouted again. 'Get out! Get out of the apartment! Get out of this office! Guard, make sure these two don't enter the factory until they have moved out.' The director would not listen to what we had to say.

"We left the office and looked at each other. We could not believe our ears.

"'All the information in the computer says liquidation, liquidation,' Paulin said very convincingly. 'Germany is waiting for us! Out of this country! I don't want to stay here with these crazy people.'

"'The sooner the better,' I confirmed, fully convinced to get into action. I was ready to leave.

"Râșnoveanu, the foreman, reached us and told us that the director was angry because he wanted to give that apartment to the daughter of the chief of the welding section. Other arrangements!

"All our joy and excitement suddenly disappeared. We had to go home with the worst news ever. We had to move to one room in the singles' block until the next lot of apartments became available. The lot was distributed every quarter, but how many lots had there already been, and how many more would be distributed before our turn came?

"We had our second child while still in the singles' block. Paulin did too. The welder's daughter, who was not working at the aircraft factory and was not even married, moved into the two-room apartment.

"One of the foremen told us that the real reason we were forced to move was because we were repentant. We did not drink, so our bosses could not expect to be invited to Poiana Brașov to drink. This was the main criterion. Corruption!

"Paulin only received an apartment three years after that incident, after I had resigned and moved to Timișoara, closer to the border, with the promise of looking for a better place to live.

"That was an incident when I was discriminated against. Any believer, irrespective of his denomination, was considered a retrograde element. The officials had their reservations about Christians. Atheism had to flourish!"

The officer listened carefully and took more notes. Then we commented more about the food crisis, and I gave him my impression about our economy, from the perspective of an economist.

"What do you think the future of Romania will be?" he asked.

"I come from a family with twelve children. Our mother had to stay home to raise the children. Father was the only one to make money for fourteen people. What chance did we have to survive? We would have done better if thirteen of us were working. I would explain the economic situation of Romania in the same way. I think that way too few people produce and many more consume. It is easy to notice the imbalance. If you talk to ten people in Romania, at least nine of them will brag about the way they cheat at work."

"Do you say people are not going to work?"

"No. What I am saying is that they do not produce. People go to work, they have nice salaries, but the production does not cover all the money people receive. This means there are many who have good salaries corresponding to good positions but who produce nothing. They work for the party or the union in a position listed in the organizational chart, but they produce nothing. This will impoverish the country very quickly. With all the 'scientific planning,' soon all the reserves will be stolen. What will follow then?"

After a pause, seeing that he had no more questions, I continued with a joke that people used to say in Romania. Somebody asked his friend where he was working. The friend replied, "I work at the aircraft factory."

"And what do you do there?"

"Nothing."

"I heard that you hired your son to work with you. What is he doing?"

"Yes, I did," the friend answered. "I hired him to help me!"

The officer interrogating me laughed. "It fits well! I have two more questions related to the transportation tickets you had. What's up with them? Why are they pierced in different places? Is that a code or something?"

"I bought those tickets as part of a package, and I forgot to throw away the used ones. They do not represent any code. The holes represent the tram station where I got on. Please throw them in the garbage."

"What is the letter you had with you? Do you need to take it to somebody?"

"I meant to mail it in Romania, but I forgot. It was written by my sister for somebody in Coldea."

"What does *Ps. 23* represent, and *Matei 5, Iuda 1–3*, and the other codes at the end of the letter?"

"*Ps. 23* means Psalm 23. It is a salutation among us, the repented ones. Instead of writing full pages of salutations, we use Bible passages, so the one who gets the letter can read them by himself in the Bible. All Bibles are the same. You can throw the letter in the garbage. I don't think it will get where it was supposed to get."

After another pause, very seriously, the officer told me that the Yugoslavian government had the power to help me get where I wanted to go. I needed to write a more detailed request with all my reasons for leaving, my intended destination, and, if I had somebody who could help me, his name, address, and telephone number. I had to sign it. Then the government would decide what to do with me.

"I will leave a model statement here, if you think you may need one," he said, showing me some pages written by somebody else. He gave me blank paper and then left.

I looked quickly at the model to get an idea, and checked the signature. It was indecipherable. I was disappointed with the calligraphy of the author. I wrote my request in what I considered a more professional way. I only took the last part of the model, knowing that there were some Yugoslavian formulas I had to include. They were more decipherable.

The entire interview and statement-writing lasted for two hours. Then I was taken back to the cell. Vasile was taken next.

"Where did they take you and what did they do to you?" Dănuț and Lucian jumped in with their questions even before the guards left with Vasile.

"One more interrogation. They need to clarify some things that were still unclear after the previous interviews. At the end, when everything is clear, they will ask you to write a request for help that you address to the Yugoslavian government. They can help you get where you want to go in the West."

"What do you need to write? I have never written such a request in my life," Lucian asked worriedly. "If it took you that long a time, what are we going to do?"

"They asked me about my military rank and about the warplanes that we built in Romania in cooperation with Yugoslavia. I had nothing else but my service record. How should I know? They will give you a model, but before that, they will ask you some questions to confirm what you have already declared. Be careful what you answer; otherwise you may have problems. Only say the truth, as you have done until now!"

The boys became more serious. They were afraid of writing the request. They were not good at writing. I encouraged them to write some general reasons concerning human rights, so often mentioned, and their desire for freedom.

"I hope it will be enough," I said. They were young and had no incidents in their pasts.

Dănuţ said, "I left the country only to help my brother cross the border. I could not let him go alone. I could not let anybody harm him."

"If Vasile heard you," Lucian said, "he would beat you. Does he need your help? It is woe to you!"

I forced myself to laugh. We were not in a mood to tell jokes. We were hanging between freedom and jail.

Vasile finished his request and returned to the cell. Dănuţ followed him, and then Lucian. They finished faster. It must have been five o'clock in the afternoon, if not even earlier, when all four of us were back in the cell. The only question the boys had been asked before copying the request was if any of them had been involved in human trafficking, due to the fact that they had been living near the border.

Another day had passed without us finding out our fate. All our predictions had been good for nothing.

## CHAPTER 15

# EASTER WEEK

W E WOKE UP very tired on Saturday morning. We had had problems falling asleep the night before, so we were quite grumpy. Insecurity overwhelmed us all. We each had our own worries, but we were concerned about those we had left at home. They would be tortured, psychologically at least, until they heard something about us.

Had the Serbian police told them anything? Who here would know if they had been informed about our situation? What would be the attitude of the Romanian policemen visiting our families when they found out about our leaving? It was an embarrassment for them. They should not harass our families, but they would, with many threats and discrimination.

The secret police were often successful in breaking up families. They came up with all kinds of lies, accusing those who left of who knew what. Usually, those who left the country were accused of secret connections with foreigners, and their families were accused of complicity. They would be "invited" to the police station.

Declarations! All four of us had expressed freely and extensively our opinions against the inhuman system in Romania, but there was nobody to listen to us.

"Friends, let's take heart and build our future from what we have," I told them after Vasile and Dănuţ calmed down. "As you see, it is already Saturday, and there has not been any decision made. It is certain we will stay here at least until Tuesday."

"How is that?" the three of them demanded. "What do you mean?"

"It's logical. On Saturday and Sunday, all the institutions are closed. They are not working, not even in Romania. If a decision concerning us was made yesterday, Friday, our case will be analyzed on Monday at the earliest. A decision made on Monday would likely be applied on Tuesday. Nobody is in a hurry. The governments have other things to do than worry about our case! We can knock our heads on the wall if we want, but that won't do any good, except to give us some bumps. If we insist on being heroes, we will change nothing except the cell. They will isolate us. They will handcuff us. If necessary, they will send us to Romania to reeducate us. I think they are working on our case. That is why they asked us to fill in the request for the Yugoslavian government."

"I feel I will lose my mind by tomorrow," Vasile said. "I will be tearing down the prison by Tuesday!"

Dănuţ pleaded, "At least cut one day from your logic. Let's give them time until Monday."

I told them a story. "I once knew a bricklayer, while I was working in Braşov, who tried to stand on his hands. He fell on his head and broke his neck. His name was Iacob. I think he was from Ilva Mică, not far from Bistriţa. They took him to the hospital.

"The first Sunday after the accident, I went to visit him. He was hospitalized in the orthopedic section. I found him in a room with several injured people, lying in bed faceup. He had his head shaved. He had a hole on each side of his head, and in those holes there was a device, like a hook with some weights hanging over a pulley at the top of his bed, pulling his head. He had been lying like that for three days. He was not allowed to stand for any reason. He had to stay in that same position until his spine recovered.

"When I recognized him, which was hard to do, he told me he would be fine. The doctor had said he had to stay like that for two or three days. Then the doctor said he had to stay like that for one more night. Iacob said he was ready to commit suicide if he had to stay in the same position for more than one more day."

"Did they let him leave the next day?" Dănuţ asked.

"They let him leave, but not the next day. They released him after twenty-three days—and he did not die! He hung in there without medication. The doctors knew it was hard for somebody to endure such a torture willingly, but they also knew what a man could do.

"The doctors used a technique. They did not scare people with the prospect of long treatment. They told patients, as they told Iacob, "One more day. One more day. The wound is not healed yet, maybe tomorrow. It looks very well, but it needs another day." This is how our friend Iacob stayed in the hospital for more than three weeks without moving, straight as a candle. He came back to work completely recovered."

"What do you mean?" Vasile questioned. "If not today, I have to find out on Monday. Monday morning! Otherwise I will fight with the director of the prison!"

"They should do something with us!" The other two also started agitating. They pulled the beds, lifted the mattresses, and shouted. We were lucky no guard heard us.

"I don't like waiting forever either," I argued. "I have more reasons than you to be anxious. I have a wife and two children still in Romania, and besides that my in-laws live in my house. How will I let them know where I am? Vasile, you are still on vacation, and these kids have regularly left home for years. Nobody is worrying about you except Lenuţa, your sister, if she has even found out about your leaving.

"I have not been to work since Monday. My wife will get my salary on the ninth, and then what will she get on the twenty-sixth? Nothing! It is winter. My whole family needs to find a means of living if something happens to me. They only have my wife's salary. That is not enough!

"These are the problems that worry me, but we do not need to go to those depths. We have the time and the will to control our thinking. Everything depends on the way we think. Our minds can be educated and adapted to the circumstances. Each person selects from the multitude of thoughts going through his or her mind—selects one thought, and then tries to put it into practice. Reason is like a filter.

"This is why people often find different formulas to solve the same problem. You get upset when somebody tells you what to do and how to do it. We say, 'Who does this guy thinks he is?' or 'Don't be so smart.' We have to use our last reserves of patience and understanding. That is what we did on Monday night. We had to hang on, and we did, but not willingly.

"I learned something in the army. We would never have jumped over a six-feet-high wall if it were not for the needle in the hand of a corporal. You tell me, Lucian and Dănuț: how often have you negotiated with dogs when you had a rooster in your hands? Fear convinces you to use unconceivable energies.

"There is a proverb that says, 'We must learn to walk before we can run.' If this government has helped others, it will help us too. If they asked us to write that request, we have more than a fifty percent chance of success. But they also need something in order to help us, something that takes time."

"How are they going to help us?" Vasile asked with sarcasm. "Will they take us in a limousine to the Romanian embassy in Belgrade?"

"They needed no request for that. Even asking the Serbian government to take us to the Romanian embassy would have required only a few days. We need to be patient. It is hard, but possible. I think the Yugoslavian government is going to help us. I will continue dreaming of Germany or the United States, and I will get there!"

I also raised my voice, more than usual. People outside could have heard me, but there was no other way to make my friends listen. I don't know if my voice or their hunger convinced them, but they were convinced—or at least they kept quiet for the moment.

Each one of us found something to do. We counted the boards in the floor, read the names encrusted on the table and the benches and the wall, or looked outside at the town. A kind of healing silence came down. None of us were bored.

The smell of food let us know it was dinner time. There was an indescribable noise in the corridor for several minutes. The other detainees were coming back from work. On Saturday, it seemed they came back at lunchtime. The noise lasted for about ten minutes and then stopped, as quickly as it had started. The same portion of food was served, without any words, just the noise of the door visor. We thought they would give us a bigger portion of food on Saturday and Sunday, but there was no difference. We were detainees too!

The afternoon went by quietly, with no news.

Sunday passed without any news either. We asked ourselves many times whether everybody had forgotten about us. We had no TV set, no news. Maybe they had said something about us on the Europa liberă (Free Europe) radio station and we did not know.

A week had passed since we had left home. My children appeared in front of my eyes. Estera, four years and six months old, played a lot. She had many questions every day. She was growing and wanted to know everything. She has been a cheerful girl since she was born. She jumped up and down for every little surprise—every toy, every candy, every colorful paper, everything.

Dariu was a true penny, healthy and diligent. At the age of one year and a half, he had already run kilometers through the house. He started walking at nine months, and he was always practicing walking through the house. I had built him a box for firewood and put it at the other end of the room from the regular woodbox. He would take the firewood from one box and put it in the other, and when he had finished doing that, he would take a break and then start all over again.

It would have been very nice if my wife could have found out from Lenuţa that we had succeeded in crossing the border without being shot. I knew Coca was watching the street day and night, waiting to receive any news. News that I had succeeded would have made her extremely happy, especially as she had been living with fear since her brother Aurel had been caught and spent a year and a half in prison. It would have been a disaster for her to find out I had been caught. Costică, my brother, had almost been eaten by dogs a few months before …

My feelings were fighting with my reason. In spite of the fact that feelings won some of the fights, reason was always victorious in the end. I was on reason's side. What good would feelings do at this time? No good. Should I ask to go home? Impossible! I only needed a few more days. They must do something with us. They could not let us stay there forever, and they could not hide us.

Sunday afternoon was noisier. All the detainees were "at home." Many doors opened, many steps passed on the mosaic-floored corridors, and many discussions were held, but at least we felt better knowing that we were not the only ones there. Time passed easier.

Sunday evening, silence again. All the commentaries ceased. We awaited Monday with great expectations.

Monday began with the regular program—nothing unusual, nothing new in the morning. We listened carefully to hear any movement from the guards, but there was nothing. They did not stop in front of our door.

We ate lunch. In the afternoon, there was the same silence in the corridor, but an increasing anxiety in our cell. Nothing new!

We had exhausted all our personal stories. I had found out almost everything about them. Their adventures comprised pilfering, small cheats, and drinking. They had nothing new to say. Boredom began to settle in our cell.

I remembered that we had studied *Eugene Onegin* during my Russian classes, a verse novel that describes, analyzes, and characterizes boredom as the most severe illness somebody can suffer from. "Guys!" I tried to get the attention of my friends. "Let's each tell the story of a book we have read. What else can we do? We all have seen the movies. Who wants to begin?"

"You begin," Vasile said after a long pause. "We have not been so passionate about reading. We had other hobbies, but reading was not one of them ..." We all laughed at that joke.

"As an encouragement, let me tell you a true story. The book is called *Papillon* or *The Butterfly*. A Frenchman was sentenced to life for a murder that he had not committed. He was sent by ship to a prison island in French Guiana. The island was very good for agriculture, and the detainees worked the land right up to their last day of life. The crops were exported back to France to be sold. The owner of the island was a very rich Frenchman. Obviously the detainees lived on the same crops. Our Frenchman had tattooed on his chest a butterfly, a papillon. That is what gave the book its name."

"Wasn't there a movie?" Dănuţ asked.

"Yes. Have you seen it?"

"No. We did not have the money. That movie was in three parts. It cost a fortune! It ran three times only in Timişoara. I wondered if they ran it a second time elsewhere. They did that with all good movies," Dănuţ said.

"Tell us, tell us," said Vasile and Lucian.

"Tell us slowly, for we do not have anything else to do," Vasile added.

I continued. "Well, they haven't run the movie a second time. Even the book hasn't been published more than once. Both the movie and the book had a tremendous impact on the country. It brought a desire for freedom.

The book sowed in each reader a spirit of independence, the desire to become free like a butterfly that flies all its life, the desire to become a papillon.

"Romania needs people to submit, to be obedient to the party and its interests. The people who felt free, especially if they said it aloud, like all the Christians who declared they would submit only to God's will, represent a great danger to a communist society.

"Nothing can force a true Christian; nothing can scare him—not even death. A Christian becomes truly free through death, because in dying, he goes home to God. This is the reason why repentant people are not in the good books of the atheist leadership and are restricted by all kinds of laws. They are despised and humiliated, with the purpose of eliminating them systematically, little by little.

"Anyway, the book was published only once. After the censor realized its effect, it was withdrawn from the bookstores. I had the chance, I don't know how, to read it. I think I read it in 1973. It was a period when I was dreaming of a true freedom. *Papillon* only encouraged me. While I was reading about his life, I grew wings. I surprised myself too."

"We grew wings in three hours," Lucian said.

"We hope they won't break in three hours," Vasile retorted, laughing loudly.

"Papillon tried to escape the island. He tried all kinds of methods. This is a true story. He was condemned in 1931. He described eleven attempts to escape out of the nearly three hundred attempts he made. Besides the guards, he had to watch his fellow prisoners. The island was surrounded by the ocean and was far away from the continent. It was impossible for anyone to escape by swimming, and besides that, there were sharks in the ocean. On the side where one could more easily escape, the security was very strong. On the side where there was no security, there was an abyss into which only those who wanted to take their own lives would jump. In a word, any escape attempt was suicidal.

"Papillon found this out on his own. Betrayed, discovered, blackmailed, sold by friends and enemies, brought back onto the island and punished more severely every time, he never gave up the desire for freedom. He got used to the hardest tortures. All the thirteen years he spent on the island, he was thinking of one thing: how to escape. He believed in himself. He believed he would be free one day, as a butterfly.

"There was nothing legally to be done. All trials had been closed to him in France. Instead of a death sentence, he had been given the alternative of working all his life on that island, along with all kinds of notorious murderers. Stabbings, beatings, starvation, isolation in the dark, torture, working day and night, and anything else you could imagine were their punishment for the rest of their lives. The dead were thrown to the sharks. All of them looked forward to that 'freedom'!

"Most of the detainees accepted that life and that end, but Papillon would not. No way would he accept a life of unjust torture nor that end: dead and eaten by sharks. He admitted he was capable of the murder he was accused of, but because he did not actually kill anybody, he never accepted the punishment. He wanted to be free at any price and believed he would be one day, even though there seemed to be no chance."

"Whom did he kill?" Lucian asked.

"He killed nobody! Did you not hear?" Dănuţ scolded.

"He was accused of murdering a judge, but even though he had not killed him, Papillon's lawyer could not convince the jury of his innocence. Papillon, I think, was under forty years old when he was condemned."

"And how did he escape?" Vasile asked anxiously.

"Did he escape?" the other two jumped in.

"He escaped, of course, because he wrote the story. That is why the book was published. It is a real case. Most books are fiction, but this was real. This man still lives!"

"Tell us, how did he manage to escape?" Vasile pressed his curiosity.

"Imagine a young, healthy, strong, tough man with criminal inclinations, like Papillon, being unjustly condemned. He became a real volcano of dissatisfaction. Treasuring his own life, he was not interested in the other prowlers' lives. He was exhausted by that torture, but he did not give up the prospect of escape.

"He stood on the ridge of a cliff, on the rocky side of the island where he relaxed from time to time. There he used to meet a friend who had been an accountant and committed fraud in France. He was caught, accused, and condemned. He had survived until that point, in spite of the fact that he was a fearful and fragile character. Those two helped each other many times.

"One day, while they were talking as usual, they watched the ocean waves hitting the rock they were standing on. Because they had nothing to do, they threw a coconut in the water and watched it break on the rocks. They watched this show for many days. They noticed that six waves broke the coconuts, but a seventh one took it out into the ocean. They repeated the experiment several times and became convinced that the waves repeated this cycle constantly.

"It is easy to guess what followed. Papillon, his mind on freedom, filled two sacks with coconuts, tied them, and threw them into the water on the seventh wave. He then jumped on the seventh wave. Pulled by the current into the sea, he found a little boat, climbed on it, and escaped.

"He finally got to Caracas, in Venezuela, where he received political asylum. If he has not died, he still lives there today, a happy ending. When he became a free man, he wrote his adventure and sent it to a friend, a writer in France. That is how we found out about Papillon and the adventure of his life."

"Stories," Dănuţ said, "have the gift of putting the children to bed. I think this story has woken us up to life."

"Even so, we have to go to sleep," Lucian replied.

Monday passed very slowly. I saved a few hours with Papillon's life story.

# Chapter 16
# THE TESTS

O N TUESDAY, DESPITE all our anxious expectations, we received no news. Breakfast, lunch, and dinner went by one by one. We were concerned not to be forgotten in that cell. They did not even take us out in the yard for a sunbath. We tried to guess the reason, but we could not find any except the fact that it took a lot of time. Time, yes, but we hoped nobody from Romania had come to take us home! That is what our reason was telling us.

We were exhausted after dinner. The worry made our beards grow faster. With our unwashed, uncombed hair, unshaven faces, and unchanged clothing, we looked awful. At least we could not see ourselves. We had no mirror in the cell.

"I think we will sleep at least another night here," Lucian said after he ate dinner on Tuesday. "Viorel! I think we owe you, but tell us something more, something new, something we have never heard before. We are all sick of this stuff."

"I thought you repentant people knew nothing but the Bible, but now I realize I was wrong," Vasile said.

"We read the Bible, but we have to go to school with our homework done too. I had an excellent Romanian teacher. I studied Romanian with him for eight years, from fifth grade to the end of high school. His name was Antonovici Clement. All the students in Suceava knew him. He knew the best way to learn a language was by reading. You could not go to his classes without reading at least a book each week. You would have been lost. He gave me this taste for reading.

"After you start liking it, you read everything you can find, without anybody asking or threatening you to. You should have seen a test written by one of his students. The entire page was colored red for a misplaced comma. He was very strict, but for our good.

"When we talk about school and exams, I remember something that Vasile concluded concerning God's protection for His children. I have been thinking of your disappointment when you said that even the repented ones are not protected. Before telling you about other books, I want to clarify that. It is seemingly true, but in reality it is not."

Vasile said, "I said it and I maintain what I said: you, Viorel, have you own experiences, and I have mine. Mother repented. It was well. Father said nothing about that. Lenuţa repented too. Well! Father thought it was right. He expected to have a good son-in-law, one who was calm, diligent, did not waste his money on alcohol, and made Lenuţa happy. You tell me. On Thursday during the week they were supposed to get married, Lenuţa and her fiancé had a motorcycle accident. He died instantly and Lenuţa lost one of her legs. Where do you see the protection?"

The three of them were all ears. They were not expecting my answer. They were looking at the beds, but the thing that stopped them from going to bed was the time. It was too early. If we went to bed early, the guards would come and threaten us with a baton.

"What kind of childhood do you think the children of presidents and kings have?" I asked.

"We wish to have such lives," Dănuţ said. "To have everything, guaranteed!"

Vasile and Lucian watched me, questioning. I knew they had not understood my question.

"At first sight, it seems so," I continued. "We would like to live as princes, but I want to assure you, Dănuţ, that their lives are not that easy. I believe many princes would prefer to live your life. Princes and princesses live lives much different from ours. They have many programs and restrictions, and many responsibilities by the time they are adolescents.

"We see or hear about only the nice side of their lives, but in reality the lives of princes and princesses are much heavier than most children bear. They are the center of attention from infancy. Their education begins when they are only a few years old and continues until they die. In school, from elementary to university, they take all the exams. Having private teachers is good and bad, because it takes more of their time. Their whole lives are a strict program: obligations to family and country, diplomatic and political meetings, and the internal and external affairs of the country.

"Besides all this, they have to be in good shape. You remember that in the old days, they had to handle a sword better than anybody. They had to be champions. Many things have changed in our day, but today's princes have to honor their position by hard work."

"I agree with you," Dănuţ said. "I never thought about their lives. You cannot know their real lives from stories."

"If you were a prince, you would be in school today, boy. You would not walk the streets or the river delta as a vagabond," Vasile said. "You too, Lucian. The two of you have lived on your own, with no responsibility."

I continued my point. "So princes live great lives on one hand, enjoying a respectable name, protection, education, power, and wealth. On the other side, the one that only they know, their lives are full of restrictions, duties, responsibilities, and, probably, continuing competition with themselves and those around them. They are very well protected, it is true, but they are not exempt from the greatest responsibilities of life.

"What life do the children of Ceauşescu have? Happy ones? Are they protected? Yes! Do they have a name? Yes! But they were not excused from going to school. They had to take tests and pass classes, year after year. They had to finish high school and university, didn't they? Only after that were they accepted to study at Oxford!

"Children born in regular families are less noticed. Whether they succeed in life or not, it does not matter. Do you notice the difference between a prince and a regular child? When you are born in a higher family, the school of life is tougher. Princes and regular children are born with the same capacities. The difference between them will be seen later in life. The prince, after years of study and work, becomes a king, and the other one ends up on the street, begging, after years and years of playing hooky."

"Well, if the second one had no money to go to school or had no connections, why would you condemn him?" Dănuţ asked confidently.

"Don't get yourself into trouble, Dănuţ," Lucian said, stopping him. "Do you want to excuse yourself for doing nothing with your life?"

"Connections and money count immensely," I replied, "but any child can do something with his life. The majority of children are born healthy, having everything they need to care for themselves and to provide for a family, if they begin their lives responsively.

"Every child begins with the alphabet, but later, depending on the school he goes to and the exams he passes, he will graduate and do something with his life. Those who pass the exams go on, but those who fail have to repeat the class or the exam. If they pass them next time, then they will go on, but if they don't pass them, they will repeat the class or the exam again.

"Passing exams brings diplomas. Diplomas prove one's level of training and are a guarantee for the positions or jobs one can have later. A child has to go to school for twenty years and only then gets a diploma. That's all! After he finds a job, he will start seeing the fruit of all those years of hard work.

"There are students who fail exam after exam. After some years, they give up school and go home without diplomas. It is obvious they won't fill in the same positions as those who graduated. Those who have no diploma will do the unqualified work!"

"I would have taken this discussion personally if we would have not been here, in the same situation," Dănuţ concluded. "I hope you do not refer to me and Lucian, for doing nothing in life!"

"You could use some lessons," Vasile interrupted. "You have done nothing in life until now."

"It was not my intention to lecture you," I reassured Dănuţ. "I was talking about God's protection for believers. It is logical to have high expectations of God as King, but we should not forget that as King, He has high expectations too for His children, His princes—that is, for us, the believers.

"Every believer, and we can use Lenuţa here as an example, is protected directly by God. God has a guardian angel for every person, angels who always see the face of God. Our protection is guaranteed. If princes, princesses, and the children of presidents have such harsh lives in spite of who they are, how much more are protected Christians trained and examined as the children of God?

"We benefit from the help and protection of those around us in childhood. But when the time to go to school comes, we are sent—and not to any school, but to the best and most severe one in the world. That's the school we have to graduate from. Christians have to pass exams in life, including the graduation exam. The exams passed guarantee the future responsibilities Christians might have.

"The school of a Christian starts with victory over one's mind, the confrontation with different philosophies and ideologies. God, right from the beginning, has put in man something special, something from Himself: reason, wisdom, and thinking. God expected man to be grateful and do His will. Everything went well during mankind's childhood. But the first man, Adam, was sent to school and had to graduate. He had to take the last exam and come home with a diploma.

"At his final exam, God allowed Satan, now a fallen angel, to test Adam's trust and commitment to God. Adam failed the exam. He was banished from the garden of Eden, together with Eve, his wife, as you all know. Adam had forgotten for the moment God's promises and the punishment awaiting him in the event of his disobedience to God. The Devil approached Eve and twisted her mind, asking her if God had really given them the commandment not to eat from all the trees in the garden. Although Eve knew for sure God's strict commandment, she questioned what God had said about eating from the forbidden tree. Both she and Adam ate. Eve and Adam failed the exam.

"The same Devil, with the same cunning or the same technique, comes to us today. He makes us question God's existence, commandments, and promises. Someone made the statement that we have an angel on one shoulder who whispers to us every morning to do God's will, and a devil on the other shoulder, who whispers to us to do the Devil's will. This is repeated every day, with every person.

"Who wins over your mind? God with the truth, or the Devil with the lie? That is the most important question in our lives. God wants us to keep our minds clean. We are directly responsible to God for protecting our minds. Alcohol, drugs, atheism, ignorance, indifference, vices, and immorality attack our minds on a daily basis. How many people succeed fighting and winning the battle against these things and instead seek God and live according to His will?

"Lenuţa passed an extremely serious exam well. The exams every Christian has to pass in life are troubles, sicknesses, accidents, material losses, mockery, and many others. We expect God's protection for believers to be absolute, seen by everybody, so all people would see a major difference, but His protection is not so.

"We are in school right now. As in a school, teachers come, teach their lessons, answer questions, explain again, and do what they can to help us understand the meaning of life. The following day they come and repeat the lesson so we get it into our heads. If we still have not understood, we can ask others about that subject. Everything is well until the day of exam.

"At the exam, you get a piece of paper, the questions, and limited time. You could ask for help before from the teacher, colleagues, or older brothers, but no one is allowed to help you during the exam. You are by yourself. If you know the subject, you pass; if not, you fail.

"The worst decision you can make is to abandon school. You give cause for ridicule in front of your family, neighbors, teachers, and colleagues. Besides that, you also spend your parents' money and waste many years of your life. Who would want to be operated on by a doctor who studied at the university but never graduated? Nobody!

"It is likewise with the Christian life. God, as a good Father, desires to make something of our lives. His care and love for every person is unconditional. It is like the care of a father and mother who love their children unconditionally and nevertheless send them to kindergarten, then to school, then to university, and then to work to produce something. Feelings of pity and compassion are overcome by reason. Feelings would make us let our children sleep and play until who knows what age, but reason makes us send them to school at the age of five or six.

"Likewise, God has sent us to school and keeps us in school all our lives. At first, as a good teacher, He listens to our prayers and helps us solve our problems. Then we all as Christians help each other, as good colleagues and brothers. But only to the day of the exam. From time to time there comes an exam in life, a time when no one can or is allowed to help, apparently not even God. It is exactly like a normal exam. We pray, but God's answer can be no, or a command to wait. This is why I said 'apparently.'

"I have prayed for years for success in leaving Romania. I have tried several times, but without any success. It is possible that this time was a yes to my prayers. I am committed to pass this exam well. I will trust in God, even if they send me back to Romania.

"The promise of a great life depends exclusively on the diploma. In the past, victors would receive a laurel crown. The Father God will give a victor's crown to all of us after we graduate from school. When we get to heaven, He will greet us with a feast.

"Every believer—and when I say *believer*, I do not mean the so-called 'repentant,' but whoever believes in the Lord Jesus and in His sacrifice on the cross—is kept forever by God, as a father keeps his child, so no hair will fall without His knowing.

"At the same time, He wants all His children to become something. Therefore, none of His children are excused from school or exams. This is why we see no difference between believers and the rest of the people.

"God has patience with us until we die. Then we will go to Him either with a graduation diploma or empty-handed. Those who stand in front of Him with a diploma will receive their promised inheritance—heaven, eternal life. It depends on what we choose. All of those who have not chosen to serve God in this life will automatically inherit hell, together with Satan, where, as the saying goes, 'All parties are canceled due to the fire.'"

CHAPTER 17

# THE CONNECTION

"VIOREL, WHAT DO you think about priests?" Lucian asked a while later. "Have they been sanctified? Are they exempt from troubles? It seems to me that they are doing well and you cannot hear them complaining."

I responded, "Adam and Eve had two boys, Abel and Cain. Even though the Bible does not mention it, it is very likely that Adam had received a law from God, a law that he passed on to his children. This law said that people had to bring thanksgiving offerings to God for all the good He had done for them, and burnt offerings for every sin they had committed.

"God's intention was to make man responsible for his own actions through these offerings. An offering was a payment for sin. You had to bring an animal as a sacrifice. The animal had to be healthy, without any defect. You had to slaughter it, shed all its blood, and put it on the altar. Then, while it was burning, you watched the smoke.

"I hope you have heard of the first offerings brought by Cain and Abel. Abel's offering was accepted by God, while Cain's offering was not accepted. Cain, angry and jealous because of that, killed Abel."

"I have never heard about that. How would they know if God accepted their offering or not?" Lucian asked.

"They knew the sign. When God accepted somebody's offering, the smoke rose directly to heaven, and when God did not accept the offering, the smoke did not rise, but spread around."

"What did Cain do that his offering was not accepted?" Lucian asked, sounding disappointed.

"The answer is not written in the Bible. Most have concluded that while Abel offered a lamb, shedding blood for his sins, Cain brought an offering from his crops. Cain did not bring an animal offering. God would forgive sin only when the blood of animals was shed. Scrupulous people brought that kind of offering for two thousand years.

"Later, during Moses's time, God chose a Jewish lineage to become priests. They were empowered by God Himself to bring the offerings of the Jews before Him, so He would forgive the sins of the people and not punish them with death. For example, for a big sin you had to sacrifice a calf, and for a smaller one a lamb. For a peace offering, you had to sacrifice a pigeon. The priests did this job according to the rules given by God.

"In those days, people used to sin, but once a year they went to the temple in Jerusalem and brought a calf or a lamb as a sacrifice. They took it to the priest. The priest slaughtered the animal for the sin, so the sinner was forgiven.

"The ritual was very interesting. The one bringing the sacrifice had to hold his hand on the animal's head while the priest slaughtered the innocent animal. The purpose was that every sinner would feel the terror of death for sin, so he would understand that he was supposed to die for his sin, but God was accepting a substitution. Instead of the man dying for his guilt, an innocent animal was killed!

"The offerings were brought once a year, during Passover. The priests did that from the time of Moses to the coming of our Lord Jesus on earth. That was more than twelve hundred years! If from Adam to Moses only a few people brought sacrifices, from Moses to Jesus the offerings constituted a law for all the Jews. The priests were mediators between God and men.

"The Lord Jesus was and is the High Priest, the last Lamb who gave Himself for the sins of the whole world. Through His death on the cross, through His blood, He has reconciled sinful humanity to God the Father. The Father gave His Son to die for our sins. We do not need to bring any other animal offerings for our sins. By believing in the sacrifice of the Lord Jesus, we are forgiven.

"After His resurrection from the dead, the Lord Jesus ascended to heaven and sits at the right hand of God's throne, interceding for our forgiveness. He has become the High Priest for us. If before the Lord Jesus's coming the priests were the connection between man and God, now we have only the Lord Jesus as High Priest."

"We go to the priest before Easter to confess our sins, and he forgives us," Lucian said very confidently. "I think it is right!"

"Lucian, how many times have you been to the priest to confess?" I asked.

"Only once in the last four or five years."

"It is not easy to go, not even once a year—is that not so?"

"Well, either I was not at home, or I forgot, or I was too ashamed ..."

"What does the priest say when he sees you? Does he rebuke you? Does he ask you how you are?"

"He does not ask me details. I think he is not interested. What would happen to him if he had to remember everything the people tell him? It is impossible."

"You are right," I answered. "The priest has chosen a very difficult job.

"Although it is late and we are tired, I want to tell you that God has abolished priesthood with the coming of the Lord Jesus on earth. After His ascension to heaven, God did not listen to priests. He taught us through the Lord Jesus to come with our own prayers, thanks, requests, or intercessions directly to Him, and only in the name of our Lord Jesus. Believers followed this teaching for over two hundred years.

"History confirms that only after three hundred years were priests reinstalled as in the old times. They were given houses, properties, uniforms, and all the other trappings of priesthood. The priests call the people to the "Mother Church." They say the Orthodox church has power and authority to give salvation, but people can do whatever they want all their lives.

"The Catholic church says something similar. There was a time when the Catholic church sold indulgences. People bought indulgences at a price according to the gravity of their sins, and the church guaranteed their forgiveness. It was a kind of payment for sin.

"Martin Luther began the Reformation. He rediscovered God's will and God's desire to have a personal relationship with every individual. It was not easy for Luther. He spent his life in such teaching.

"The Bible says very clearly that by living in a direct relationship with God, by faith in the sacrifice of our Lord

Jesus, and by changing our thoughts, our words, and our deeds every day, we will be saved. It is very possible that many good people will end up in hell, not because they have done only bad things, but because they refused to believe in the Lord Jesus.

"God, as Father, wants to have a personal relationship with us, with each of His children. What would happen to those children who, after going to school, refused to answer in any way to their parents? As children, we need to be in a permanent connection with the Father.

"*Repentance* means to be sorry for your sins and not do them again. Believers are called the repentant because we do not continue to commit sins. But I want to tell you that no believer is repentant enough. Every believer still has sins and mistakes that he or she needs to repent of every day. Repentance is a lifetime process. It is the school you've been sent to and where you will study year after year until you graduate."

"I have changed my impression about the repentant ones and their church," Lucian said. "I thought there was indescribable boredom there, the same things repeated over and over: prayers, cries, mourning songs, and so on."

"It is true that all these things are being repeated," I agreed, "but there is nothing bad about it. 'Repetition is the mother of learning.' We learn. We encourage and help each other, as in a real family. Isn't it nice when all the family is at home every night and discusses what has happened during that day? Next day we start over, each in his own way, and then in the evening we are back again.

"The Bible tells us how the Jews left Egypt and went into the Promised Land, a land flowing with milk and honey, the precursor of modern Israel. They were a people of nearly three million, and the road led through the desert. The journey lasted forty years.

"Those who went out of Egypt had many memories, while those born during the journey had nothing interesting to see. They woke every day, picked up food, ate it, took down the tent, and set out on the road. They were on the road all day. In the evening they stopped, set up the tent, ate, and went to sleep. Next day the program was the same, as well as every day. On Friday evening they prepared for the Sabbath, which lasted until Saturday evening, and then they repeated the same cycle every week for forty years.

"They did not sow, reap, build, make clothes, or make shoes. Nothing special happened. It was tiring and boring, but that was the only way to get to the Promised Land. If they had turned back to Egypt, they would have turned back to slavery. If they had stayed in the desert, they would have starved. Going toward the Promised Land was the only alternative, and this is the only alternative we have.

"The only way to God is through faith in the Lord Jesus. Christian life resembles very much that journey through the desert to the Promised Land. We repeat every day the same activities, but with every day we get closer to the Promised Land, which is now the kingdom of God and the promise of eternal life."

"What shall we do with the priests?" Vasile asked. "Are they good for something?"

"In some religions, priests still have a lot of work to do, if we can say that, but they do not have more favor before God than we do. As long as priests or pastors teach others to believe in the Lord Jesus, they have a role, but what if they do it only for money? Priests are in the same situation we all are. They too need the same intercessor between man and God: the Lord Jesus Christ. The Bible encourages us to pray for each other, so we are priests and intercessors for one another too."

"As I understand it," Vasile said, "priests are like a union. They are the organization that keeps the connections between God and us. Our fate depends on them. If they want to take our problem to the leadership of the factory, we have a chance, but if they consider it is not worth doing so, our request has no future."

"Something like that!" I exclaimed. "There is another condition: if you are not a member of the union, nobody listens to you. Even if you are a member, but you do not pay your fees, things are the same. In Romania, all employees are union members and pay a monthly fee. Christians, the children of God who believe in the Lord Jesus, have a personal relationship with God the Father. We do not need to go to the union, to the priest. We address the Father directly by praying in the name of His Son, the name of the Lord Jesus. Our connection with God or the fee, is faith in the Lord Jesus.

"Actually, symbolically, God established in Moses's time a fixed amount of money, silver, for every Jew over the age of twenty to bring to the temple as a gift. God did not command the rich to give more and the poor to give less. Everyone gave the same gift.

"We are asked to bring exactly the same gift, the same fee that any man has: faith in God's existence. No one has the excuse that he did not have the required gift for the temple, or that he could not get it. Even the thief on the cross brought his gift in the last moment of his life.

"Likewise, the question Jesus asks is very important: 'When the Son of Man comes, will he find faith on the earth?' Faith! Faith! Nothing else. In the same way, at another time, the Lord Jesus told His closest disciple and friend, the apostle Peter, the one who walked on water and the first disciple to truly recognize Jesus as the Son of God, that Peter's life circumstances would change dramatically. Peter's faith was going to be tested. In spite of all his promises to follow the Lord Jesus, Peter would deny Him and swear he had never known the Savior. That was going to happen on the night the Savior was arrested, judged, and sentenced to death by crucifixion.

"The Lord Jesus knew that His disciples would be terrified by what was going to happen that night, and that all of them would flee to save their lives. But the Lord Jesus prayed for His friend Peter that in those moments when many hopes would be broken, his faith would not be lost. The Lord Jesus is doing the same thing for us now. He is praying that we do not lose our faith in Him."

"What happened to the apostle Peter? Why did he deny Jesus?" Lucian asked. "Why did all the other disciples run away?"

"The disciple expected, probably, that the Lord Jesus would perform a miracle, disappear, and save His life. They were convinced He could do that. But when they saw Him arrested, tied, and put into prison, they started trembling. They got scared that they would be caught, condemned, and crucified with Him. So they scattered. All their hopes of becoming somebody, of earning positions of leadership in the new kingdom, crumbled instantly. Even so, each disciple would come to his senses, except Peter. The only thing Jesus was interested in about him was his faith."

"It makes sense," Dănuţ said. Lucian and Vasile, who were listening very carefully, agreed with him.

There was a moment of profound silence. My friends were contemplating. The sleep that heals had not conquered us yet, but it was not far away.

Wednesday passed by without news. Thursday morning we continued our regular program. None of us was in the mood to talk. We were dumb. Hours passed without any word said. We were like ghosts. Our beards continued to grow; our hair became oily. We did not even try to comment on that situation.

In the morning we were all ears. We waited to hear the lock of our door open, but nothing. However, the guards eventually took us out for a walk. In the yard, there was the silence of the grave.

The evening brought some noise for a few minutes when the detainees came back from work, but otherwise there was quiet. The silence tortured us. If the guards had not brought us food to eat, we would have thought we had been forgotten.

When we were sure nothing more would happen that day, we breathed deeply and relaxed a bit, ready to start all over again the following day. Our discussions were limited to those we had left back in Romania. If we, who knew something about ourselves, were so anxious and uncertain, what were our families feeling, knowing nothing about us? We could have been dead somewhere in the snow for all they knew. With our white sheets, people would have found us only after the snow melted. We were convinced that those in Romania had even bigger nightmares than we did.

"Time solves everything," we often said. We depended on time, but time seemed to have stopped. When evening came, we were exhausted. We had nothing else to talk about. Thursday we fell asleep with the same questions in mind: what is going to happen to us, and especially when?

We felt better when we woke up on Friday. There were great expectations for that day. We checked our clothes carefully. We watched our words, thinking the guards might speak some Romanian. Usually, we wanted justice every morning. We mentioned "human rights" so maybe somebody could hear us.

The noise of the door silenced us, but it was only our daily walk. After the walk, we were back in the cell, like all the other days.

"Viorel," Vasile opened the discussion, "we hope you do not predict that we again have to give up the desire to leave until Tuesday."

"I say nothing more. I just hope that they finish our documents this week. They hold us here like parasites. They have to get rid of us somehow."

We laughed a little bit between hiccups.

There was no noise at the door after lunch. The only noise we heard was that of the detainees coming back from work. We could not stand the idea of waiting two or three more days in the prison. All our calculations led to the same result. We began to see everything as dark: "Long illness, certain death!"

The turning off of the lights interrupted our reading of the names written all over the cell. We had the custom of finding a discussion subject in the afternoons, something that helped time pass quicker, but that Friday, as on the preceding evening, we could find no subject to talk about. Our future concerned us more and more. We lost our vigor completely.

Saturday morning found us in the cell. They escorted us for a sunbath in the morning. After lunch, the same exhausting silence took over. We expected no news. Not until Monday, at least. We had two long days of torture before us. How would we pass them?

I was really worried. Vasile and Dănuţ were becoming more aggressive. Lucian was encouraging them. I could not be responsible for them, and neither could I try to play the boss among them. We were only acquaintances, but I had to share the same fate with them. We were the same group.

Their attempts to get the attention of the guards, with all the "Romanian adjectives" they used for the Romanian and Serbian governments, were futile. They calmed down after two hours. They were upset with me, and I knew why. I had not made noise as they had. If I had helped them, maybe something would have happened—not necessarily what we wanted, but for sure what we deserved!

We were exhausted before the evening meal. Sunday was near. It was the second Sunday we would spend in prison in a foreign country, as if it mattered where we were locked up.

"What are you going to do tomorrow?" I asked them, joking.

"You could not ask a better question," Dănuţ said with a smile from ear to ear. "I am sure you are going to go to church, and we are going to stay in the house until lunchtime. After lunch we will go to the meeting hall to see what's new. It is good we gave up drinking and smoking, but we need to meet our friends and talk. We play cards and backgammon. This is how we'll spend our Sunday." We laughed out loud.

"As usual!" Vasile confirmed. "As usual!"

## CHAPTER 18
# THE PREPARATION

WE LIGHTENED UP after the evening meal. The food tasted better as the days passed. I don't know if we were getting used to the Serbian food or if the food really was better, but it seemed to be enough.

"Viorel," said Dănuţ after a while, "tell us something from the Bible. I never believed that there would come a time when I would like such stories, but these stories from the Bible are more and more interesting! Tell us how the journey of the Jews to the Promised Land ended. Did they get there all right ?"

"Exactly; I haven't finished that part of the story. I can tell you now because we have had our meal. We are having the same experience as the Israelites. We eat for free. We have done no work, but we get food on time." We continued to smile for a while. We were in the land where if something flowed, it was anxiety.

"The Jewish people left Egypt and went to the Promised Land under the leadership of Moses, a Jew chosen by God for this special purpose."

"Excuse me, but how did the Jews get into Egypt?" Lucian asked. "And why did they need to be delivered?"

"How did the Jews get into Egypt?" I intentionally repeated the question. "The question is short, but the answer is a long one. I have to begin with the father of the Jewish people, Father Abraham. I think you have heard of him. Abraham was a man who lived three or four hundred years after the flood. Abraham's father used to make gods, wooden statues, and sell them. We call those gods *idols*.

"This was a good business for Abraham's family. Abraham was very intrigued, seeing people buy wooden images made by his father overnight and worshipping them immediately. The stupidity and naïveté of the people made him ask very seriously all kinds of questions about man's life and if it was worth living.

"Abraham began to search for the true God, if He existed, and tried to establish a relationship with Him. In his sincere search, he met God Himself, the Creator of heaven and earth, of the universe. The coincidence was that God was also looking for an honest man among all the people. Since the flood, God could not find a man who would seek his Creator by any means necessary.

"God, who knows the heart of man, revealed Himself to Abraham, talked to him, and then became Abraham's friend. God made Abraham many promises, among which was the promise that Abraham's descendants would possess Canaan after being delivered by God from Egyptian slavery through signs and wonders.

"Abraham lived in Canaan, but the times changed. Many years later, Joseph, the great-grandson of Abraham, brought his family to Egypt because of a famine that had been affecting the country for many years. Joseph brought the eleven brothers he had, together with Jacob, their father, their wives, and their children. There were eighty-five people who escaped death by starvation. They had a good life in Egypt as long as Joseph was alive, but later they were enslaved for four hundred years."

"These are the Abraham, Isaac, and Jacob that many mention in their prayers when they say 'the God of Abraham, Isaac and Jacob'?" Vasile asked.

"Yes, they are. Joseph was Jacob's son, Jacob was Isaac's son, and Isaac was Abraham's son. All the Jews come from Jacob, whose name God changed to Israel. Jacob had twelve sons, and the last but one was Joseph.

"After four hundred years of harsh slavery, the Jews began to cry to God, so God remembered His promise made to Abraham, Isaac, and Jacob. God delivered the people from Egypt with great miracles, led them, and provided for them for forty years of journey through the Sinai desert until they got to the border of the Promised Land, which was the River Jordan. They had to arm and train and prepare to conquer the land.

"Moses was 120 years old. Even though he was still in good health, God told him to hand the leadership of the people to Joshua. Joshua and Caleb were two survivors from the approximately three million Jews that left Egypt. Only the two of them had their dream fulfilled while all the rest died in the desert—not because of old age, but because they did not believe God's promise.

"After handing over power to Joshua, Moses died without entering the Promised Land. All the rest of the Jews were under the age of forty. Only those born in the desert were left. Joshua had to take the lead, cross the Jordan with them, enter the land, and conquer it.

"A great surprise awaited them: instead of simply entering the gates of the Promised Land on flowers, God told them, 'Get your provisions ready. Three days from now you will cross the Jordan here to go in and take possession of the land the Lord your God is giving you for your own.' God's promise was not fulfilled without a fight. The Jews were not welcomed with tables laid, not even with bread and salt. They had to fight to the death to conquer the land, but they did!

"This is the answer to your question, Dănuţ. All of those delivered from Egypt, with the exception of two people, died in the desert, and those born in the desert had to fight and conquer the land."

"Everything is well when it ends well," Lucian added as a conclusion.

"We are now like those Jews before the River Jordan. Back to Romania means back to slavery. To conquer the Promised Land, we need to take all the risks. If we want the Promised Land, we need to get prepared and conquer!

"Actually, we began the fight from the moment we were born. 'The child who does not cry does not get food,' people say, and reality demonstrates that things do not change later in life. In order to survive, man needs to fight.

"A child needs to be at least fifteen years old to be able to care for himself. He starts with the fight for his life—the fight against hunger, thirst, cold, and all kinds of sicknesses. He fights for education: to learn to speak, to walking, to tie shoelaces, to ride bike. He goes to school, finds a job, and provides for a family. Not to mention those who carry on their shoulders the responsibility of a country, or scientists who risk their lives for ideas. Every year Nobel prizes are awarded for scientific discoveries to those who persist in finding something new for humanity.

"You need to fight for any objective, and do it in such a way as to conquer it. People need to fight even when they intend to do evil. The Bible says that God punished the world through the flood because every inclination of the human heart was evil, all the time. When you intend to steal, you set up a plan. Then you start fighting, acting, doing something stupid in order to reach that goal. Then you try hard to find a lie that people will believe.

"Right now, we are fighting our impatience, generated by our desire to find out what is going to happen with our request."

"It is true," Vasile said. "Most people obtain what they want by working, but there are quite a few who receive everything as a free gift. I was not one of them, for sure! I left my village and went to work in a mine, heavy work. I worked as a slave for good money, but I was afraid that silicosis would hit me and I would kick the bucket before my time."

I responded, "To those who have everything they dream of, the proverb applies most of the time: 'Easy come, easy go.' I have set a goal in life to earn as much as possible. I armed myself to succeed and then started fighting for the best promises. My final decision is to conquer all the possible promises I have heard of for this life, and also the promise of eternal life—the future life. I don't want to miss anything."

"Are you convinced there is life after death?" Lucian asked.

"I am one hundred percent sure!"

"That's hard to say and hard to prove."

"The Bible gives us a very good example," I argued. "A wheat grain cannot sprout if it does not die first. Each seed carries in itself the germ of a future life. Why should man not have that same germ of a future life? It has been proven scientifically that blood never dies. We carry in our blood the immortal embryo of eternal life.

"Think of the way a chicken comes out of an egg. The chicken comes into being, grows, and develops in the egg. At exactly twenty-one days, the eggshell breaks and the chicken comes out. He begins a new life once he's out of the eggshell, we could say, but actually he continues the life he had in the egg. We can say the chicken was born again.

"This example tells us that we go through the same process. We are born here on this earth, but we do not live here forever. We will die one day. I heard people who have witnessed a death say that before the person died, the person saw those in his or her family who had passed away long ago. I compare this to the chicken that breaks its shell and sees another world. Man breaks the shell of this first life, gets out of the egg, and continues his life in the new world he has entered.

"The same happens with children, who live in another world before they are born, and change their old world for a new one when they are born. The Lord Jesus told us about the death of two people, a believer and an unbeliever. The angels took the believer on the day of his death to Abraham's side, but the unbeliever ended in the fire. The one in the fire, in hell, cried to Abraham for help. Father Abraham told him he could not help, and nobody was allowed to help him.

"The one in hell was thirsty. His tongue was dry and he had no water to quench his thirst or the fire that burned him. He remembered his brothers who were still alive on earth and who were not believers.

"This story tells us very clearly that there is something after death. Our conscience and senses do not die. We will recognize each other after death. People will feel thirst and heat, hear the cries and the mourning. We won't forget those still alive, how we treated them, and how we refused salvation given by grace.

"If we put our trust in God while we live on earth, we will be rewarded with an everlasting, happy life. Those in the flames of hell will see those in heaven enjoying eternal happiness, but those in heaven won't see those in hell, because the Lord Jesus will wipe away every tear and they will forget any trouble. There would be no absolute happiness for those at Abraham's side if they were able to see their loved ones in hell. The most certain evidence is the fact that the Lord Jesus rose from the dead and is alive. Likewise, all people will be resurrected, and they will be judged by God for their works. He will separate them according to their fates. This is what the Book of Life, the Bible, guarantees."

"If man comes from monkeys and everything ends in the grave, what good is the fight?" Lucian asked.

"If man had come from monkeys, he would be a monkey too! God created, before He created man, all the creatures in the air, on the earth, and in the water, and none of them has changed. Every species has a form of chromosomes that characterizes it, and today's science confirms that these chromosomes cannot change. That means the monkey's chromosomes never change.

"The atheist school cannot demonstrate that evolution is the real source of life. But as it is said, if somebody wants to believe that nothing gave way to the monkey, the monkey gave way to the ox, and the ox became a communist and an atheist, nobody can stop him.

"Somebody said that the crab created by God should move backward, with its tail in the front. It has not evolved at all. The attempt by scientists to cross species has not resulted in a new generation of those species. A very strong argument against evolution is the fact that monkeys never change their life partners, while people do, and quite often!"

"Very interesting," Lucian said. "I have to think more about this. I admit I had no time for philosophy until now. Our school in Romania did not consider the Bible. I have heard at funerals the statement that what is from dust goes to dust, and what is from God goes to God, but I have not paid any attention to it."

I said, "We who live in communist countries, with an atheist education, have been exposed to an ideological slavery, in the sense that there has been imposed on us one philosophy, the materialistic one. We have not been given the opportunity to choose among different philosophies. We have been taught evolution, and we had to believe what they said.

"I know that not all nations are convinced that evolution is true. Hindus believe in reincarnation or metempsychosis. They believe the soul has seven lives. Life goes from one being to another at death, and after seven transactions it goes to rest. This is why they do not kill animals, because they do not know whom they are killing. The social status of a Hindu in a later life depends on his current way of living. The future life can be better or worse. You can be born as a prince or an insect or a mouse. It all depends on the character you develop in this life.

"This is how they explain the fact that sometime when you meet somebody, and you are sure you have not met him before, he still seems somewhat familiar to you. The explanation: you must know him from a former life, during which you must have met him somewhere. Hindus will never accept evolution as explained by Darwin."

"As I said before," Lucian reaffirmed, "I will set some time to meditate on these things."

"I hope you won't get too much time to meditate on the purpose of your life from the Serbians or the Romanians," Dănuț told Lucian after a while.

"A year and a half is the minimum time Romania will give you," Vasile said.

"I believe we need to consider this matter seriously for our entire lives," I said. "I believe this is how Father Abraham began to search for the meaning of life. He found God. The one seeking God sincerely will find Him. The battle for our minds is a lifetime battle, but we will not be able to conquer much if we do not arm ourselves with the most modern and effective weapon: knowing the Word of God. You have to read the Bible. 'Theory is a theory, but practice kills us' is the proverb everybody knows, but what can you practice if you do not know the theory?"

Sunday went by as any other day. The multitude of detainees who stayed home in their cells gave us another feeling, although we could not see or hear them. We were not that alone anymore. It was better with the cells full. We spent the whole morning with that feeling.

We reviewed all our future possibilities. What would happen to us if they sent us back home? What should we do after getting out of prison? How were we going to meet and try to leave Romania again? If one of us succeeded, he should not forget the others and should try by any means necessary to get us out. We realized that the strongest friendships are born in difficult times.

"Tomorrow I should be at work," Vasile said, a bit worried. "If I do not get there in three days, they will fire me."

"I do not have that problem. They fired me a week ago. The ink has already dried on my documents," I said wryly.

"Are we not doing better?" Dănuţ said, laughing out loud. "Nobody can fire us. We live with one worry less. That is the advantage when you do not work—you have nothing to lose!"

"We have to tell them the truth," I emphasized after a long time of negotiation concerning what we were going to say to the judges in Romania. "We should not avoid the truth, even if we don't like it. You are brothers, friends, but they will compare every answer. If we hide something, we will drown ourselves."

"This is what I told the boys too," Vasile said. "Actually, they do not have that much to lose, but things become complicated if they catch us lying. They can assume anything."

"You can count on us," Dănuţ said. "Why should we lie? They must have realized we do not like being in the country without us telling them. We did not like the free life in Romania any more than being in prison. If they lock us up, they will lose. They will never be able to reach an end with us. We want freedom!"

"Now I like it," Vasile said. "Now I am starting to believe you. I believe you because there is nothing to influence you. If you had told me this in Romania, I would have said that I did not believe you because you were drunk. But now I do believe you."

We considered all kinds of ideas before lunch, and then we continued with the things that would happen the next day. Was something special going to happen? We interpreted some of our dreams, as if we could count on them. We would have clutched even a straw, as one who drowns, but we did not have it. We had no hope for Monday.

"It is obvious we have no idea," I said. "Probably our fate is in the hands of someone who does not know what he is doing. We have to be ready for anything. It is said about Decebal that he was one of the greatest leaders in history. He knew how to win even when he lost a war."

"How could he win when he lost the war?" Lucian asked indifferently.

"After he lost the war with the Romans, he asked them to build cities on the Danube to protect the empire against an invasion of the Tatars coming from the northeast. The Romans listened to him and built very strong cities. Later, when the Romans retreated, the cities were left for the Romanians.

"There is always another chance. If we cannot find any solutions, there is still one door we can knock at. Let's do what the Jews did in Egypt: ask God's help. We are Christians, aren't we? Christians have held on to their faith even to death."

## CHAPTER 19
# THE GUIDE

"WE ARE CHRISTIANS! We can admit it here, but it was an embarrassment in Romania to say you were a Christian, not to mention anything about being a repented one," Lucian said. "You were humiliated, mocked, and stepped on by the last atheist. You had to endure embarrassment! I am praying to God too, but in secret. I do not want people to know I pray. I am embarrassed!"

"I never admit that I pray," Vasile said, "even if I do pray when I have problems. I want to seem independent. I manage by myself, but embarrassment makes me admit it."

I said, "I don't know if it is true or not, or if it can be attributed to a modern Caragiale, but someone said Romanians have been Christians for more than two thousand years. (Christians are followers of Christ, and they did not exist before His coming.) Atheism has destroyed the best in the history and soul of our nation. It broke our soul and stole our most precious and holy thing—it stole God from us.

"We studied in high school a poem written by an anonymous poet, with the title 'Dan, căpitan de plai.' Dan was the captain of a military contingent. Captain Dan was taken as a prisoner by the Tartars. In order to regain his freedom, he was asked to renounce Christianity and accept Islam. Captain Dan preferred to die rather than renounce Christianity. Before his death, he asked for a last wish, something I often remember. As a conclusion to all the threats, he said,

> Christian Dan, the old man with a bright soul
> Rises his stature and majestically says:
> 'The mount Ceahlău would not become a heap!
> I, Dan, never a pagan will be in any circumstance.
> I will not agree with a life cowardly preserved,
> Nor with the sign of injustice on my forehead.
> Shame is rust on a warrior's sword,
> A worm that eats the white cheek.'"

"Beautiful! Beautiful!" Vasile admitted.

"Beautiful, but what's our reason for pride today?" Dănuţ added.

"Now we take pride in our shame," I replied with no hesitation. "We are ashamed of being Christians. This shame makes us lie to others and even to ourselves. No wonder. Shame has played a role since the birth of our Savior. I am sure you can remember something from last Christmas. When Joseph, Mary's fiancé, found out that Mary was pregnant, he wanted to leave her in secret, so he wouldn't be ashamed. To save the situation, God sent an angel to Joseph and told him in a dream not to leave Mary, because what was conceived in her was from the Holy Spirit. The Lord Jesus was to be born from a virgin.

"Mary found herself pregnant in a miraculous way. God brought His Son into our world through an unheard-of miracle. This birth from a virgin was prophesied hundreds of years before. It was supposed to be a sign for our Savior's birth.

"Shame almost won. The same happens today too. People think they are their own masters, and they are ashamed to admit they depend on God. Due to this shame, they won't accept the Savior into their lives. But those who have, won't leave Him again. He has created us, He provides for us, He gives us the heaven He prepared for us before the creation of this world. Why should I be ashamed? What would our world look like if all people were true Christians?"

"It would be great," Vasile said, "but that is not possible for now. Everyone wants to cheat someone else."

"Is that not a shame—to do wrong, get caught, and be punished by the law? The Communists want to scare us using shame. The first punishment mentioned in the regulations of the Communist Party is the public reprimand. You should be ashamed for what you have done.

"Mary, the mother of the Lord Jesus, was not ashamed to be a mother, even if she got pregnant before she was married. She was only engaged; she risked her life. She brought our Lord Jesus into this world and raised Him with all the passion and love of a mother. If she had been ashamed, we would have no Savior.

"If we are ashamed of the Lord Jesus, He will be ashamed of us in front of the angels and the Father. We will end up in an everlasting fire of conscience, a fire that burns forever. It will be the place of remorse and regret that you could have been saved, but you were not … because of shame.

"People are ashamed of the Bible, but they have forgotten, or never knew, that God has used the Bible not only to save the world from sin, but also to civilize and educate it. The first book printed in Romanian was the Psalter, and then the Bible! The Bible was and still is at the foundation of the civilization of other nations too.

"Today, the church sends missionaries to other countries, especially to undeveloped ones, and God changes the face of this world through the church. The human spirit makes developed countries try to help economically undeveloped ones, but it seems they do it only to exploit them …"

"I think we have been deceived in many ways," Vasile said. "Everything we hear all day is money, drinking, politics, and football. When do we have time for the Bible?"

"Before I forget, I would like to understand something about the Holy Spirit I heard of in church," Lucian said. "'In the name of the Father, the Son, and the Holy Spirit' is what we hear as a conclusion every time we go to church."

"This morning Dănuţ sent me to church, but it happened as in Mohammed's case, when he gathered a crowd on a field by saying he was going to do a miracle. People awaited him expectantly. Mohammed spoke to them. Then he prayed and commanded a mountain to come to him. The mountain did not move. Seeing the mountain would not come to him, he said, 'If the mountain will not come to Mohammed, then Mohammed will go to the mountain.' They say that Mohammed left to go to the mountain and never came back.

"So with me. I did not go to church today; the church came to me! The greatest miracle is that the mountain came to us. We can have church here."

We had some fun with that.

"The Father, the Son, and the Holy Spirit form the Holy Trinity. They are three persons. A well-known preacher, Saint Patrick, who preached in England, Ireland, and Scotland, carried a clover leaf with him. He explained to people that the Trinity was like the three parts of the leaf united on one stem. Free countries have a holy day in honor of this preacher and wear something green on that day, the color of the clover.

"God, as the Father, creates us, sends us to school, tests us, and punishes us for our mistakes. He does this with love and understanding, because He wants to make us into something.

"God the Son brought us good news from the Father and gave us, through His life, an example of holy living. Through His death on the cross, He forgave all our sins, with the exception of one: unbelief. He is our older brother who came to tell us and to confirm all the Father's promises written in the Bible for the faithful ones.

"God the Holy Spirit is the third person in the Holy Trinity. The Lord Jesus, before His ascension, promised the disciples (and us also) that He would not leave them alone. He would send the Holy Spirit, who will be with us and in us, who will teach us, guide us in all the truth, and reveal to us new things or future events.

"Abraham, as we have talked about, had Isaac when he was one hundred years old. As customary in those days, when Isaac was supposed to get married, at the age of forty, Abraham sent his most trustworthy servant, Eliezer, to his relatives, far away in another country, to bring his son a wife. Abraham did not want his son to get a foreign wife, but one from among his relatives.

"At that time, people married a relative, for various reasons. One of them was the wealth; another was the power of the tribe or the preservation of the name. Eliezer prepared ten camels and went to the relatives of Abraham to look for and find a wife for Isaac.

"The journey was long and dangerous. Bedouins were looking to catch, attack, steal from, dishonor, and kill any traveler or caravan. They were the shepherds of the desert, very mean people. Eliezer was aware of that.

"We don't know how many people he took with him, or if he had a confrontation with the Bedouins. The only thing we know is that Eliezer arrived well at the home of his master's relatives after a long journey. There he saw a beautiful and diligent young girl, talked to her, and proposed to her to become the wife of his master's son.

"After discussion with her parents, her brothers, and the girl herself, the proposition was accepted. Only then did Eliezer open the sacks on the camels and give her and her family rings, bracelets, expensive clothes, and many other gifts. Then they prepared for the journey and went back to his master.

"This diligent and beautiful girl, Rebekah, would never have known about Abraham, the rich man, or about Isaac, Abraham's son, if Eliezer had not stopped at her door. When she found out about Abraham and his riches and his son Isaac, she could have refused such on unusual offer. But as in the fairy tales, Rebekah said farewell to her mother, father, brothers, and sister and, together with her female servants, got up on a camel and followed Eliezer to meet Isaac. When Isaac saw her, he loved her, and she became his wife."

"It is a nice love story," Lucian said. "They had other customs in those days. In our day, I would not accept others planning my marriage."

"It happens though. There are arranged marriages, but most of them are unsuccessful," Vasile added.

"In those days," Dănuţ said, "men could have more wives at the same time, and it would not cost them six thousand lei to divorce, as it costs today."

"Times have changed, but people often change the rules in life," I said. "Since democracy appeared, the power of the people and voting have been introduced. The people vote, and with their votes established majority law for all people, even for those who do not agree with it.

"God does not submit His law to a vote! His law is based on responsibility, among many other things. Anyone can marry, for love or as an arrangement, but once married, he needs to take all the responsibility for his family. There are many irresponsible parents who, after giving birth to a lot of children, leave them in the care of others—family members, government, orphanages, or even for the church. Isaac and Rebekah loved each other. That mattered."

"If love ends after a while, then we return to other interests," Lucian said. "How can you know that it is love and not a passing fancy?"

"Lucian, real love never ends! If someone says he really loves, he needs to be ready to give his life for the loved one. In the moment you are ready to give your life for a girl, you are sure you can marry. It is ideal to meet a girl who would be ready to give her life for you. This is valid for every person."

"Are you ready to give your life for your wife?" Lucian asked.

"This is what I do," I declared. "I have crossed the border, risking my life, because I want my wife and children to be happy. I cannot get out of my head the idea of leaving my parents, brothers, and sisters in Romania. I thought I would be able to do something special for them there, but the system would not allow me. 'Money does not bring happiness, whether you have much or little!'"

"What did Isaac and Rebekah do?" Lucian was interested.

"They had twins: Jacob and Esau. Jacob was the father of the twelve tribes of the Jews. He married for sincere love, serving his father-in-law for fourteen years for his wife, Rachel.

"The story of Isaac, Rebekah, Abraham, and Abraham's servant is a perfect parallel with what the Holy Spirit has done and is still doing today. If we replace the elements, like in mathematics, we solve the equation. We replace Father Abraham with God the Father, Isaac with the Lord Jesus, the future bride Rebekah with the church, also called the Bride of Jesus Christ, and the trustworthy servant Eliezer, who found a wife for his master's son, with the Holy Spirit. It is simple!

"The Holy Spirit is the third person of the Trinity. He works with the Father and the Son. He does what the Father says. As I told you before, the Lord Jesus promised to send a comforter after His ascension to heaven. That is the Holy Spirit. The Holy Spirit, like Eliezer the trustworthy servant, has the mission to seek us among the nations, find us, tell us about His Master and His Son, and propose to us that we marry the Prince of universe.

"The servant of the master was looking for a diligent girl. The Holy Spirit still has the same mission: to seek diligent people! I don't believe there is a girl who wants a lazy husband, and I do not believe there is a man who wants a lazy wife. What company would hire lazy people?

"God has been always searching for diligent people. Abraham worked in his father's shop, making statues. Noah built an ark, and David protected his father's sheep and fought the wild animals, bears and lions. Gideon hid in the wheat from his enemies, another great prophet God found while he was plowing the field with ten pairs of oxen. The disciples of Lord Jesus were fishing, and they were not doing that with pleasure—that was their means of living. Dănuţ and Lucian know how fish is caught on the Danube. There is no guarantee!

"Everybody hates laziness. Do you remember the story of the lazy man who was taken by the village people to be put to death? On the way, a rich man asked the people where they were taking him. When the rich man heard the people had sentenced the lazy man to death because he was lazy and not working to earn his living, the rich man offered to let the lazy man eat crackers he had in a storage room. The lazy man asked him if the crackers were soft. You know what happened after such a question—they put him to death! If Rebekah had been lazy, the servant would have not talked to her.

"After we accept the Holy Spirit's proposition, He will give us the gifts from His Master. The gifts confirm a reality: on the ten camels were brought a multitude of gifts, but this was not all the wealth of Eliezer's master! When somebody comes from Germany and brings gifts for his relatives, he does not bring everything there is in Germany, only a small part. Though we know this, our hearts are ready to burst for joy. How would it be if a relative were take us with him or her to Germany and tell us that everything we see belongs to us?

"The same is true with the Holy Spirit. After we accept the proposition, after we say good-bye to our families, we begin a new life. We immediately attach to the Servant, without whom we cannot get to the Groom who is waiting for us.

"I need to mention here that none of Rebekah's family members were invited to go to Isaac, only Rebekah. The family was satisfied with gifts. It happens today that many Christians are satisfied with a simple gift, but do not take the decision to go to the Master, who is extremely rich. Only the Holy Spirit, the Servant, can lead us to the Master. Besides that, because the road goes through the desert, dangers await us on the way: wild animals that can eat us, thieves who want to rob and kill us, hunger, thirst, weariness, wrong directions, winds, heat, illness, and many other dangers. He guides us through all the perils and will bring us to the final destination.

"It is easy for us to imagine that the servant had with him all the provisions necessary for such a journey: an elite guard for protection, clothes, food, water, medication, and a doctor with a first aid kit. He also had the duty to encourage the fiancée every day, telling her about his master and his son, something she enjoyed listening to. This is what the Holy Spirit does today in our lives. He tells us about God. He confirms things we have heard before and raises our eagerness to meet Him. If we listen to the Servant, we will meet the Groom who awaits us. If we don't, we will get lost in the desert, like the Jews on their journey to the Promised Land."

"Where is the Holy Spirit now?" Lucian asked.

"The Holy Spirit is with us and has the same mission. He guides us, He encourages us, He shows us the perils on our way to God. Many people read the Bible, but without the help of the Holy Spirit, they cannot understand what they read. Others read the Bible with all honesty and want to understand the true meaning of life. The Holy Spirit helps them to understand and then convinces them who God is and what His purposes for man are.

"Nobody can get to God without the guidance of the Holy Spirit. We have left Romania without a map, without a guide, and do you see where we ended up? In jail. If we had had a guide, we could have gotten to Germany and been happy."

"It is crystal clear," Vasile said.

"So the Holy Spirit should be in our minds?" Lucian asked, very interested by the subject.

"Yes. He has His residence there, if we can say so. Abraham meditated and sought God with his mind, and found the real God. We, through our prayers and meditation on the Word of God, will meet the same God. God promises to reveal Himself to the one seeking Him.

"The book of Job speaks about the Spirit that breathes into our understanding. We could call Him 'holy understanding.' Since all your thoughts are holy, you are holy too.

"The Holy Spirit helps us and guarantees protection until we reach the destination. Our Groom will be waiting for us, as Isaac waited for Rebekah. The shame of being a Christian nowadays, at least in most Communist countries, takes unbelievable proportions. Some of those who have accepted the invitation begin on this way with enthusiasm, but after a few days or years give up everything and turn back to their own things. It is a big mistake. If somebody turns from his way, he takes all the risks.

"There is only one alternative: to die on the way. As long as we hold on to the Holy Spirit and obey Him, we will not miss our way. True believers will not give up the promises made by the trustworthy Servant of God.

The Father, the Son, and the Holy Spirit work toward our happiness. It all depends on our will. Everyone has to decide today. Tomorrow is not promised to anyone."

"In the name of the Father, the Son, and the Holy Spirit," Lucian repeated. "The Trinity."

"Viorel, you should have become a priest, if you are not already," Vasile said very seriously.

I replied, "If I were a priest, I would have taken all the money you have for the long service today."

We all laughed at that good joke.

"Too bad the Romanian authorities took all the Bibles away," Lucian said. "They took them out of the libraries and from everywhere. I have never seen a Bible in my life, and I think I would not be able to lay my hand on one. I have seen one from the distance, in church ... that's all!"

We all bitterly confirmed that sad reality.

The discussions had the gift of diluting the worries and thoughts that made our hearts ache. There were moments when it was hard to find something interesting to talk about and when every one of us was overwhelmed by his own worries.

If we were sent back to Romania, we would be considered losers. Usually, the Romanian government, celebrating of the expulsion of the king on December 30, would pardon those who had prison sentences of less than five years. But because we crossed the border after December 30, we could not enjoy such a pardon now. We would have to stay in prison for at least one year, with the hope that at the end of 1979 we would be pardoned and set free.

We panicked very easily. Our agitation increased quickly. I thought it would be nice to encourage my friends with some new stories about people who had overcome greater difficulties in life than we had.

"Have you seen the movie *The Count of Monte Cristo*?" I opened a new discussion subject right after dinner.

"We have," all three of them replied.

"Do you remember how long our hero had to stay in prison before he escaped?"

"He stayed for twenty years," Vasile said, "and escaped by getting into a sack in place of the elderly neighbor from the next cell who had died. The sack was thrown into the sea."

"Oh yes," Dănuţ and Lucian confirmed. "It was a nice movie," Lucian continued.

"The movie was good," I agreed. "The time he lost in the prison could not steal from him the hope of being free again one day. There are many sentenced to life who lose their hope of becoming free again and also lose their minds. Papillon was careful not to lose his mind. Our count had unusual patience and strong ambition for twenty years and never gave up his escape plan until he finally put it into practice.

"Do you remember how he was arrested on his wedding day? He had been a young and nice knight, but after long years in prison, people could not recognize him. In the meantime he found something to do. In order to make time pass more quickly, he dug a secret tunnel through the thick stone wall into the cell of his neighbor, an elderly man who had been given the same sentence. After a while the older man died. The count pulled the body into his cell, and the count entered in the sack instead of the corpse. That was how he escaped."

"He risked very much," Lucian commented. "He could have frozen to death in the water. He could have been drowned or eaten by the sharks …"

"Everything was possible, but he succeeded," I answered. "My Romanian teacher, Mr. Antonovici Clement, used to ask us do many analyses and syntheses according to a plan. We wrote our conclusions and what we learned from a book. We learn from *The Count of Monte Cristo* never to give up and never to bow before current destiny. There is always a possibility that the future will be brighter. Things can change overnight.

"A similar situation was that of Jean Valjean in the book *Les Misérables* by Victor Hugo. Do you know it?"

"We have never read any book," my friends admitted ashamedly. "I think there was a movie with that name," Vasile added, quite unsure. "I think I have seen a movie, but I cannot really remember."

"Well, that Frenchman, Jean Valjean, stole a loaf of bread because he was hungry, around the age of twelve. He was caught and sent to prison. There he was involved in more problems, so his sentence grew. He ended up spending eighteen years in prison. Eighteen years of forced labor for stealing a loaf of bread!"

"How did he manage to get out?" Dănuţ asked.

"He finished his sentence. He got out of jail with the desire to get his revenge. He was right. The social system had wasted eighteen years of his life. He could have become something during all those years. Anyhow, he met a priest who helped him completely change his attitude toward life. Valjean started working and helping those around him."

"What was with that priest?" Vasile asked.

"Valjean asked a priest to accommodate him for a night. But Valjean, at midnight, woke up and left without the priest knowing, taking a lot of expensive things from the priest's house. Valjean then encountered some guards who used to watch him in prison. They recognized him and searched him. When they saw all the valuable things, they arrested him. Questioned about the silver, the poor thief, afraid of ending up in prison again, said he got them from a priest. The gendarme did not believe him, so they went back to the priest to find out the truth.

"This unusual priest knew Valjean had stolen all those objects, but when he saw the gendarme behind him, he sent his wife to bring a silver chandelier. He gave it to Valjean in front of the policeman, asking Valjean to forgive him for forgetting to give it to him when he left. Javert, the gendarme, had to let Valjean go. After that incident, Valjean changed his life. He became a good man, especially to those with an unhappy fate. He became a patron and even the mayor of the city."

"What is the moral?" Dănuţ asked.

"You guess! In spite of all the troubles that come into our lives, even if we cause them, we learn never to give up. It is possible that we will be sent back to Romania and spend some months in prison. Let's take care of our health; we will need it. If other people have done so many things after decades in prison, we will do something too. Time flies. We forget trouble as we forget happiness. Let's not panic. Life can give us a second chance."

"If they send us back home and condemn us, won't they send us all to the same jail? Lucian asked. "I don't want them to separate me from Dănuţ."

"It is more than certain they would separate us," Vasile said. "How can you believe they will put us in the same prison? Never! They will never create the conditions for us to make plans to leave together."

I said, "In the worst case, even prison educates people: some one way, others the other way. Most people get out of jail with new perspectives and are ready to do great works. I worry so much for you. Let us not lose our tempers and do what Jean Valjean did, wasting our time in prison."

"I hope we will be free and not stay behind bars," said Lucian, meditating.

"So be it!"

We spent the rest of the evening mixing courage with fear. What tomorrow would offer us, nobody knew. Despite the careless expressions on our faces, we were all worried at the prospect of returning to Romania. For the last few days, we had not been able to change the subject of our discussion. We had forgotten we were one step closer to the West. We were in Yugoslavia. A dream almost fulfilled.

Monday morning brought the regular routine: washing, break, breakfast, and another break. The walk in the fresh air was canceled, probably due to ugly weather. Tension rose until lunch, when we hoped to find out new things. The boys walked around anxiously, talking with no control, saying whatever went through their minds about Romanians and Serbians. Had they forgotten us? How could we get in contact with the Europa liberă radio station? There was no way! Nobody knew where we were hiding.

We received food at lunchtime and nothing else. Monday afternoon was very tough. Early sunset made the day seem shorter.

This is what the weather was like every day. The clouds were dark and very low. The darkness outside matched the darkness inside us.

Good news would have made us come alive, but it delayed coming. The evening meal was as usual; the same taste, the same portion. After dinner we expected nothing but sleep. At least we could lie in bed. We continued to plan for several long minutes with our eyes open and fixed on the ceiling.

# CHAPTER 20
# THE FEAR

TUESDAY MORNING WAS not different from other mornings: the same guards, the same faces, the same orders that we already anticipated. We followed the routine with precision. After having breakfast, we went out for a walk. After fifteen minutes in the yard, we were led to a large washing room situated on the ground floor, full of mirrors and sinks. We each got a razor blade and some shaving cream. We realized we had to shave. This was a surprise.

When we saw ourselves in the mirror, we were shocked, astounded. We had not seen our faces for more than two weeks. Unshaven, unwashed, uncombed, we looked like real immigrants. We seemed to have come from the other end of the earth.

We had problems shaving with those razors. They got stuck all the time. I washed my hair with a soap that would not make any foam.

After we refreshed ourselves and came back to life, we heard guards speaking Romanian. We opened our eyes wide. We lost our voices. The boys, who used to slip some adjectives into their Romanian outbursts, changed immediately. Their mouths dried up. The guards waited patiently for us and then led us out.

"Where are you taking us?" Vasile asked one of the guards. The corridor seemed longer on the way out. We wished to get out as soon as possible.

"I don't know," the guard answered. He seemed to speak Romanian better.

"Are they going to send us back to Romania?" Vasile asked.

"We know nothing about what they are going to do with you," the same guard replied.

When we got to the office where we had emptied our pockets and left our laces and belts, we found the same officer, who did not seem to be in a hurry. We were given back our stuff, and after we signed an inventory, we went out. The entrance door opened. Two cops were speaking to the director.

"Where are you taking us?" Vasile shouted in Romanian. "Are you Romanians?" He continued to demand information from the policemen standing next to the police van. No answer.

The director said something calmly to the policemen. Vasile recognized that theatric voice, so he switched to German and asked the same thing: did the director know where they were taking us and who the police with the van were. The director was a nice-looking man in his sixties, wearing officer pants and boots with a short, thick coat. He answered calmly that he knew nothing about where they were taking us. However, he asked the policemen with the van, who told him they had orders to take us to Belgrade.

"Are you turning us in to the Romanian embassy?" Vasile asked? His face red and very angry-looking because of the forced shaving.

"No," they answered briefly.

Vasile asked the director some more questions and got "I don't know" answers. After the director wished us good luck, he departed.

When we got into the van, it started. We could not see outside, as the curtain in the cabin stopped us. We tried to guess where we were going, but it was impossible due to the clouds. We could see only walkways through the ventilation of the van. Because we had gotten used to being without watches, we could not keep track of the time. We had other things to worry about. Time did not matter anymore.

"Why haven't they told us where they are taking us?" Vasile continued with the questions after we got into the van.

"I was curious too," I said, "but don't you like surprises? Let's say they are taking us to Romania. Why would they not have told us? What good would that be to us? Just to cause trouble for the policemen? If they take us to Belgrade only to put us on a train, it will not make any difference."

"If they had told me they were taking me back to Romania, I would have run away with the van too."

We were determined to run away, with the van if it was necessary, but their calm answers made us give up. We had planned for a movie-like escape. I don't know where and how everything would have ended up if we had tried it.

"We are going to Belgrade. Let's hope we won't end up at the Romanian embassy," I said.

We looked at each other. I don't know what happened to our courage. We were paralyzed. The van continued speeding along. We would already have arrived in Jimbolia if we had been going in that direction. We could not see much, but we could hear cars around us. We were in a large city.

It took time to get out of the heavy traffic, and then we continued to go for a while. The van left the noise of the town behind, something we enjoyed. After more minutes, very long ones, we stopped again. The van backed up a few meters. The driver came and opened the back door. We got out, looking toward the large building in front of us and at the white field around us. It was the railway station, not the embassy nor Jimbolia.

Before realizing where we were, we had to enter into a building. The door of the first office opened and two officers came out of it. They exchanged some words in Serbian with our policemen. They invited us in and asked us to empty our pockets. We empted our pockets and took off our laces, belts, and watches again. They wrote an inventory of everything we had and put the things into a large plastic bag. Then the guard asked us to follow him.

We said not a word. It was hard to guess what the four of us were thinking. I thought we were at the Romanian border, being turned over to the Romanians. Later I found out that my friends thought the same.

We crossed a sixty-foot inner yard and entered a three-level building on the other side. On each side of the yard were buildings, some large, others small. All of them had three levels. They seemed to be strong, made of concrete. We could see no fence. The buildings enclosed the entire yard.

We followed our guide without asking any questions. We entered the building in front of us and went up to the second floor. There was a complete silence. Once we arrived, we turned right, into a large corridor, and then into a large room filled with lots of beds, as in the army. It looked like a morgue, twenty-four beds aligned from left to right, with a long aisle on the right from one end to the other of the room. We could see no nightstands at the sides of the beds, something that made us wonder if everything was all right. Each bed had a white sheet.

At first sight, the dormitory seemed deserted, but when we looked more carefully, we noticed a man under each sheet. Nobody was moving. The guards abandoned us there without our noticing. Even if they had tried to tell us in Serbian where we were and what we were supposed to do, we would have understood nothing, being completely lost at the sight in front of us. We looked at each other with eyes wide open. We noticed on the left a small dining room, some toilets, and probably three showers.

"Hey!" Vasile shouted. "What's this? Do any of you speak Romanian?"

We all thought we were in Romania. Our first impression was that they had taken us back into the country and that we were about to be picked up by the Romanian police. We looked instinctively at the kitchen window, thinking of running toward it, but we gave up when we saw the solid bars.

"Is somebody alive here?" I shouted. "Does somebody here speak Romanian?"

"These are the dead!" Dănuţ said, scared to death.

As we got used to the dim light, we got more and more scared. Vasile ran to a bed and tried to pull off the sheet.

Then a crowd of people jumped out from under their sheets, laughing, amused by our fear.

"Hey! Look what we did it to you! Ha-ha!" All of them were laughing, almost to tears.

It took us some time to recover from that fright. We knew nobody, but all of them were friendly, full of compassion toward us. We understood from what they said that it was a farce they pulled on all the newcomers. We came to our senses after a few minutes, but still had wide eyes and pale faces. We did not know if we were supposed to be happy or worried, seeing the thick window bars.

"Who are you?" Vasile said when they quieted down. "Where are we?"

We watching them closely. All of them seemed healthy and rested. We were somewhere between ecstasy and reality.

"Don't be scared," said a boy of about twenty-five, with an athletic constitution. "We are in Padinska Skela."

"What are you doing here, and why have they brought us here?" I asked.

"This is a kind of concentration camp," the boy explained. "We are waiting to be sent to Italy, Austria, or Australia."

"Who is going to take us and when?" I asked. "Are you sure they are taking us to the West? How long have you been waiting here?"

One of them, older than the others, said, "I have been here for six weeks. I came one week before Christmas. Unfortunately, I had to spend the holidays here. They told me all the transports to the border were interrupted for at least two weeks, but I saw some transports leaving the week before Christmas. Somebody leaves every morning, almost. One good thing is that they do not split up groups of friends if they want to go to the same place, no matter how large the group may be."

"Those of German origin go to Germany in two days," another said. "They get passports prepared and leave with the first train. If someone wants to go to Australia, he is brought out and accommodated in a hotel in Belgrade, where he can write letters or make phone calls home, if he has family. In two months, he is ready to leave. We, all the others, have to wait our turn. I don't know how long, but they eventually send us where we want to go."

"Do they also send people back to Romania?" I asked to make sure.

"Only if you insist," someone from the crowd answered while the others were laughing.

I smiled. "I have no desire to ask to go there, because I know how hard it is for the Romanian government to let you leave—very hard, and only if you are well connected!" All of them laughed.

We got used to this new group of friends quickly. They seemed like brothers. Their happy faces made them pleasant people. Most were between twenty and thirty years old. One or two of them seemed older than forty, and three of them seemed younger than twenty. We fitted in well.

"You say we cannot write home?" I continued my preliminary interrogatory.

"No, we are not allowed to write any letters, because they are hiding us here," somebody replied. "Nobody is allowed to know where we are. Not even the Romanians know anything about this place. This is a Yugoslav prison, but they arranged a place for us too. Nobody would search for us here!"

"Has anybody left this year from here?" I asked my last question. "The New Year may bring new laws; this is why I ask."

"Good question," the one who had been there for six weeks answered. "Yes, since last week they have begun to reduce our numbers."

"The two weeks they told you became four," I deduced.

"The Serbians respect the old rite," the same person said. "They keep the holidays two weeks later, so it is understandable. Anyhow, you will see somebody come after lunch and tell us who should get ready to leave tomorrow morning. In the morning, at six, those who are to leave will be picked up."

Discussions continued. Each of us associated with an inmate who was close by and collected all the necessary information. We were allotted a bed on which we put our winter clothes. We could see the garden through the prison window. A curtain of trees continued the fence for about sixty feet. It resembled the tree curtain we had seen on the border, so we started wondering if we were not on the border. All of them assured us we were far from Romania. A few of them who could speak Serbian had talked to the guards. We found out where we were from them.

We got plenty of food for lunch, big portions, and those who wanted could have more. We had plenty of bread. We ate only a little, as usual. We were still afraid. Dănuț and Lucian ate well. Vasile also had enough. After eating, the guards left us more bread for the hungriest.

We recovered after lunch. We soon realized what the concentration camp was all about and began to believe everything the inmates said. We were all in the same situation. Morale was good. All of them thanked God for being able to cross the border.

We had to take care of our health and wait. The conditions were very good—the warm room, the food, the toilets, the showers— but that time of endless waiting made us sick. When were we going to leave?

Thinking of those I had left at home was killing me. For how long? All of those who had wives and children quickly lost their patience when talking about those at home. We were overwhelmed by the thought. We changed the subject. Every man told his adventure. Everyone spoke about those waiting for them in the West. Most of them had relatives somewhere and were anxious to get there, or at least let their relatives know they had left the country.

The four of us, and some others, had nobody there. Was there something we could do? Nothing. Vasile spoke German, and that was our only hope. We were making plans to go to Germany; that was why we had asked to be sent to Austria.

I knew nothing about Vasile Tepei, my friend and Dănuţ and Vasile's brother-in-law. We thought he might be in America. How were we supposed to find him?

The inmates agreed that repented ones were the luckiest because they helped each other; they looked out for each other in the camps. They assured me I would have no problems in the West, not anywhere I'd might go.

Some of them came to me and told me they were from believing families, but they had not been believers because they were ashamed. Now, in the free world, they wanted to repent, so they asked me all kinds of questions about the Bible, the church, and what it meant to be a Christian. Four of the young men had a pocket Bible or New Testament and told me they were convinced that only the Bible had saved their lives and would get them where they were heading.

Time passed quickly. Sharing and listening to each other's adventures, we did not realize how quickly the day went. With difficulty I escaped the questions to go wash some clothes. Those I had on me—my socks, my shirt, and my pants—were still dirty from crossing the border. I also had a good shower, after three long weeks. I put my pants under the sheet after they were restored to their natural color, for some "ironing." My friends did the same.

Before dinner, an officer entered our dormitory and brought us the good news of a new group that was leaving, among whom was the one left over from the preceding year. There was a fuss and joy for those who were to leave the following morning, but also for the rest of us because this meant our turn was coming soon.

"Are you sure they won't take us back to Romania?" Vasile asked once more.

"Sure, as long as we do not do anything stupid," a young man from Jimbolia, who could speak Serbian, said. "They say Romanians pay a salt wagon to the Serbians for each fugitive, but the UN gives four for every immigrant sent to the West, and especially for those who want to go to Australia. The UN intends to populate Australia, which needs shepherds. This is what they say."

"This is why we see so many advertisements about life in Australia," another confirmed. "If you want to go to Australia, you can leave directly from Yugoslavia."

"We told them we want to go to Germany," I said. "Do you think we can change?"

"We don't know," more of them said together. "They asked us nothing here, but gave us the order to be ready to leave the next day, and there we go."

None of them were 100 percent sure where they were going, but we all hoped the authorities were not sending us back to Romania.

The evening meal was very rich. We ate as much as we needed. They told us we would get enough food and nobody would ask us to follow any program. We could lie in bed, sleep, sing, play, whatever. The only restriction was we could not leave the first floor. We were free, but only in the dormitory.

We could not sleep. We were too many, and life was becoming full of events. We heard all kinds of new, important things. We listened to some who had relatives in America and spoke about life there. From others, we heard about life in Australia. Encouraged by the success we had had so far, all of us were ready for the next step: leaving Yugoslavia.

Time passed quickly while we talked with each other. We made friends easily. After two days we were like brothers.

We played games just to change somewhat the boring life we had. One of the games was called "thick milk." We chose two teams of five or six members each and then drew lots. The short-straw team had to build a bridge. The man in front bowed from his middle and held on to a table or a bed. The next also bent from the middle and put his head between the legs of the first man. Then the others did the same.

One at a time, the members of the second team would run and jump, saying "thick milk," on the backs of the first team. If a man on the first team fell or knelt, then the first team lost. If all of them were still standing, then the teams switched places. It was a relatively dangerous game, because those who were jumping often jumped on the back of the same person, but none of them complained of any back pains.

Since January 30, when they transferred us to Padinska Skela, the days had passed to our advantage. After a few days, there were so few men left in the dormitory that we started to panic. Nobody new came except a Bulgarian and a Romanian. Our companions agreed that, as winter is not a good time to cross the border, very few people do. The summer and especially the fall, when the grass was tall and the trees had leaves, were the seasons when many people crossed. In fall, they could find something to eat in the trees.

The following week seven boys from Vărşeţ came. We heard them coming, so we played the same farce on them that had been played on us. After they were scared, we told them what it was all about.

CHAPTER 21

# FEBRUARY 8, 1979

O N WEDNESDAY AFTERNOON, when the guard came to announce those who were to leave the following day, we heard the names of three others and then our names. We shouted with joy. We hugged. We were alive as never before. The blood coursed quickly through our veins. Our faces became red with joy and excitement. We promised to look out for each other and then began to prepare for leaving … What was there to prepare? We had nothing to prepare—some clothes and empty pockets! We shaved and washed our socks, and we were ready. Vasile also washed his shirt; he was very clean.

Being more cautious, I had not worn my shirt after I washed it when I arrived. I had a T-shirt that I wore instead. I abandoned that when I left because they said it was very warm in the car. All of those who had left had thrown their thick clothes into the garbage. I kept my plaid coat because I could wear it in February too, as it was not very thick.

The following morning, around six, we were escorted by two guards through the long yard to the office situated at the exit. After a few steps, I was sorry for abandoning my T-shirt. It was a beautiful morning, with stars still in the sky, but really cold. We each received a bag of our stuff from the office, and when we got out of the prison, we saw only one van. There were seven of us squeezed into a four-seater van. It was good, considering the cold, but it was not really comfortable. What a comparison to the polite way they had treated us in Padinska Skela!

We thought we would get somewhere quickly and change cars, but when we tried to look at the road between the front curtains, we realized we were leaving town, heading west. We left the sun behind. We were doing well, from our perspective. Not long after, the daylight became full. A sunny day! A beautiful day!

It was Thursday, February 8. The joy and novelty of our situation made us forget the conditions we were riding in. The hard bench, the lack of room, the insufficient air could not make us complain. From time to time the policeman on the right, who might have been the exchange driver, pulled the curtain back to check on us. Sometimes he left it open, to our joy. We could see the road. We were heading west.

We got to Zagreb by noon. We had the chance to see the name of the place through the pulled-back curtain. We had made no stops until then. The van had no heating in the back. Our legs had frozen long before, but what was worse was the fact that we could not stretch our legs. We were packed in like sardines. When one moved, we all had to move. Then another would move, and so on.

When we had given up hope for better conditions, the van pulled over, finally, at a gas station. The policemen opened the back door and let us out. The driver let us know we could go into the store at the station. There were other people there too. We were surprised they encouraged us

VIOREL BILAUCA

to enter, and without any hesitation we did. We showed them Romanian money and they nodded, answering that it was good.

Then we started picking chocolate and biscuits from the racks as if we had never seen anything like that. With my eyes on the van, I left four hundred lei there. The salesman counted it out and tried to explain it to me, tried to give me back some change, but I refused. I paid for all four of us. My friends told me they had around two hundred lei, but could not find the money in their pockets.

Happy that we could buy something with our money, we went out, ready to leave. We saw two mechanics changing a wheel on our car. That gave me enough time to open a foreign chocolate and taste it. The taste was the same as Romanian chocolate, but the writing was different. I wanted to keep the paper, but I had some more, so I threw it into the trash bin.

We got in the van, refreshed by the stop. We drove for a few more minutes and then pulled over to the right again.

"What happened this time?" one of the other three asked. We were out in a few seconds, to realize we had stopped at a restaurant, a summer garden type. The policemen went to eat something. We stayed outside, looking in, and then we went into the restaurant and looked around. I got a lemonade and drank it. Vasile, Dănuț, and Lucian disappeared into the bar.

We walked through the restaurant. Then, to use up time, we went out and looked at the fields around. That restaurant was situated outside the town. Probably this was a better place; the police might have lost us in the town. Before we left, two of the guys got a beer and shared it with the those who wanted to taste it. They had no money for more.

In less than an hour, we were back like sardines in the van. The weather was nice, a sunny day. It might have been two o'clock in the afternoon. We continued to go west. The sun was trying to go by us.

"Let's smoke a cigarette. Whoever does not have one should not ask for one," Vasile said unexpectedly. He pulled out a cigarette and, trembling, lit it up.

"Are you going to smoke in this crowd?" I rebuked him.

"Let's be fair," one of the other three defended him. "Some die because they smoke and others because they don't." I had not heard him speak until that moment. He also pulled out a cigarette and lit it up immediately.

In less than two minutes, six of the seven of us had a cigarette in our mouths, and we could hardly see each other through the smoke. All of them became pale few seconds later, ready to throw up because of the pollution, but even so, none put out his cigarette. What could I do? No one vomited on me. That was the last thing I needed! I hoped they would finish quickly so we could breathe oxygen.

"You said you had no money," I grumbled.

"We had, but not for chocolate," Dănuț answered. "Chocolates are for children." They all laughed.

I said nothing. This was their joy and revenge after three weeks of jail. After the first cigarette came the second, then the third. Even though they felt bad, they did not give up smoking. Each of them had two packs of cigarettes. I forgot everything else for two hours. I was only thinking of how to survive the cigarette smoke.

We started going up the mountains. We felt it as the gears changed rapidly. When we reached a certain altitude, we continued our journey on the same level for another half hour, and then stopped. The guard on the right opened the door and took the other three with him. He locked the four of us in the back. After a few minutes, we continued our journey without the other three.

"What have they done with those three? Dănuţ asked when the van was back on the road.

"They have been abandoned for attempted murder," I answered jokingly. "They tried to suffocate us."

"I think they left them there so we would not be too many in the same place," Vasile tried to explain. "From what they said, they also asked to be sent to Austria. Are we at the border with Austria, or did we stop at the border with Italy?"

"If we had stopped at a border, then it must have been the one with Austria. The sun has been to our left all the time, and that means we were going to the north or northwest, toward Austria. Italy is exactly the opposite way, to the south."

"Let's see where we end up, at what border. They were left in a forest," Dănuţ said, mostly to himself.

Weariness was beginning to show its signs. We had more room and also less smoke, reduced by half. Three of the six smokers had left, so we had double the volume of oxygen!

After an hour and a half and many serpentine curves, we arrived at a town. We began to hear the noise of cars. We went round several times on the same streets before we stopped at a public phone booth, where the companion of the driver talked for several minutes. The policemen were very tired too. We had been on the road for about ten hours.

After the phone conversation, we went on. Before it got dark, at five in the afternoon, we stopped in front of a prison. Completely terrified, we got out without saying anything. We wondered to whom the policeman had talked on the phone. Had the orders changed? We had stopped at the prison in Maribor. Why? We were so close to Austria!

They had just turned on the lights in the prison when we got out of the van. After stretching ourselves, we followed a new guard to a room with a one-person bed.

"What is this?" Vasile jumped as if he had been burned. "I told you to run away at the restaurant, but you did not listen to me," he said to Dănuţ and Lucian, who were looking at us speechlessly. We were shocked by this turn of events. The other three had been left in the forest, on top of a mountain, free, and we were back in prison. We could not understand it!

We were called into an office, where we again had to empty our pockets and take out our laces, belts, and watches. They wrote another inventory. I saw again the tram tickets I had forgotten to throw away and the letter to my mother-in-law which, instead of getting to Codlea, had gone from prison to prison. We bit our tongues and lips out of frustration at the imprudence we had shown.

Once the inventory was finished by the patient bureaucrat, he led us to a large dining room. We were served polenta with cheese. This was our evening meal— not much, but good enough. Shortly after that, we were asked again, very politely, to follow the guard to his office. We obeyed once again, without any complaints, and nervously entered the office.

The guard sat at his office desk, took out the bags with our personal stuff, and gave them back to us. I accepted the plastic bag. Looking at the trash bin, I took out all the useless papers and threw them away. The guard looked at me and told me to pick them up. I could have thrown them anywhere!

After putting our things back, we went to our van. It was waiting with its engine running. Before we got in, we looked around to see what the prison in Maribor looked like. We had heard bad things about it. Many Romanian immigrants had been sent back after being caught in Maribor. The stories were terrifying!

On the other hand, the prison looked very nice, like a premium hotel. The rooms had a bed, a steel toilet, and a sink with hot and cold water. There were hidden lights in the outward corridors. The yard was clean, with traffic signs at every intersection, even the smallest one. Everything was enchanting at that time of the evening.

We left all that beauty behind as if it were a dream. As night came down on the city, we headed north on a curved road. We drove for more than half an hour without saying a word. We were not sure what was happening. We did not know where they were taking us. We were waiting to see the surprise. We could not communicate with the guards, and that was a serious impediment. They might have told us if we could have understood them.

We could tell we were driving on a national road, because it was well traveled. Through the thin curtain, we could see the lights of cars coming from the other direction. After a few short maneuvers, we stopped behind a huge building. We got out of the van and faced a long and tall corridor. A high officer, wearing a uniform, came to see us and began talking to us in German. We were not taken into another office.

Vasile spoke to him for a few minutes, so he could tell us what was going on. The instructions were these: First, we were to give him all our documents from the prisons we had stayed in, keeping only our personal stuff. Then we were to take some cans and bread the officer had prepared and put into Serbian bags, which they were going to give us. Then the officer would help us cross the border personally in two groups, two by two. On the other side of the barrier, about fifteen feet away, we could see a two-foot white milestone. Beyond that, we would be in Austria.

Once we were in Austria, we were to walk about two kilometers to the first village and present ourselves at the police station, saying we were Romanian immigrants and wanted to go to Traiskirchen. We should tell them we had crossed Yugoslavia on our own, not that we had been helped by the Yugoslavian government. If necessary we should show them the food and say we had bought it in Serbian stores. The Austrians should never know that Yugoslavia would help immigrants get to the West.

Once Vasile translated all the instructions, the officer, with a very serious face, looked at us for a few seconds, and gave each of us a bag with food, receipts included. Vasile and Dănuț followed him to the border, which was within a stone's throw. Lucian and I watched them go past the long and beautiful trucks, clean and shining, until we lost sight of them on the other side of a barrier that was letting the trucks pass one by one.

Watching these new things, we did not notice when the officer came back. We had the impression he returned through the building behind us, using a shortcut. We followed him quietly. We walked as if flying. We stayed close to our guiding officer, as to an angel. He was not looking back to see if we were following, as he was crossing the border legally. The noise of the truck engines stopped us from hearing our own steps.

The officer knew what he was doing. He was very confident and, in fact, was following a government order. It was too much for my reason to comprehend. The government of Yugoslavia was helping us, even though we were nobodies to them. They helped us as if we were the children of a king! They had picked us up on the roadside, they had saved us from freezing to death, and they had spent a lot of time on us, from the first policemen who caught us. Then there were the officials who got involved in our case, the food, the guarding, the transportation—all to care for us, some illegal immigrants! They had behaved so nicely to us, in spite of the fact that they had heard and understood all our complaints. Look what humanity had done for us! Would we have an occasion to give them something in return, and when?

With these thoughts in mind, we crossed the border to Austria, following the officer. He showed us the milestone situated a small distance beyond the customs building, and then left us. I could hardly say *danke schön*, overwhelmed by emotions, wondering how I even remembered that much German. I don't know if I had ever heard those words before. He left without looking back at us.

We wasted no time, but with big and confident steps, eyes on the milestone, we hurried to catch Vasile and Dănuț. Nobody followed us. We did not want something to happen when we were so close to happiness. Vasile and Dănuț were waiting for us. We met on the side of the road on which the beautiful trucks continued to run in multiple lanes.

Vasile and Dănuț had begun rejoicing. They were jumping and shouting for joy. We approached them and joined in the dance of Zorba the Greek, a dance by those who had nothing in their pockets, no future, no past—but who were free. Free at last!

Full of the joy of freedom, we shouted, yelled, and jumped up and down. We kneeled and kissed the ground. The stars in the sky were brighter than ever. The half moon watching over us was cheerful. The snow had melted almost completely during the last days, while the sun was shining. We were glad to see the frozen ground. The snow would have spoiled our joy in stepping on the free ground. Nothing could happen to us. I cried out to God and thanked Him while jumping like some crazy person on that freeway. We hugged and wished each other well, whatever the future held for us.

I was surprised by this outburst by my friends and me. I hadn't anticipated such a wild expression of our feelings; I would never have believed we were capable of it. Up to that moment, to the extent we had come to know each other, we were very self-controlled. Now we gave in and proved what we actually were: children. Our joy was the joy of innocent children in front of a great and pleasant surprise.

The dream and hope of being free was fulfilled. More than seven years of plans and actions had borne fruit on February 8, 1979. I would have been so happy to have had with me, besides these boys, Costică, my brother; Aurel Ciuriuc and Ionel Ciuriuc, my brothers-in-law; Paulin Martinuc, my friend and the cousin of my brother-in-law; Teofil Maga, a friend I had made many plans with; and Dimitrie Cantemir, who "had made plans from cups and knives" (a metaphor used by the Romanian poet Mihai

Eminescu in his poem "Epigonii"). I would have given anything to have with me my classmate and good friend, Dan Isapciuc, with whom I left home to work as a porter in the harbor, dreaming big dreams.

I was the only one, the first of all my relatives, the first of my friends to succeed in leaving Romania. I was the first to taste freedom that evening.

The thought of bringing all my family to the West one day gave me courage and joy that I tried to experience in that moment: meeting my mother and father, if they wanted to leave the country; and then my brothers Ioan, Costică, Gheorghe, Cornel, and Cătălin, the youngest of us; and then my six sisters, Lenuţa, Vica, Rodica, Violeta, Lidia, and Doina.

I was overwhelmed thinking of the joy and pride of my wife when she heard I had succeeded. I was so glad she was a friend of Lenuţa Tepei. They fitted with each other so well. Their destinies had already changed. Estera and Dariu were to know only the free world. That was my most important gift in life to them. I already knew their lives would be totally different from mine. I would consider myself a happy man, living accordingly every day!

I needed more time for these new dreams. How much? How would it happen? I was already prepared for that, and it added to my joy that night. I had the impression the whole universe was rejoicing with us. The sky, the moon, the stars, shining so eminently beautiful, as natural splendors crowning our special celebration. We were celebrating liberation and freedom. There was not a cloud in the sky, not a worry in our souls!

A short distance in front of us, to the left, on the other side of the road, we saw yellow mixed with white lights, as if nobody had heard of saving energy. It was only a gas station. We were in another world!

We calmed down only when we approached the first village, situated a couple miles from the border. We walked manfully, joyfully. We did not feel the cold, the freezing temperature. Among the first houses in the village, we saw a plaque marked Police. It was not a special building, as in our country, but a regular house. There was a Romanian SUV parked in the yard. We hesitated when we saw the SUV.

"What shall we do?" Vasile asked. "Is this a trap? Shall we go to the next village?"

"We fear even our own shadows," I told him. "I don't believe that after the experience we have had in Yugoslavia, somebody will send us back to Romania from here. I have never heard of anybody being sent back from Austria. Let's knock at the door, even if it is past eight. Let's do what the Serbian policeman told us. I am sure the people inside know what they are to do."

Vasile, who could speak some German, approached the door and rang the bell. A German dressed in a thick bathrobe came out and asked us what we wanted. Vasile explained to him what we were looking for. He sent us to the railway station, where there was a police office. Otherwise, he said, we should come back the following morning.

The railway station was not far; we could see it from the policeman's house. We got there in less than an hour. We looked around. Nobody was there. The station was completely empty, but the entrance door was open. From a back office came a German dressed in civilian clothes, who had probably been talking on the phone with the policeman at the house. He asked us what we were looking for. Vasile explained to him who we were and that we did not know what to do or how to get to a concentration camp. He asked for our documents and started filling in all kinds of forms.

Meanwhile, the three of us looked at the TV set in the office. It was on and it was a color TV. We did not have color television. There were only two channels in Romania, for those who could receive them, and only black-and-white. For the first time we also saw that shows were interrupted with advertising. That was something new for us. The adverting was more interesting for us, because we could see landscapes, cars, bathing suits, vacation resorts, and other new things.

The man put the completed forms into an envelope and returned our identification documents, but not before comparing the document with its owner. Then he asked us to go to the waiting room, in the building situated in front of the platform, and go to sleep until somebody came to wake us up and take us with him. That would happen around two thirty in the morning. We had three hours for sleep.

We went out of the office and quartered in the waiting room. The man from the station opened the door for us. It was warm inside. We were the only ones in the whole station. We did not know if it was the end of the line or if trains would come from Yugoslavia, but the station was small and deserted at that hour of the night. We closed the door and lay down on a soft leather couch, as if in business class. We fell asleep immediately.

I suddenly felt somebody was pulling my feet. I jumped and saw a real German policeman in front of me: tall leather boots, a belt hung with revolver, flashlight, communication devices, and baton, and a leather jacket with fur. I had the impression we were on a different planet. He looked too perfect for a human like me.

He asked me something I could not understand, so I answered in Romanian, "We are Romanian immigrants." This was what the Serbian officer had told us to say to whoever asked us who we were. I thought he understood me right away because he asked no more questions and left after examining us one more time. He was a member of the night patrol doing the rounds. We tried to go back to sleep, but we could not.

About two thirty in the morning, as we expected, a civilian in a long leather coat came and asked us to follow him. We got on a train, composed of several cars. As in the movies, it was very luxurious. There were a handful of other passengers on board. The train moved right away, and after a few stops we understood the next station was Gratz. We got off there. We had expected them to take us to a concentration camp near Vienna, but we got off far from Vienna.

We followed our guide, who walked faster than we expected. We were convinced we were trying to catch another train, but we got out behind the Gratz station, where an open van was waiting for us. We got in quickly, but before we had much opportunity to realize how comfortable the seats were, the trip was over and we had to get out.

The Germans were not speaking much, as if they were radio controlled, but maybe it was too early for a discussion. We got out of in the center of the town. The streets were illuminated and very few people were about. The stores were closed. We looked around only once because we were asked to enter a building in front of us. We did not know who had picked us up from the station or where they were taking us. We just did what we were asked to do.

We entered the four- or five-story building and then went into the first office on the left. A policeman was waiting for us with the yellow forms that had been filled out at the railway station. Vasile talked to him and found out we were about to be sent to a camp, but we had to wait for a bus that picked up all the immigrants once a week. The bus had just passed by a day before. If we had come one day earlier, we would have left the same day.

As it was, we had to be accommodated for a week in the jail in Gratz. Great! With no hesitation and with much experience, we emptied our pockets and took off our laces and belts. We pretended to forget about our watches, but it did not work, so we had to turn them in too. They would have kept us company.

We went to the fifth floor and entered our new cell. There were six cells on each floor. It was not an ugly prison, but the doors were iron and the small windows were so high that we could not see outside. We soon settled down. We each chose a bed and were inspecting the racks of old magazines in the corner of the cell, hundreds of magazines, when the door opened and a cook brought us some food and put it on the table.

"This is different, a detainee served as in a restaurant," I said when the cook left.

"Another life, but we are still in prison," Vasile added through his teeth. My friends were upset again.

"A bit of bad luck," I said. "If we had come one day earlier … What would we have said if we were in a Romanian jail? I don't know if they would have served us as in a restaurant! Rotten polenta? Pearl barley? This is what they serve in the cannery."

The atmosphere changed instantly. The boys woke up from their dreaming. The smiles came back on our faces, and we started eating our breakfast, a relatively small one.

We began working while we were still eating. We took a pile of used magazines and looked at the pictures. They had advertisements for all kinds of clothes, perfumes, watches, and cars, some of which I had seen before. I soon realized the models changed every year, in comparison to our models, which were built for several years without any change.

There were also ads for hairstyles for women, men, and children, as well as for motorcycles, hotels, restaurants and everything you could want. There were new magazines and some older ones, older than twenty years. We had no television, but during those first days we spent our time looking through German magazines. It was special.

Vasile translated some things, but there were not too many things to translate; we were limited to looking at the pictures. We developed a system. Vasile sat next to a pile of magazines. He opened one and told us about some of the advertisements. Then he handed the magazine to his neighbor and started with another one. This way we studied every magazine.

The meals were served at eight in the morning, at noon, and at four in the afternoon. We soon realized the cooks were civilians who went home at five. We would have had no problems with that if we had not had to fight killing hunger pains from eight or nine in the evening until eight the next morning. We had no alternative; that was the program.

We started to complain. Vasile talked to the cook on Sunday at lunch and told him that the young men were saying the food was not enough. The cook recommended that we take more food at lunch, especially bread, which he had in abundance.

"What do you have to say?" Vasile asked the two boys after he talked to the cook. "You said you could manage by yourselves. You would die of starvation without me. Don't be so arrogant."

"You saved yourself," Dănuţ replied. "You've been complaining twice as much as we have."

"What? You complained twice as much because you are a glutton."

"No, you were doing that, both in Romanian and German—"

"Now, after our stomachs are full, we are in the mode of joking," I said, trying to interrupt their fight.

"Hunger makes people less human!" Vasile said.

"There is nothing more nourishing than bread," Lucian said. "I have never had bread with cumin, but this smell makes you so hungry that you faint."

"This is why I said that the best thing is we are here in Austria, even locked up. Compare the prison conditions. In Zrenianin, we had a toilet bucket in the cell. In Maribor, closer to the West, to the free world, we had a toilet in the cell. Here we have a toilet in a separate room, we have a sink, and we have magazines, so we do not forget the alphabet. Plus they give us as much bread as we want."

"We are on the good road," Dănuţ concluded.

"Exactly," I said. "I think it will be even better in the German prisons, but I do not want to visit those too."

"When you stay in prison, you forget what freedom is like," Lucian said.

"On our journey from Zagreb in the van, I would have preferred being in prison to that cigarette smoke. I wondered how I would make it. Here it is much better. I can breathe."

"We were not feeling well either," Vasile said, "but we cannot tell you the torture we had to endure for a month without cigarettes."

"You can get used to being without cigarettes, but in that awful smoke you pass out! Man cannot live without air, water, food, and heat, but he can live without cigarettes, alcohol, and swear words."

"I am sure you are right," Vasile said, "but what good is life without these?" My friends laughed.

I replied, "That's why we have jails. The fun costs. A priest once was asked to name the smallest sin: drinking, murder, or sexual immorality? The priest answered, 'Drinking.' Then they gave him something to drink. After the priest got drunk, he approached a woman. When somebody saw him doing that evil, the priest killed the witness. This is how one evil brings another, and you end up doing all of the things."

"Humph," they answered.

"All is well if you do not lose your temper often," Lucian said calmly.

"Lucian, you hit the nail. You are perfectly right," I answered. "Anger, the Bible says, is the root or the starting point of all the other sins. When they are angry, people swear, fight with each other, do not communicate, separate, beat each other, and kill each other. We got angry with Ceaușescu, for example, or with his dictatorship, so we left. You can get angry about injustice, small wages, big taxes, and bribes. You cannot go to the school you like if you do not give a bribe, which is corruption. I also got angry about evil things: lies, injustice, and many others. Even a 'good' man like me can get angry."

"Ha, ha, ha." They all laughed with tears.

"If I had not gotten angry, I would still be a robot today in Romania. I've also read in the Bible that if you are a slave and get the opportunity to become a free man, you should use it. That is what I did. I don't need to tell you the injustice and humiliation some of us, the repentant, have had to endure. We have been the object of their mockery. The members of the party, the atheists on the other side, have been the most advantaged, even if some of them did not even know the world they lived in."

"I have to agree with you here," Vasile said. "They wanted to enroll me in the party. I and the party! They wanted to make me a member who would turn in those who spoke against the party."

I said, "I remember a joke about party members and Jews. One rainy and cold fall day, when many people had been waiting in line at a meat store since four in the morning, the manager came out at about eight and said he had just received a phone call. Those from the meat transport unit said they had no more beef, so those waiting for beef should go home. When they heard that, all the Jews went home.

"Later, at about one o'clock in the afternoon, the same manager came out and said the people from the meat transport unit called again and said there was a little pork. It was reserved only for members of the party. They had to identify themselves with their red Communist Party cards. When they heard that, all of those who were not party members went home.

"After four in the afternoon, the same manager came out and apologized, saying all the meat had been sold at other stores, so everybody should go home and come again the following morning. Those who had stayed to the end on that cold day went home complaining, 'The Jews have been favored.'

"The party members were not only favored and protected, but they also discriminated against all the others. We, the repentant ones, have been considered the lowest people, according to their mockery. I cannot say how glad I am these days for my children. They will escape that humiliation."

The days passed awfully slowly. We got bored with the magazines. We spoke about Romania as a past experience. We had some fun thinking what the reaction of our acquaintances or the police would be on hearing we were in Austria. We named the people who would be glad to hear the good news, but also those who would not be glad. Only a few people would really rejoice for us.

We moaned, thinking of how difficult it was to send a telegram or a letter to family: wife, children, parents, brothers, or sisters. We had been gone for almost a month and nobody in the country knew anything about us. It was true they would rejoice on getting the good news, but we also knew the terror they had been undergoing. Fortunately, the children were too young to realize.

"Let's hope we will be able to send a telegram from the concentration camp," I said in a show of optimism.

"Let's hope," Vasile said, "but if that camp is a kind of prison, as its name suggests, I don't see how we can let them know."

"What, the camp is a kind of a prison?" Dănuţ jumped. "No way. All of those in the camp have sent home telegrams and letters. How could Lenuţa have gotten the telegram about Vasile if they could not send one?"

"It's good you remembered our brother-in-law," our Vasile said. "Is he still in the camp? If he gets the news that we left the country, he is going to get scared. We did not part on good terms last time. I am sorry. I hope he has forgiven me."

"I have no problem with him," Dǎnuţ said, "but I don't think we'll get into the same place. He dreamed of going to America; we dream of Germany. November is a long time ago. It is possible we won't catch up with him in the camp."

"I would be glad to find him in the camp," Vasile said.

There was noise in the corridor of the prison all that day. We had the impression we were hearing all the detainees at once. We could not understand anything. There were voices, but their echo seemed to mix, so Vasile could not understand a word.

Tuesday morning, they let us out for a walk. We went down the stairs and walked for a quarter of an hour in the courtyard. We could walk freely. We met more detainees. They were speaking among themselves, not paying any attention to us. We realized the language barrier. We could understand nothing. We had to learn German! How long would it take me to do that? How would I learn it? Vasile understood and spoke German, but we were dumb. If only I had studied German in school! Anyway, I had to learn German; it was not a choice.

Tuesday went by and Wednesday came. We read the names scratched on the walls. They were many, but most of them were in German. We could find no familiar names. We wrote ours in plain sight, with the date too, so those coming after us would be encouraged.

The Germans were very loud, though there was no sign of a riot. They acted like they were in a motel. It was clear the prison was not for dangerous prisoners, but nonetheless it was a prison. I don't think the authorities sent them to work, because we could hear the same voices talking to the guards.

We became more anxious. We wanted to leave the prison sooner, even if the camp was not promising us much freedom.

When we woke up Thursday morning, Vasile asked, "Can you tell me what you dreamed of last night?"

"I cannot remember," Dănuţ said, "but why do you ask? Did someone speak while sleeping?"

"No, nobody spoke while sleeping. I want to know if you believe dreams can predict the future."

"Dreams predict something," Lucian said, very convinced. "I believe in dreams, but I have dreamed of nothing, or at least I cannot remember. But you, what have you dreamed?"

"I dreamed we ate grapes," Vasile said. "They were so nice, white and red, and I could sense their taste. They were extremely tasty. What can that mean?"

"Dreams may signify different things," I answered after a while. "They may have different sources too: worries, fatigue, health issues, medication, and who knows what else. I think the morning dreams are more important because the body is already rested."

"I had that dream before I woke up, so ..."

"And what do you think your dream means?" Dănuţ asked.

"The old people used to say that when you dream of eating fruit, it means you are going to cry."

"Were we also eating grapes with you?" Lucian asked.

"You are self-centered. I retract my words," Dănuţ said. "If it is about crying, then you can cry alone."

"I was convinced," Vasile said.

"People can also cry from joy," Lucian said, trying to save Vasile.

"I hope we leave today," Vasile said, upset. "Then they will be tears of joy. Otherwise we will have to stay one more week here, and then they will be tears of sorrow."

We expected to leave in the morning, thinking that we would need a few hours to get to Vienna. If the employees of the camp had to leave at five, we should at least be away before that.

Breakfast came as usual, at eight. We awaiting transportation, with our pants ironed under the sheet, but lunch came and we got no news. We had lunch and then sat on the chairs, waiting for the cell door to open. The beds were tightly made, so we did not sit on them. We walked anxiously through the small cell. Time seemed to have stopped.

"What are they doing?" Vasile burst out. "What are they going to do with us? It is going to be midnight by the time we receive our inventories and get to the camp."

"I am glad I don't understand German," I said. "I don't know what they said when they put us in here. Have they mentioned anything about the bus?"

"They said nothing about it. Supper is almost here! When is the bus going to come? It is too late!"

"Vasile," Lucian intervened, "I think you've started eating the grapes. I don't know which: the white or the red ones?"

"I think you will eat with me too," Vasile answered, discouraged. We were discouraged too.

"Let's have dinner first," Dănuț said.

He was the first to hear the usual noise of the plates in front of our door. We had dinner, but we only ate half. We needed no extra, even if they had some. We looked through the small window to see darkness coming down rapidly. We would have extended that Thursday if we could until the coming of the bus. One more hour passed without any news.

"What are you thinking, Viorel?" Lucian asked, seeing me contemplating.

"If you want to know, I am praying. I pray for patience. I am thinking of the things we have been through lately and the fact that we are here, healthy and safe. We only need some more patience."

"You are lucky you know how to pray," Lucian said. "Do you take prayer seriously?"

"If I did not believe in prayer, I would not waste my time. I know God answers our prayers, and through prayer we entrust our lives and futures into His hands."

"It is easier to count on what you can see, isn't it?"

"Yes, but you only see the present. Through prayer, we secure our futures, the futures we don't see."

"Can one foretell the future?"

"Yes, you can foretell it, but foretelling is nothing sure. Some depend on foretelling, others on dreams. Vasile's dream told him something, as you see, but the interpretations can be very diverse. We will know if his dream had any significance much later. In the Lord's Prayer, we address the Father. I hope you remember how we should pray, as the Lord Jesus taught us: 'And lead us not into temptation, but deliver us from the evil one.'"

"Don't you also pray to the saints to intervene for you?" Lucian asked.

"The Lord Jesus taught us how to pray, not to waste time and have nobody listening. Prayer has a purpose; it is not for the sake of religion. Liturgy is religion.

"You cannot play a game if you do not follow its rules. Every game has its rules. Soccer has its rules, handball other rules, chess other rules. You cannot play rummy following the rules for soccer, nor soccer by following the rules of rugby, and so on. So we need to come to the Father with our requests, addressing Him in the name of His Son, in the name of the Lord Jesus Christ.

"It is interesting that the Lord Jesus prayed and always mentioned the Father's name, because He was addressing the Father. On one occasion, while the disciple Peter was to face a big trouble, the Lord Jesus said, 'Satan has asked to sift all of you as wheat. But I have prayed for you, Simon, that your faith may not fail.' He Himself prayed for Peter's faith, even if, being together, the Lord Jesus could have protected him. But advice does not always help, while prayer has a guaranteed power. The Lord Jesus intervened for Peter then and can intervene for us today."

"How shall I know how to pray if I am not a priest?" Lucian asked. "Who can teach liturgy but the priests?"

"We pray according to circumstances and needs. We do not need written prayers. Liturgy is a nice church service. No child comes to his mother saying poems when he needs something. He will ask for what he needs as it comes to him, and his mother will give it, if she considers it good. His mother and father will not remind the child of all his mistakes. Parental love is unconditional. As parents always love their children, our heavenly Father loves us, listens to us, and even gives us what we ask for—at the right time, for our good. He gives rain to all people, even if not all of them ask for it. So He shows His love and care for us, even if some do not admit it. Imagine how our Father would feel if all people acknowledged Him and thanked Him.

"It is completely different when you go to the director of a factory with a request. You have to write it as nicely as possible, or even ask some professional to do it, so it will be correct, concise, clear, and include a slogan: 'Long live the Romanian Communist Party!' or 'Long live the Socialist Republic of Romania!' This is how you go to a foreign person, but to your parents you go directly and simply, especially since your parents already know your needs.

"There is a big difference between the way a three-year-old asks and an eighteen-year-old asks. You don't need a special talent to pray. Every person can pray. You cannot sing if you have no voice; you cannot paint if you are not talented. But every person can pray, no matter how much talent he has or has not. Only pride can hinder a man from praying, and the one who has the most to lose is the child who does not get what he needs."

"We have to agree with you on this," Vasile said. "A man does not want others to see him kneel."

"I remember a good example told by Pastor Lăcătuş, from Braşov. He told us about a history teacher, Ion Popescu, who, being very sick, asked some visiting pastors to pray for him to be healed. He was in terrible pain, and no medication could help him. All the people who knew the teacher also knew he was a convinced atheist.

"The pastors went to his home, but before they prayed, Pastor Lăcătuş, a special man of God, endowed with the gift of speaking with conviction, talked to the professor for few minutes and told him about the power of prayer to open heaven. Then he took the Bible and read, with some changes, a passage that would make the atheist understand nobody was perfect. He read from Romans 3:10–12: 'There is no one righteous, except Ion Popescu, not even one, except Ion Popescu, there is no one who understands, except Ion Popescu. All have turned away, they have together become worthless, except Ion Popescu, there is no one who does good, except Ion Popescu.'

"At that point, Ion Popescu kneeled and cried out with the last strength he had: 'Enough! Stop reading, please. It is not true, I am not the most righteous. I need forgiveness and repentance, for I am not better than all the others.' From that day, the history teacher Ion Popescu repented."

"In trouble, the one who is drowning hangs on to even a straw," Vasile said. "I believe it happens often that people begin praying in their last moments of life."

"That is true. People turn to prayer and use it as a weapon, a secret one. But why don't we use it from the beginning? Why do we have to exhaust all the alternatives and then, finally, realize we could have won the battle from the beginning?"

It was becoming late. Vasile approached the sink and washed his socks one more time, hanging them on the edge of the bed to dry. Ten minutes of silence. Contemplation? Weariness? Boredom? Prayer? I don't know what the others were doing in those moments, but in that silence we heard the rushing steps of a guard approaching our cell. When the door opened, I saw the guard, who told us to get our stuff because the transportation to Traiskirchen camp had arrived. You should have seen Vasile putting on his wet socks.

In less than fifteen minutes, we had our pockets full with the personal stuff we got back from the downstairs office. With no other comment, we left the prison in Gratz.

The engine of the bus was running. The driver, an older German, followed us after he finished drinking his coffee (or who knows what) with the guards. We left the prison at night, as we had arrived. The white, yellow, blue, and violet light that invaded Gratz, its streets and windows, gave us the feeling we had come back to life in another world. We had the impression we were in a Christmas movie. In our country, they saved energy; it was gloomy.

Vasile asked the driver how long it would take to get to the camp and if we had to stop somewhere to pick others up. The driver told him we were going straight to Traiskirchen and that we were only three hours away. We were surprised that nobody else was on the bus and that it came so late for us.

The police bus was very comfortable: soft, folding chairs with seatbelts. It smelled new. The painted windows did not bother us, because it was dark outside, and the winding road through the forested hills would not let us see too far. We were going to the camp we had dreamed of for years. They said that once you got to the Traiskirchen concentration camp, you were free.

I broke the silence. "Vasile, Vasile, tell us again about that dream of yours. You were eating grapes. What else have you dreamed of?"

"You see that dreams do foretell the future?" he replied. He was happy.

"Are you crying?" I asked him.

"Why shall I cry?"

"Well, you said that if the bus came, you would cry tears of joy."

"No, I am not crying, but I thank God for today. I have no words to say how happy I am."

"We are happy too," Dănuţ said. "You see how quickly has God answered our prayers? We are free once again. This bus usually carries murderers, but today it does the special service of transporting us, four Romanians, to freedom, at somebody else's expense. It is a genuine miracle for us!"

With the driver, who was driving carefully, we exchanged no words, for two reasons: most of us could not speak German, and he could not speak Romanian. Besides, in Romania, we were not used to talking to the driver while he was driving. Otherwise we would have had thousands of questions for him about living in freedom.

We left Gratz around quarter past nine in the evening. We looked at our watches from time to time, but could only guess what time it was, due to the dim light in the bus. After midnight, our impatience grew. We could not talk to each other. We were all looking ahead, even though we could see nothing in the dark. Through the transparent curtains that separated the driver from us, we could only see the trees on the roadside.

## CHAPTER 22

# TEMPORARY RELAXATION

A FEW MINUTES BEFORE two o'clock in the morning, Romanian time, according to our watches, the bus stopped in front of an automatic gate. Two or three minutes after that, it exited the freeway, the main road. From a booth on the left came two guards. We got off the bus and stepped into a large courtyard, with green spaces and well-kept sidewalks. The courtyard was surrounded by many massive buildings. The fence, made with a concrete bottom and wrought-iron top, surrounded the elegant camp where we had to stay. We had expected the camp to look more like a prison, but its fences, without any barbed wire, showed us a much more civilized picture.

Four guards—very well equipped, as in the movies, with leather uniforms, belts with perfect diagonals, and shining boots and caps, traditionally decorated—led us to the right, onto the main street that divided the courtyard into two. We entered an inner yard, almost the same size. This one had some smaller buildings in the middle that looked more like barracks. They probably looked smaller because of the huge building, like an old casern, that surrounded the yard. Everything was beautiful, clean, and quiet, at least at first sight. Under the spotlights, all looked much better than in the daylight, when you can see too many things.

We followed our guide into the building on the left, which seemed the biggest. We climbed the stairs to the first floor. The building, built centuries before, had a very high ground floor, as high as a fourth floor in the more modern buildings, and a first floor similar to the ground one. From the first floor, you had the impression you were on the fifth floor.

We went up another floor. When we arrived there, the guards rang a bell, which was in an office type of room. A woman came immediately with blue bags full of personal hygiene supplies. She gave us plates and cutlery and led us through a large, tall corridor to the right into a dormitory.

We left some dormitories behind to the left. She told us that because the camp was in the process of being remodeled, we had to squeeze together for a few days. We would have to stay only on the third floor and the dining room until our last interview. Then we would be moved to other rooms. We would get a camp ID and be free to go out into the town if we wanted to. Meals were served on the ground floor. While we were in quarantine, separated from the rest of the camp, somebody would take us to the dining room.

The second dormitory on the right had its door open. We were showed in. The room was full of bunk beds, as in the army. There was a little table with four chairs at the entrance, and on each side of the door, there were two big trash cans full of cloths and leftovers. The room smelled of oranges and bananas. The light was on.

Some of the men were in bed, sleeping, but most of them were awake, talking to each other. It must have been around three o'clock in the morning. They were not surprised when we entered. We were four more people, something normal. They looked at us only to see if we were people they knew, and then continued telling their stories or listening to each other. We looked at them, but we saw nobody familiar. We hoped to find the three that the police van had left in the forest before we got to Maribor, but they were not there.

There were some bananas on the table that we would have eaten, but we had no courage to ask whose they were. The iron beds looked very familiar. We chose two sets of beds side by side. The vocabulary we heard that night made us sleep very carefully. However, we fell asleep immediately, in spite of the insecurity. I thought, and also told my friends, that we had nothing to lose; we had no more money to spend in Austria.

We woke up at six thirty when the news that it was breakfast time spread from one to another. We went down and stood in line to get our breakfasts. We had not yet begun any conversation with the others. They all had somebody to talk to. We followed the crowd, guessing what we were supposed to do.

It was very noisy; all of them were speaking at once. They spoke very openly about Ceauşescu and the party, expressing loudly their hatred for the tyranny under which they had been raised and educated. Most of them were making plans of how to get their families out of the country. I was convinced that these men in quarantine had arrived recently, but I was surprised to see how quickly they were arming themselves to go back into Romania and start a revolution. I was shocked at the open way they were speaking, cursing Ceauşescu and his family. They were revolutionaries.

We went back to the bedroom and had a better look at those around us. Some had come with friends, others alone, but all of them had become friends in a few hours. We began to talk to them once we were completely awake. All of them were ready to listen to a new story: who you were, where you were from, how you had crossed the border, who helped you, where you were going, who you had in Romania, what job you had done there, whether you were a party member, and other things. They said there were some among us sent by the Romanian secret police, so we should be careful, as they could kill us. When I told them I was a repentant, none of them had any doubts about me. If you could not prove that you had a serious reason for leaving the country, you were suspected of being a traitor. The most quiet ones were looked upon with suspicion for a while.

Among the Romanians in quarantine, there were some Albanians too. An older Albanian raised some suspicions due to his daily ritual. He prayed at certain times, something that was not a problem, but he had an even more interesting ritual during the meals. He ate from a bag, and then put all the leftovers back into it. Later he ate again, and the food he could not eat, he put back. We watched him and were all scared of him to a certain extent. We were not sure everything was all right, but that was his religion.

I asked if there were other repentant people, in order to find out if I could talk to somebody and also if I could get a Romanian Bible. They told us we had to stay in quarantine for at least two weeks. Then, after the interview, we could go into town and send a telegram home.

I was completely ruined at the thought we had to wait two more weeks. I wished I could use that available time to read the Bible. We had no television in the quarantine to watch a soccer match, and we could not go out to work yet. Endless talks, sometimes with the same people, made us forget about ourselves.

The food was sufficient. We counted the days. The weather in February was cold and foggy. We looked through the window from the corridor into the yard of the camp. It seemed deserted, too quiet.

One person crossed the yard in a hurry from time to time. After some turns at the corridor window, I saw a man who seemed to be a Romanian. He was wearing a Romanian cap. I opened the window and asked, "Hey, are you Romanian?" The fog hindered me from seeing his face.

"Yes!" a voice answered. "Is that you, Viorel? I recognize your voice."

"Vasile, is that you?"

He approached the building so I could see his face. He was still smiling as always, and he still had the joy in his voice that was so characteristic of him. You never knew if Vasile was upset. His voice always had a joyful ring.

"How did you get here?" he asked. He took off his cap to enable me to see him better, even if didn't make much difference at that distance. His rich, black, curly hair looked exactly like a cap.

"Last night, about two," I cried.

"Who helped you cross? One of our people?" he continued

"Yes, of course. I crossed with two of your people," I answered, though I knew he was referring to my brothers-in law and my brother Costică, not his brothers-in-law.

"With whom? Are they there with you? Get them to the window for me to see them!"

There were at least ten people in the corridor who had gathered when they heard me talking. Most of them wanted cigarettes. The smokers were panicking. I called Vasile and Dănuţ, Vasile's brothers-in-law. I thought they would be happy.

"What are you doing here?" Vasile from the ground apostrophized them.

"It is not your business!" said Vasile from the top. "Can you get us some cigarettes?"

"I don't have money for cigarettes," he shouted from the ground.

"We will give you money, just buy some for us. Can you go into town?"

"Definitely. I will see."

"Vasile," I called to him, "can you send a telegram home to Coca?"

"I can. What shall I write her?"

"I arrived well in Vienna. I am with Vasile Tepei. Your husband, Viorel."

"Do you have any Romanian money? I can exchange it. If you don't, I will pay for you and you can give me the money later."

"I have about six hundred lei, but I don't think that will be enough."

"I think it will, but if it costs more, I will put some of mine in. Throw the money."

I rolled the money, put it in some paper, and dropped it to the ground. "How long does it take for you to send a telegram? Can you send it today? Is the post office far from here?"

"I will send it today, after I eat. It must be lunchtime by now."

"Okay, Vasile. Thank you. I owe you!"

"Don't forget about the cigarettes!" his brothers-in-law shouted.

"I will see," Vasile said. He picked up the money I'd dropped.

"He won't buy me any cigarettes, you will see," Vasile behind me said. "He does not like me very much."

Dănuţ and Lucian had already made new friends to tell their adventures to. Vasile was surrounded by new friends once they saw he had somebody outside who could bring him stuff. The others in the dormitory, more than thirty people, had nobody out there. Some complained that they had given money to a person to buy them cigarettes or something to drink, and then the person disappeared with the money.

We went down to lunch. It was a hullabaloo. Everyone spoke at the same time, and I think there were more than a hundred people in the dining room. What if all the people in the camp had come at once for lunch? My guess is there were more than a thousand detainees.

I heard somebody shouting at around four in the afternoon. We all gathered around the same window. We could see the window of another dormitory to the left, and that of a bath one level lower.

That building was huge, the biggest in the whole camp. On the ground floor it had a dining hall, and above that were dormitories for men. On the other side of the building were dormitories from bottom to the top, only for men. Women and families were accommodated in other buildings. In the building at the back of the yard there were Polish, Bulgarian, Hungarian, Czech and Albanian detainees. The Albanians were moved to another camp because they were very dangerous.

"Who else has come?" I heard a bass voice from the window on the lower level.

"Four of us came last night," I said. People customarily gathered around that window to see some familiar faces.

"Where are you from?" the same voice continued. I could see through the thick fog a face with a blond mustache.

"I am originally from Suceava, but I left from Timişoara."

"What's your name?"

"Viorel Bilauca, along with Vasile Magda, Dănuţ Magda, from Uivar, and a friend of Dănuţ, also from Uivar."

"I have never heard your names," came the answer in a few seconds, after they asked each other about our names.

"I saw and talked before lunch with Vasile Tepei, whom we know," I said. "Do you know him?"

"Yes, of course. We stay in the same dormitory, but he is not here right now. We will tell him when we see him."

"He might be at the post office. I asked him to send a telegram to my wife."

"Maybe. The post office is not that far."

"Where is your wife from?"

"From Vicovul de Sus, Suceava, but now we live in Utvin, near Timişoara."

"I was born in Vicov, interesting!"

"What is your name?" I asked, though I did not know many people in Vicov.

"Gig, Gheorghiţă Gheorghe, but we moved to Galaţi when I was one year old and then we moved to Banat."

"I haven't heard that name, but it does not matter. Here we all are brothers—Romanians! How long have you been in the camp?"

"Since the fall."

"How long do people stay here?"

"It depends. Those who have somebody to be a guarantee for them may leave in three to four months. Those who do not have anybody must find someone, and that may take time. Generally you can leave in six months. Those who wait for their families here may stay up to a year. I, together with some other people here, would like to wait for my family, and then we will leave for America. I have just come from Germany, from a protest in front of the Romanian Embassy. We asked the authorities to approve passports for our families. We will see what happens. We will talk about this more. Tell me if you need anything."

"I don't know how long we are going to stay in this quarantine. Do I want something? Yes. Can I find a Romanian Bible around here? I did not bring my Bible with me. I did not know I would leave as I did, and even then, I would not have wanted to take a Bible from home ..."

"There are Bibles in any language here. Something else?"

"A notebook and something to write with. I will pay if there is some money left from the telegram, and if not, I will pay you later."

"You do not pay for the Bibles here; there are plenty. Christian missionaries bring Bibles in any language. On Sunday there will be somebody looking for you up there. He will bring you everything you need."

"How long are we going to stay in quarantine? We are so crowded."

"Usually around two weeks. Do you need any food?"

"No, we have plenty of food. We want freedom! We stayed in Zrenianin for two weeks, one week in Padinska Skela, one hour in Maribor, and another week in Gratz. Now we face another test of our patience here. Should I expect something else before being free?"

"They will take you out for a medical visit and then the first interview. After that, you will be free."

"Is there any work around here?"

"Normally yes, but not now. There is not much to do in winter. Next month there might be some work in the grapevines. After leaving quarantine, you will come to stay with us. We are many and time goes fast. Look for me!"

"I look forward to that."

The others listened to our conversation and collected the information they wanted.

While I was speaking with Gigi, I looked anxiously for Vasile Tepei to find out if he had sent the telegram. That was my heaviest burden; I wanted to get rid of it as soon as possible. I had no idea how long it would take for an international telegram to get to its destination, but once it was sent, it would get there faster than a regular letter, which took longer because of the censor.

Vasile, Dănuț, and Lucian made new friends from among the people in quarantine. They told their stories and listened to others'. We were excited by the new world we had arrived in. Vasile had an advantage because he could speak German. He had some problems with the Austrian accent, but we counted on him.

All the people in quarantine were newcomers, and there were not a few of them, in spite of the fact that during the winter it was more difficult to cross the border.

Most of them were Romanians. Of the four dormitories in the building, we were squeezed into two, because during the winter the Austrians did their cleaning and fixing.

Another hour passed. I looked through the window many times for Vasile Tepei. I knew he liked talking with people, so I was not surprised he was late. The most important thing was for him to have sent the telegram.

After a while I saw him coming. I recognized him by his Romanian cap. I did not think he needed a cap for his rich and curly hair, but I was glad of it. He was the only one wearing something Romanian.

"Vasile!" I called to him from a distance. "You did it?"

"Of course, of course!" he answered. "If I was able to cross the border, sending a telegram is a piece of cake."

"Was the money sufficient?"

"Yes. There were seventy lei left. I exchanged them for schillings. You have six schillings. You got lucky today; a schilling cost only twelve lei. Normally it is more expensive."

"It is good you sent it. That's all I am interested in. When is it going to get to the country?"

"She should get it tomorrow or the day after tomorrow, at the latest."

"Do you think it will have to go through the censor?"

"I don't think so. It is open, and I think there are some laws that even Romania has to follow, especially concerning telegrams."

"Can you call into the country? How much does it cost? Do you have any idea?"

"You can. You can call with a phone call notice. It is not that expensive. It depends on how long you want to talk for, but you need at least thirty to forty schillings. You pay per minute."

"It is good you can call," I answered, feeling relieved of a heavy burden. "Vasile, I owe you. Thank you."

"How come you did not cross with Ionel or Aurel or Costică? I was expecting to see them here before you."

"I would have preferred to be with them, but that is life. I hope to see them sooner or later."

"I hope that too," Vasile said.

There was a cluster of curious men around me trying to say something, to ask about somebody, so, after I found out everything I needed, I left without setting up another meeting with Vasile.

This time I had with me my watch, a Prim watch, made in Czechoslovakia, that I had bought after working a whole summer at a farm when I was fourteen years old. It was different, very fashionably made. I wanted to buy myself an Atlantic watch, very popular at that time, but I had to be satisfied with what I had. I had other priorities, and a watch was not among them. Nor were gold, diamonds, or cars.

I wanted freedom, and I was beginning to think I'd gotten it, in spite of the fact that I was still a prisoner in a free country. I easily accepted the idea of waiting in quarantine for two more weeks. It was normal for them to get to know who I was, where I was coming from and where I intended to go.

It was dark already. You could not see anything outside. Shadows were going in all directions, but I was not interested in who they were or where they were going.

My head was hot. My wife and children were about to receive, finally, the telegram I had dreamed of for years. The vision that one day I would be in a concentration camp in Vienna and would send a telegram home, saying that I had succeeded, had invaded my mind for many years.

Today, on Friday, February 16, 1979, a Good Friday for me, I wrote in the calendar of my life the phrase "mission accomplished." It was not a dream, it was reality.

There was nothing more important to me than for the people I loved to find out I had gotten to Austria well. I was so excited knowing that the following day, my family would shout joyfully upon receiving the telegram. That telegram was about to change many things in my family's life, beginning with my wife Coca, with Estera and Dariu, our princes and our hearts, as we often called them. Other lives would change too: my in-laws, my brothers and sisters, Paulin and Teofil Martinuc, and Dan Isepciuc, my colleague and best friend during eight years of school. I was the one who would get him out of the country. I would do that!

I tried to compare myself to Joseph in the Bible. Would I get my family out from under communist dictatorship? I also had eleven siblings. I was convinced that I would be able to get them out in due time. I was not expecting any change of government in Romania because the system was very well set up. The Communists dreamed of conquering all the countries in the world. Russia, China, Chile, and Cuba, together with Russia's satellites, had been propagating the idea of a democracy based on socialist principles. They wanted to convince every country that a communist society, based on central planning in all economic sectors, was the best society.

Who knows what we had for dinner that night? Under the appearance of calm and complete satisfaction at what we had realized so far, new battlefields opened in my mind. You have to fight for the Promised Land if you want to conquer it. That was my slogan, the flag I was fighting under. I was not bothered by the ongoing noise in a dormitory full of rested and satisfied people. I have always enjoyed being among people.

I remembered a dream I used to have with Dan Isepciuc. We enjoyed sitting at an isolated table in the cafeteria and watching the people. It was the perfect relaxation for us. We used to order a cake, a lemonade, and a coffee, and watch as people came and went. Now, instead of getting tired, I was relaxing. I had no friends, no enemies, but I felt safe.

Saturday passed by without any news. I looked at my watch often, waiting for three or four o'clock in the afternoon when the postman would go through Utvin. I thought of the joy my family would have reading the telegram from Vienna.

## CHAPTER 23
# NEW AND OLD FRIENDS

S UNDAY, AFTER ONE o'clock in the afternoon, I was called by a guard to go to the upstairs office of the quarantine sector, where a Romanian pastor was waiting for me.

"Peace of the Lord," he welcomed me, examining me from head to foot. The night before, Saturday night, I had shaved my head because my hair had begun to fall out, and because we did not have very good conditions; we could take a shower only once a week. There were many men who shaved their hair in the quarantine. Many of them shaved their heads once they got to the camp. That took advantage of the fact that nobody knew them. By the time they arrived at their final destinations, their hair would have grown back thicker.

"Peace of the Lord," I replied, looking at him very attentively. This pastor had dark hair. He was of medium stature and carried some pounds more than the normal weight.

"What is your name, brother? Are you a repentant?"

"Viorel Bilauca. Yes, I am a repentant, a Pentecostal."

"When did you repent?"

"I was born into a Pentecostal family, but I was baptized when I was fifteen. Is there a reason why you are asking me?"

"Yes and no. Some say they are believers just to get to America, but they are not."

"Is this an official interview?"

"No. I came to bring you a Bible. Gheorghiţă told me you need a Bible. Also, here is something to write with. Nobody can come up here but pastors."

"Thank you. What is your name, and where are you from in Romania?"

"My name is Toma, and I am from Mediaş."

"I met Brother Pleşa, Ionel Pleşa. Are you an immigrant or do you live here?"

"We went to Şamu, if you heard of him. I am an immigrant and I arrived here in the fall, more than six months ago. Where are you from? I cannot recognize your accent."

"I am from Suceava, but I left Suceava years ago in search of a better place to live, so here I am."

"And where do want to go? Do you have somebody waiting for you somewhere?"

"I have nobody. I know Vasile Tepei. He is my sole connection. I crossed the border with two of his brothers-in-law. One of them speaks German, and I stick to him for now."

"I have met Vasile. He is here, but he does not have many connections. He is waiting for approval to go to America."

"I already talked to him on Friday. He sent a telegram to my wife in Timişoara, but I have not talked to him about other things. I hope we will meet again after I am able to go down from here."

"Sure, we will meet again. We, the repentant ones, stay in two dormitories, but the one I stay in is bigger, so you will be able to stay with us. We have a prayer service in the evening, when all the brothers come."

"I am looking forward to leaving this quarantine, but people say we have to wait for two weeks until the interview."

"It depends on how many of you are here. Anyway, we are so glad you made it here, and we are awaiting you downstairs."

"Thank you again for the visit."

We separated. He went down, and I went back into the dormitory with a Bible in my pocket, a notebook, and some pencils. The Bible was brand new, with a brown plastic cover. I had found my main food. I was happy for that Bible, which was also free. Since I had left home on January 13, I hadn't worked at all, and still I had had food to eat daily. Now I also had a Bible and sufficient time for reading and study.

It was unbelievable to me that I could read the Bible in the dormitory and nobody was offended. Every person was respected, whatever he said or did. In Romania, most people would have mocked me if they had seen me reading the Bible, but here I was respected. What a joy! I started reading Exodus. The book of Exodus fitted me perfectly.

Wednesday morning, around 10 o'clock, the guards asked us to go down for a medical check-up. Fifteen of us lined up to go down. On our way to the doctor's office, which was in the opposite building, we came across Vasile Tepei. The brothers-in-law had a chance to meet face-to-face. They exchanged some words in a cold manner. I did not want to intervene in their discussion; I only greeted him. I left them with their thoughts and memories, unpleasant ones as it seemed.

Vasile was the same. This time he did not have the cap, and his rich and long hair, uncut for two months, compensated for it perfectly. He smiled at me, probably because I had shaved my head. We shook hands, and he told me we would talk after the interview. Then he left with his hands in his pockets.

The medical check-up went fast. I think they looked at our birthmarks or our tattoos. They took some blood from our fingers. They looked into our mouths. That was all.

It was cold and foggy outside. It was much better in the dormitory. We returned to our stories. I sat at a table with the Bible and the notebook as my best companions. The friendship and respect I was shown were unbelievable. I was surprised to see that none of the others were interested in the Bible. Their problems were solved, so the only thing they did was spend time joking and making future plans. We enjoyed heat, food, drinks, and good beds to sleep on. We could not go to work.

The days passed quickly. Many of those in quarantine left immediately after the interview and were replaced by new ones. I hadn't spoken with Gigi or Toma or Vasile Tepei.

Friday, after lunch, a guard called the four of us to go for an interview. We had been awaiting this for a long time, but we never thought they would call us so soon. I realized that Friday was to be our best day.

The interview was long. There was a lady who spoke Romanian, German, and English, but it took the officer a long time to write everything in English. They asked me all kinds of questions, starting with myself and my family. They asked questions about persecution, religious or political affiliations, activities with organizations (willingly or compulsory), membership in the union or the Romanian Communist Party, titles or positions held, leaders, propaganda, discrimination against sectarians (especially the repented ones), mockery, and humiliation in general.

Then they asked about our motives for leaving Romania illegally, and where we wanted to go. In spite of the fact that I had left the country with the idea of going to Germany, I now said I would like to go to the United States if possible, but I had no guarantor. That was the suggestion of Vasile Tepei.

"If you want to go to America, you can. We will have your name written on a waiting list for the United States, and we will let you know when we find a guarantor for you."

"How long can this process take?" I asked.

"It depends. Sometimes three to four months, other times sooner," an older and thinner officer answered with the help of the interpreter. He had not been paying much attention to me when I was answering the questions he asked, and I did not know whether he could understand Romanian at all.

"What happens if I find a guarantor before you find me one?"

"If you find a guarantor, a person you know or a friend, let us know immediately. That is good, but you should leave your name on this list. The churches in the United States establish guarantees on the basis of the documents we make and our recommendations. I personally handle this matter. I am an American."

"In the worst scenario, may I stay here in Austria?"

"Obviously," he answered, "but it would be better to go where you are headed for from the beginning."

"I had thought of Germany, but they say it is not that easy …"

"This is your choice. We need to know as soon as possible; otherwise we will put your name on the list for the United States."

"I will go to the United States."

After the interview, they let us gather our things from quarantine and look for a dormitory. I chose the dormitory with the believers, number 65. I met Vasile, Dănuţ, and Lucian two days later in the courtyard of the camp. They had made new friends and moved in with them. I had been convinced they were not going to come to number 65 dormitory to stay with Vasile Tepei, their brother-in-law. When I met them, they told me they had completed documents for going to Australia.

"Australia?" I exclaimed. "I would never have thought you would do that. Vasile, you who speak German? What has Australia to offer to you?"

"State guarantee," Vasile said. "They keep us in the school until we learn the language. That is from two to three years. In the meantime we rest or …"

"We have made friends who have somebody in Australia. They say there are much better prospects than in America, at least at the beginning," Dănuţ said.

"Besides that, we leave in about three months," Lucian added. "We will start doing stupid things here if we stay for too long."

"And you, where do you want to go?" Vasile asked me.

"I put my name on the list for America. All the repentant ones go there. They promise us lots of advantages. America very seldom offers a state guarantee, and I do not think that I would qualify for it. You have to be a scholar for America to buy you!"

"Good luck, Viorel! It was a great pleasure to know you," Vasile said with a tremble in his voice. He looked into my eyes. "We would love to be like you. You are very optimistic. You will succeed anywhere you go! Without you we would have been dead in those barracks in Yugoslavia."

"I wish you the best of health and hope to see you well! I am sure you will do well, especially if you stay close to each other and help each other. The fact that you make quick decisions and go into action without fighting will help you succeed, as long as your decisions are positive," I concluded, smiling my wish for them.

"Same to you."

We separated after saying good-bye one more time. I hoped we would see one another again in the camp, but we were to see each other seldom and only in passing. Then we greeted each other from a distance. We had been friends for two months, from December to February, but we would continue to be friends in my mind forever. We had experienced a revolution, and we had won. I could not have done it without them, and they would not have made it without me. Their fiery temperaments combined with my calculations had helped us make it. We fitted together perfectly in all our risky and important decisions, and we made it.

## CHAPTER 24

# PARTIAL STABILIZATION

LIFE IN THE concentration camp became normal after a few days. My first visit to town was so emotional, it was indescribable. Traiskirchen was not a large town, but it had a great impact on us, newcomers from Romania. We heard people speaking only German. We looked at anything: people, cars, shop windows, buildings, and especially the sky, toward God. We thanked Him for this surprisingly great blessing, for living and breathing freedom. Everything was different. Our spirits were revived. We thought better and spoke more honestly. Friendships were sincere; people were better and happier.

We were in a foreign country. We had many things to do, but as the saying goes, "Even if a man falls from the tree, he still waits for a moment." We had so many new territories to conquer, but at the beginning we enjoyed doing nothing. A few days of rest were the best treatment for the mind of any immigrant. Between leaving Romania and getting to Traiskirchen as free people, we had accumulated a lot of weariness.

Number 65, where I found a bed, was full with simple people like me. Most of them had families in Romania.

The usual discussions revolved around our families. We became friends very quickly. Everyone was following the same route: expecting somebody to become a guarantor for them, expecting to receive approval from the American consulate in Vienna, expecting to be put on a transport, expecting to arrive in America. There were no shortcuts. Even those who had a guarantor had to go through the same steps, which could take from three to eight months.

The end of February was cold and we had no hope of immediately finding work. I would have worked in order to send something home, but the work season would not begin until mid- March. The weather would be warmer then, and we could probably work cleaning the grapevines.

I met Gigi one day. He, with another married man, had just come back from a protest in Germany, organized in front of the Romanian embassy in Bonn. They had been asking the Romanian government to issue visas for their families.

"What was it like at the protest?" I asked. "Who organized it, who participated, how did you get there, who paid for everything, and what did you achieve?" I fired off all my questions without waiting for an answer. I was anxious to find out everything at once. I expressed my regret for not getting to the camp earlier, so I would be able to go with them.

"First of all," Gigi began in his low but certain voice, "you should have come last year. We who went to Bonn last year got our *beshainic*—that is the Austrian ID. Vasile Tepei could not come with us because he arrived in the camp too late.

"There were many Romanians in Bonn, and not only from Austria, but also from other European countries. We had a serious message to send to those in Bucharest.

Costică Apetroaie, Tiberiu Coşa, Toma, Ghiula, Lazăr, and I had built a coffin and wrote on it: *Human rights in Romania are in the coffin!* That coffin was carried by two men in front of the Romanian embassy for several days. Others of us offered information to whoever asked us—newspapers, radio, or TV stations—about the situation in Romania and about the flagrant violation of human rights by the Romanian government."

"How did you carry that coffin?"

"We chose two men of the same height and put the coffin on their heads. The coffin had no bottom, and it was made of light plywood. We made two holes in it so they could see where to walk. It looked real and had a great impact."

"Do you think it will cause any reverberations?"

"We don't know yet, but we will find out if our wives get a visit from the secret police."

"Will there be any other demonstration in the near future? Why don't they do one here in Vienna?"

"Austria is a neutral country. I think such a demonstration here would not have the same impact, whereas the situation in Germany and France is completely different. I don't know if there will be another such demonstration in the near future. This time I think the Gypsies, who are well organized, helped us. Some Gypsies from France came with money and all kinds of help. Some Romanians went back to France with them."

Vasile Tepei came into the room later. Almost all night, we shared memories. Vasile had already received an invitation from America, from California, and was waiting to be put on a plane.

Vasile was still the same person I had known, always with a smile on his face. He was full of enthusiasm and optimism. He hoped to take his family to America in a very short time. He dreamed of seeing his wife and children in less than a year. I was really happy to hear that. It made my mission and promise to Lenuța, his wife, already seem to be fulfilled. With her help, I had seen my dream come true. The fact that Vasile had not even thought of abandoning her, as I had previously assumed, made me sleep well, at least from that perspective.

On the first Sunday out of quarantine, we went to church. The church met in a Rathaus club rented from the town hall. There were about one hundred believers there. I met some other Romanians whom I had not known: Nicu Matei, who had changed his name to Daniel; Viorel Torj; Vasile Ghergheș; Iulian Rusu; the Gherman family; the Suciu family; Mitru Moldovan; Medve; and Bruder Paul, an American missionary who was translating Christian books and sending them into all the communist countries. He had a printing shop not far from Vienna where many Romanians from the camp worked as volunteers. He came every Sunday to the Rathaus, preaching both in the morning and evening services.

Bruder Pol, as we called him, spoke many languages, and he preached in Romanian. He had an accent, but we got accustomed to his Romanian. We used to listen to him carefully.

Some Russians and Polish believers also came to the Rathaus, and in spite of the fact that they understood nothing, they were happy to be in a church. When we celebrated Communion, Bruder Paul served it to all those present who believed that the Lord Jesus was the Son of God who came to earth, lived among us, taught us the Father's will, rose again, and ascended to heaven. He also made an altar call in Russian and Polish.

All of us there took Communion. The main condition was that those who partook should remember the sufferings and the death of our Lord Jesus. Some of us Romanians hesitated at first to take Communion with such a diverse group—Russians, Poles, Orthodox, Catholics—but the truth was at home among us. We gave up some of the rules and prerequisites we had learned from other people, and almost all of us shared Communion.

On our way to the camp we sang songs one after another. It was beautiful. There were many singers, so we formed on the spot a complete choir. We were truly in a free country. My heart was filled with joy. I began to dream about singing on the street with my wife and children. How wonderful it would be for them to be free! I was convinced that all of those present who had families in Romania shared the same wonderful dream. Most of us were alone. There were some families in the camp: the family of Ghiță Nicolae from Ploiești; the Gherman family from Oradea; the Suciu family; the Tache family from Bărăgan, Unirea village; and other families. They all had different worries from the ones we solo men had.

Ghiță Costescu, a very diligent young man, approached me. We became friends very quickly. He wasn't married, but he was the only one looking for a job. He asked me to work with him when he found a job. I could not speak German, so I hung out with him.

After a few days he found a job, digging a hole for a pool for the mayor of the town. We worked for several days. The wages were good. I sent a telephone notice to my wife. We talked very little because on the other end I could hear only a few words and much crying. We could hear each other after two months. All of us were well. I promised to send her money as soon as somebody had money to exchange. She would have to resign from the glove factory where she was working.

A few days later, I saw Sandu Ardelean among the newcomers. He had come from Syria. He had been sent to Syria by the Romanian government to work on the roads, and at the first opportunity he escaped. That was how he got to the concentration camp.

"Where are you from in Romania?" I asked him.

"From Oradea. And you?" he asked, looking at my shaved head.

"I am from Suceava, but I lived in Timişoara during the last year. Do you know somebody in the country who could exchange some money? I need to send money to my wife, and none of those I've asked has money in the country."

"I do. Actually, my brother-in-law has money. How much do you need and where?"

"Around 25,000 lei, if he has that much. I think my wife can go to Oradea to pick it up. She might go with her brother-in-law, if it is necessary."

"Oh, you say your wife is in Timişoara? She could go and stay with my wife—and encourage Anuţa to apply for passports. She is so scared. Is your Coca courageous?"

"Coca is very courageous, enough for two at least. She also has the support of Vasile's wife, Lenuţa. She began to work on documents earlier, because Vasile crossed the border at the beginning of November. How shall we do the transaction?"

"We make a phone call to Romania. Coca will go and get the money, and if she has some time, she can help Anuţa submit the documents."

"So I will give you the money here, but I don't have all of it yet."

"You can give it to me when you have it. I don't need the money right now. For me it is more important that Coca go and help Anuţa as soon as possible."

In just a few days, Coca was with Anuţa, applying for her passport in Oradea. They had a very, very good time together and they remained friends.

That was good news for us. We went out to the *platz* (this is what they called the place where we were picked up to go work for the Austrians), and a farmer came. He gave us work to do on his chicken farm. I went with Sandu and Gigi and won the Austrian's trust. We worked like bulldozers, digging a tunnel that was supposed to connect two buildings. Sandu and Gigi worked hard. We formed a perfect trio. We were optimistic, healthy, and afraid of nothing. We had a lot of work to do, so we earned some good money, enough to pay my debts to Sandu.

Meanwhile, we also worked on cleaning grapevines and other digging. It did not matter what work we were given to do. There were very few trying to avoid work, probably only those who had relatives sending them money.

Time went by slowly. I was waiting to hear some news about a guarantor from America, but I was convinced it was going to take a long time before I received an answer.

I made friends with Florian Gherman. He was with his family. The girls worked during the day in the printing shop. I found out that the fiancé of one of their daughters was still in Romania; they were hoping to get him out as soon as possible.

Gigi had his wife and three children in the country. Sandu had his wife and two daughters. I had my wife and two children. Vasile Tepei had his wife and two children. There were many more like us. We were ready to do anything to have our families with us. The only thing we talked about was our families in Romania and what they were doing.

I met a young man in the camp, my age, and because I was open to anybody, we became friends. His name was Gheorghe Ardelean. He told me how he escaped the country and what made him leave.

"Why did you apply for a passport?" I asked him once. He had told me his story in a hurry the first time.

"I applied for a passport, and I got it because I threatened that I would blow up a gas station if they did not give me one."

"What did they promise you that you did not get?"

"Viorel, I want to tell you that I was not a saint. I have made my share of mistakes. Hungarian policemen caught me and beat me black and blue. I was also beaten in Romania by Hungarian policemen who spoke no Romanian. I could not stand it anymore! I did things to them, but they found my grandfather, who is Gheorghe too, and almost killed him. They said they were confused by the name, and they were looking for me. Then I threatened them with blowing up the gas station, and I ended up in prison for a while. I learned many tricks in prison that I used when I escaped to Austria. Now comes the part that will interest you the most. You are the only one I can recommend."

"Recommend to whom? Hungarian policemen?"

"Well, we won't go back, only forward. Let me tell you what it is about. It is something very serious if you want to take it into consideration. I was selected for an elite army unit in Germany. It is similar to the French Foreign Legion, if you have heard of it."

"I have heard of the French Foreign Legion. Sounds risky!"

"It is very risky, but if you survive, you will be an accomplished person when you reach forty-five!"

"Tell me what it is about," I encouraged him. I was all ears.

"There is a school in Germany that trains a special army, the elite. If you qualify, you work for fifteen years and have no future worries—and not only you, but all your family. In one year you get German citizenship. You will have your family with you in Germany, and everything will be as in the stories. I was accepted into the school. I learned German in two months. That is school! They have some great teaching methods. I speak perfect German without any accent. Then what happened? I had a small accident and broke my ankle while disembarking from a plane. I was disqualified. They offered me a job in their office, but I refused. I want to go to Australia and take my father there with me. This is his lifetime dream, and I promised to fulfill it."

"How did you find out about this? How did you get to their door, and what did you need to do to be accepted?"

"I found out by chance, from an advertisement. They have an office here in Vienna. I went with an acquaintance who speaks German, and I got some information. I thought for a few days, and after weighing the benefits with the risks, I decided to change my life completely. You have to be half crazy or very smart to accept the risks, but if you believe in yourself and you risk everything, you have a unique chance to resolve your future and the future of your family forever. It is worth it. Your life is guaranteed for a hundred years. Who knows what tomorrow holds?"

"It is said that there are dead and living heroes," I responded. "We also need some living heroes among us."

"Well, I believe you cannot do anything great in life without risk. Anyhow, I went to the recruiting center for the initial preparation. They told me I would not be able to return to the concentration camp if I accepted the conditions. After passing the physical tests, I would go straight to Germany for instruction. I accepted, I passed the medical check-up and the physical tests, and then I went to a military base in Germany.

"Once I arrived there, I saw a nice building with all kinds of top-class automobiles at the entrance: Jaguar, Mercedes, BMW, Porsche, Ferrari, and others. I began my first day of German classes. They used different audio and video teaching methods that helped control my pronunciation. There was also physical training. Everything had to meet a certain standard. The Romanian army was nothing in comparison to that one. In two years, you had to become a real ninja; otherwise they would send you to some other kind of work."

"How many passed the tests along with you?"

"We were fifteen to start, but after a week we were thirteen. Two Bulgarian brothers were released. They were too slow."

"The selection was done very quickly."

"Yes. Nobody wanted to leave that casern after seeing the luxury there."

"What missions could you engage in after the training period?"

"All exercises have as their target the Russians. Maybe it is easier for the German people to train with the Russians as their objects. The mission: be merciless. Duty and only duty. You become a machine, simply! This is what they say from the beginning. They recruit up to the age of thirty, and they release you at the age of forty-five."

"If you reach that age."

"Exactly. If there is peace, no problem, but if a war begins, the chances of survival are small."

I thought of all the advantages. It was difficult to say no to such a tempting offer, especially when it came from nowhere. Gheorghe Ardelean found me, and I was the only one he wanted to do that favor for. In his opinion, I would have qualified without any problems.

I refused the offer, but I remained friends with Gheorghe. He had some unusual ways of treating the Romanian government, even from a foreign country. One of them had to do with getting his father to Australia. He knew what he was doing. He had to obtain a medical certificate from Australia proving that he was very ill and that his last desire was to see his father. That "last desire" would be published all over: newspapers, radio, television, humanitarian agencies, human rights organizations, and so on.

One day he found out that the president of Romania, Nicolae Ceaușescu, was about to make a visit to Egypt. Gheorghe came up with the idea of sending the comrade a "congratulatory telegram" that Ceaușescu would get in Alexandria, Egypt.

What to congratulate him for was the question.

"Everybody knows that Ceaușescu does not receive letters from the Romanian people; the censor throws them in the garbage. Some responses may come from officials on a lower level, but not from him. However, when he goes out of the country, he receives everything people send to him. I found this out in the prison. The smart guys linked me up with the greatest and most intelligent politicians. I learned from them some rules that you could not find out anywhere else. That is how I learned the Morse alphabet in a few days. It is very helpful to me.

"So now was the perfect moment to ask for approval for our families' passports. I want to send a special telegram to Ceauşescu on behalf of those in the camp. In the first part we will congratulate him for the Romanian policy concerning international relations ..."

"The message of peace, disarmament, and noninterference in the internal affairs of other countries," I continued.

"Very well! Then we will ask him in Romanian to approve the issue of passports for our families. We will all sign the telegram. It will cost some money, but it is an exceptional occasion."

So said, so done. All of us who were willing to take risks that could result in trouble for our families gathered and wrote that telegram, signed it, and then sent it. President Ceauşescu received our telegram. We did not find that out immediately, but the idea was good, and we hoped it would speed the process for our families.

At a certain point, Gigi planned to return to Romania and steal his family and children. He asked me for my family's address in Utvin and a picture, so he could steal them too, but I did not agree to risk that much. I had no picture of my family on me. I had been afraid of being caught on the bus to Uivar with it. That could have been a blow to my intention to leave the country. I was not searched, but I could have been.

Gigi applied for a visitor's visa for Yugoslavia. Then, prepared with an inflatable boat, a gun, and some light supplies, he went fishing on the Danube. Fortunately he caught nothing, but he was caught by the Serbians. After only a week, we saw him back in the camp. The mission was not that easy to accomplish, but we were glad to see him well.

Time passed. A good singer came to our dormitory, Toge. He not only sang but could also play the accordion and the piano. He was very secretive. He had changed his name. He did not want to have any pictures taken, but otherwise he was friendly and knew very well what he wanted to do with his life after getting to America. He had some arrangements made. After many requests, he recorded an audiotape with songs that I kept for a long time. Unfortunately, we recorded it on an old tape, and after a while the older recording interfered with the newer one.

My *beshainic* came in April. The actual word in Austrian was *Bescheinigung*. I became an Austrian resident with my new ID. The same day I also received political asylum.

We could find work, but not all the time. I returned the money I had borrowed from Sandu, and I started saving. The camp food was sufficient, even if it was not like home cooking. I was not that picky.

I communicated with my wife by phone, although I would rather have corresponded by mail. We had no urgent matters to resolve by phone, which cost much more. For my wife, who thought I had everything, money was not a problem! I was glad to hear her on the phone, especially when she had to submit the immigration documents. That was not easy. I focused more on the problem ahead of me: getting to America. She wanted to begin filling out the immigration documents, but she had no address in the States.

After I sent her money, she quit her job, something that gave me peace. I wanted to know that she was at home with the children. The children were small and needed their mother's full attention.

With my ID in hand, I went to a lawyer's office to make a mandate to send to my wife. With that, she could go to the ISIM factory, fill out my liquidation documents, and sell the cabinet of my tools. After she received the mandate, she went to ISIM, and then we talked on the phone.

"How were you treated?" I asked.

"Awfully! I could never have imagined anything like that. The laboratory chief, or the ex-chief, jumped on me like a crazy woman when she saw me. We had never seen each other before. I had no chance to say a word before she jumped on me like a hyena. I think somebody had told her that I would knock on her door."

"You should have left her alone and simply walked out. That money does not matter anymore."

"It was not a matter of the money. I have my own personality too. She was not your master, nor mine. I let her calm down, because she was not listening to me. She told me you had destroyed her career and her future, and because of you she cannot go outside the country."

"What career have I destroyed? She was about to retire."

"Her reputation. When she hired you at ISIM, she promised the party she would cure you of the West, but you left right under her eyes."

"Now I understand why they would not give me work to do, but kept me in the office, discussing mainly the disappointments of those who had gone to Germany, and their regrets for abandoning Romania."

"Anyhow, I had to sign your liquidation papers in order to submit the application for a passport."

"Have you finally finished my liquidation?"

"Yes, I did, a few days ago. I went with Aurel through the shop and sold all your tools and the cabinet. I made some money. They also gave me six hundred lei for your last days of work, and the painting tools I sold to Aurel."

"Anything else?"

"I met Fritz, the miller in your laboratory. He asked about you. He was so happy you made it, and so excited for the day when he will get there too. He has submitted the legal documents to leave. Paulin and Lidia came from Braşov for a visit. Paulin told me about the postcard you sent him from the World Cradle of Music. You made him go crazy!"

"I just wanted to wake him up, that's all. I did not want to think of him being happy with the way things were and with what he had. He can do better. I am glad that my postcard had the anticipated effect. I hope to see him here soon."

"What news do you have about a guarantor in America?"

"It takes time. I have sent the documents to Louisiana State, to an American church. I am waiting. They say I will get approval. I also received the 'immigration with political asylum' letter, which people say will help very much. We are praying and waiting. In the meantime, I am working. When possible, I will send you more money."

"Right now I have money for several months. We do not owe anything, and we have plenty of food. Grandpa takes good care of the six sheep we bought, so we will manage."

"I am sorry I left the pictures with you at home. Can you send me some recent pictures?"

"I will go to town with the children, have some pictures taken, and send them to you. The children are doing fine. They have your pictures. Any time they see a plane, they tell all our neighbors they will go to America in that plane that flies that high."

The next month brought new things. I sent my documents with the Gherman family to a man named Doru Sărac in Louisiana. I did not catch Doru in the concentration camp because he had left for America in January, but he promised to help all of those who had nobody in America. There were many who sent their applications to him for a guarantor. I received the answer that a church from Louisiana had deposited a guarantee for me.

I was not sure what I was supposed to do: rejoice or worry. Vasile Tepei had left at the end of April and I had heard nothing from him. I had no other acquaintances, so I simply sent my documents to the United States. Germany seemed nonexistent for immigrants. It was a destination for ethnic Germans, but all others had to wait a very long time to be accepted—not because of discrimination, but because processing the documents took such a long time.

Almost all the people I knew in the camp were going to America. Most of them left in May: Ghiță Costescu, Suciu, Medve, the Gherman family, Viorel Torj, Nelu Militaru, Drina, and others. I was left with Sandu Ardelean and Gigi.

Others came in the meantime, among whom were Nicu Ciurculete and his brother-in-law, Gheorghe Coajă; the Apetroaie family; the Coşa family; Doina, Nicu

Matei's wife; Iosif, Doina and Ramona's brother; and Nicu and Doina's daughter.

Nicu Matei had a brother in Germany who was working for a Bible mission and who wanted to go to America. I think he asked for the help of the printer missionary. At least, he was about to go to Houston, Texas, to the home church of Paul, the missionary. Why hadn't he gone to Germany? Nobody would ask.

## CHAPTER 25
# THE HISTORY

THE BEGINNING OF June 1979 brought two warm waves into my life. The first was caused by the weather. Everything was green outside. The cold winter rains had passed. I was speaking a little bit of German, just enough to find some work. I was very confident in myself. Only the fear of a new world war made me want to leave Europe. Europe did not seem too stable, especially because of a very aggressive communist system.

Communism claimed to develop a society without any worries, but in reality proved to be a monster ready to devour everybody. The first phase of communism, socialism, had the task of creating a new man, responsible and aware. Every man was to do what his conscience dictated. Whoever consumed should also produce. The distribution of goods had to equal to consumption.

Once man achieved this phase, he was supposed to go to a second phase, in which everyone produced for society, and goods were distributed according to needs. In this second phase, communism, money would disappear.

There was no sign of a communist society advancing in that direction. On the contrary: because of the lack of competition, the quality of products disappeared. Care for the assets of the country was neglected. Since everyone worked for a salary, he made sure to check his time sheet in order to secure that salary and his children's allowance, and not be fired.

The Austrians had a completely different mentality. The owner was directly interested in the care, quality, advertisement, and warrantee of all the things he made. Owners worked alongside us and were a real example of diligence. Everything they possessed was very well taken care of and functioned as new.

The second warm wave came upon me when I received a telephone notice from Detroit, Michigan. The notice was from Ioan "Nelu" Enciu, a boy from Suceava, who had married Lenuța Filip one week after my marriage. I had never met him in Romania, but he had heard from the Ghermans that I was in the concentration camp, so he sent for me. I waited anxiously to hear a voice from America for the first time.

"Here is Viorel Bilauca."

"Here I am, Nelu Enciu."

I heard very clearly the voice at the other end of the world.

"I am sorry we did not know each other before, but thank you for the phone call."

"I know you," Nelu said. "I found out a few days ago from the Gherman family that there was someone from Suceava in the camp. Man, I am so glad you made it out of the country. To make a long story short, I deposited a guarantee for you to come to Detroit. There is no life in Louisiana for immigrants like us. The Gherman family came to Detroit after one week of heat, humidity, lizards, and unfamiliar people. We have a Romanian church in

Detroit. You can easily find a job, and you will have somebody to talk to. We help each other here."

"It does not matter for me where I end up. I know nobody; I have no relatives. What do I need to do? Can you give me your address to give to the office people to change my destination?"

"I have called the organization that helps you get here. I gave them all my details, and I asked them to send you to Detroit. Don't go to the office to change anything, because it may take you six more months to redo all the documents. That's if they don't mess them up … When you arrive in the airport in America, give the authorities my phone number and they will send you to Detroit. Have you received approval for America?"

"Yes. I have already done the medical check-up, and I went to the consulate in Vienna two weeks ago. I am waiting for them to put me on a plane."

"Great. Send me a letter with the date of your arrival, and I will arrange for you to come to Detroit. Keep my phone number and give it to the connecting agent in America. Ask him to call me. Otherwise they will send you to Louisiana, and things will become complicated."

"I perfectly understand. Thank you again for everything you are doing for me. I owe you. Nelu, for how long have you been in America?"

"For a year. Lenuţa will go to Romania and stay for the whole month of July. She misses her family so much."

"Well, I will take into consideration everything you told me."

I left a completely different person. Security replaced probability. I was thinking of what the apostle John wrote in his epistles, when he changed the phrase "we believe" to "we know." It is a long way from believing to knowing.

I knew now that I was going to America, something I hadn't dreamed of.

I knew very few things about America, in comparison with the European countries. General Motors had been used as an example of reinvested capital in our finance classes. I also knew something about the car industry concentrated in Detroit: Ford, General Motors, and Chrysler. I also knew that California was situated on the fire chain of the Pacific Ocean, along with the Andes Mountains. I had suddenly become very interested in the physical and economic geography of America, and also in the English language.

With the money I earned, which seemed like nothing in comparison with what I thought I would earn in America, I bought a suitcase and a briefcase. I had the attitude of a soldier spending his last days of duty. I was waiting for release orders. I had stayed five full months in the camp, and my documents had been sent to America three months before.

In Romania, everything was going well. My sister Rodica sent me a wedding invitation. Her wedding was going to be held on the fourth of July. Unfortunately, I would not be there. I was on a totally different orbit. I would only be able to return to Romania after many years.

I was meditating a lot on my life. If God had not been on my side, what would have happened to me? But I was overwhelmed with all the blessings I was experiencing. I thought again and again about Joseph. I saw more and more new fortresses to conquer.

Costică, my brother, had enrolled in the army in February. For one year and four months I would not be able to do anything for him, but the chapter would not end there. I was preparing, at least theoretically, some plans for getting all my family free as soon as possible. I had everything in perspective. I hoped my best friend, Paulin, would get to the West. He had the advantage of a sister-in-law in France.

My open temperament and the fact that I enjoyed multitudes of people helped me make new friends. I was what many would call a good listener. All the new people who came into my life trusted me. But friends from childhood were irreplaceable. History was written differently at my age. I did not like to think of time passing so quickly, knowing that my mother and father would get to America so late in life. They deserved better, without the worries of daily life in Romania.

That spring, I heard of a Christian conference being held in Vienna. Some of us attended it. For the first time I sat next to the president of the Pentecostal Union, Brother Bochian, and exchanged some words. He told me he knew about our family and about the interview my mother had given to a magazine. He told me he was proud of my mother's answers to the interview, for thanking the leadership of Romania for the care the government had shown for children.

"I know nothing about that interview," I told him.

"It was published in *Zori Noi* magazine. *Scânteia* newspaper republished the article," Brother Bochian told me. "It was good she did not complain, as most people do. Most Christians would bring shame on us!"

"I hope my mother knows about that interview," I answered, more as a joke. "It is good they got the interview before finding out I had left the country illegally. I hope they won't ask her for another interview asking for the reasons I left the country."

Our discussion was interrupted because Brother Trandafir was about to preach. I had no opportunity to talk to Brother Matache. He gazed at us and probably, seeing my head shaved, reached his own conclusions. I think Brother Bochian had the same impression. They saw me as a fanatic. It might have been their opinion. I was a fanatic, but not for traditional religion—for God and faith in Him!

Time was passing slowly, dreaming and waiting. I looked for work and accepted anything, for the sake of passing the time faster. I wanted to go to America, to be established in a certain place, to find a job, and then to invite my family. Coca was asking for a stable address to mention on her application.

The Pentecostal brothers, who came back from France after a long stay in Paris, brought some money to buy a car, so every immigrant would learn how to drive. Once you got to America, you had to know how to drive. We took turns, so I had the chance to drive the car several times. I drove for four and a half hours in total. That was all. I wasn't worried. I was convinced I would learn that too. In Romania, you had to go to school for several months and then take an exam, which many passed at the first attempt.

My biggest problem was the English language. You could not learn English in the camp. We were preoccupied with so many things that nobody paid attention to the most important problem we faced. We were more familiar with the German language. We could communicate after a relatively short time. But English seemed an insurmountable obstacle. We understood nothing about a language that you write one way and read it differently. Apparently, you had to learn every word separately, and you would get the meaning only after listening to the whole sentence. It was complicated! Consequently, we left it for later, as we used to do in school when we had many exercises to do. We always left the hard ones until the end.

In mid-June, I saw my name written on a list of those scheduled to leave for America on July 12, 1979. I read my name several times, standing astonished in front of that notice board. I looked again and again before I was sure it was real.

I don't know if anybody saw me or not, and I would not have cared, but I suddenly felt my eyes fill with tears. I think if I could have seen myself, I would also have been surprised. I was crying. I could not control myself. I was looking at my name on that list and crying.

I was celebrating a great victory all by myself. I celebrated something I had never dared to dream. It was different from the moment when we celebrated crossing the border into Yugoslavia. Then I had been dreaming of Germany, in secret. I had risked everything to get to Germany.

America? It was much more than I had ever imagined. When I saw my name on that list for America, I was happier than when I saw my name on an admission list for a coveted school in Romania. I considered myself very blessed, very special. The United States of America had accepted me, so I would be put on a plane.

Who was I? I reviewed my biography and realized that what was happening was like a fiction, like a fairy tale. Reading those stories, people always ask the same question: how is it possible for a poor child to fall in love with a rich and beautiful princess, marry, and live happily ever after? The answer is simple: the poor child wrote the story from his perspective, not that of the beautiful and rich princess.

Likewise with the story of my life. I was convinced that only God could have brought about such a miracle in my life. It was not an accident nor a coincidence nor by chance that I, Viorel Bilauca, was going to go to America. It was a miracle, a destiny directed solely by God. It might have been good fortune or an accident for others, but for me it was a destiny I could not have dreamed of.

I spent some hours standing around that list. Though I could read it clearly, I kept looking to see if somebody had changed it, as often happened in Romania.

Nothing changed. I was extremely happy. I wrote a letter to my wife, telling her the good news. I had one more month before leaving. I paid the required $235 the same day and received the necessary confirmations.

The days that followed were days of contemplation, of future planning. As in Timişoara one year before, when I was planning to bury all my childhood memories and leave the country, I reviewed my whole life. I had to leave Europe behind this time, with its rich history of thousands of years: so many nations with their successes and failures, prosperity and declines, civilization and misery, revolutions and wars, troubles and government changes. I had to archive everything, along with my memories from Romania. The path of my life was taking unexpected turns, up and down.

I remembered some of the prophecies I had received a long time before, which I was living now. One came through a prophet in Dealul Mare, near Dorohoi, who told me something like this: The Devil has prepared a high place he wants you to climb to and from where he wants to throw you down, but I, says the Lord, I want you to go up higher and stay there.

I received this prophecy through Vasile Bilauca (we are not relatives; it is only a coincidence that we had the same name), a neighbor and friend I grew up with. I paid a short visit to Suceava, and stopped by the home of his brother-in-law, Teofil Martinuc. Viorel came up from nowhere and told us the Holy Spirit had told him to leave work two and a half hours early. On the way home, he stopped by his brother-in-law's house without knowing why.

I had just arrive there from Braşov. The Spirit of God told me, through the gift of prophecy, that He had prepared some unbelievers to help me go to new and unexpected places. I should not wait; God had prepared them for me at the right time. I was making plans about leaving, but Vasile Bilauca had no idea about my intentions.

Three long weeks of waiting followed. Gigi kept asking what was wrong with me when he saw me crying from time to time. I was very strong usually, but during those days I felt overwhelmed by the situation. I was happy about my unexpected future, on the one hand, and on the other hand I had to say good-bye for a while, or even forever, to all my memories, my friends, and especially my parents, brothers, sisters, and other relatives.

I remembered in that moment a drama I saw with my friend Dan Isepciuc at the cultural hall in Suceava, *Our Uncle from Jamaica*. The drama was about a high school boy who had to choose between spending the summer with his girlfriend or visiting his uncle in Jamaica. He chose to stay in the country with his girlfriend, but he told his uncle that he had failed a mathematics class and could not go to Jamaica. His love for Romania and for his girlfriend was greater than the desire to pay a visit overseas.

In spite of the fact that life in Romania was not a dream, some found it hard to break the emotional connections. The stormy history of Europe, with its wars and revolutions, the uncertain present, and a future even more uncertain, all encouraged me to give up those feelings and hope for a better future.

I envisioned my whole family in America. Communism had failed to create the new man. The communist conscience had failed to reach its goal. Even the most ardent communists were as selfish as everybody else. There was nobody working for society, only for themselves. The second phase of communism, during which all the money was supposed to disappear and everybody would be paid according to their needs and not their capacity, was nowhere on the horizon.

There was the possibility of another world war. Espionage was everywhere. Socialist countries were permanently fighting with capitalist countries. Who would win? Socialism had destroyed competition and quality, and care for the means of production had ended up in the hands of day laborers. The owner, the government in a socialist society, was not there every day to ensure that everything functioned well. Workers only cared about their salaries and not about quality and productivity, as elsewhere in the world.

When friends used to ask me why I was leaving for America, I always said that I wanted to live in a country that was at the top of the pyramid. I had lived the first part of my life in a developing country. We were considered to be the generation who had sacrificed for a better life for those coming after us—for our children and grandchildren. My opinion was that socialism looked nice as a theory, but practice would say differently.

How long would socialism live? Where would it get to? Nobody had the courage to say. It was clear that many people were eager to try other alternatives.

A story I heard a lot as a child spoke about a woman who complained to everybody, saying she was afraid. She was afraid that the cat would pass by the salt block on the stove and push it off. She was afraid it would fall on the child sitting next to the stove. Her husband, seeing her so clumsy (she could have moved the child or the salt), left home to find if there was somebody more stupid than his wife.

In his travels, he met a man who was trying to get a bushel of light from the outside into the house he had just made. The house had no windows to light it. The story says the husband crossed himself, took an ax, and cut a window so the light would go in. But he did not turn back home.

He continued on his way and met another man, who tried to lift a cow onto the roof of his barn. The wind had just blown some hay up there while he was putting the hay in the barn. After the husband took the hay down from the barn's roof, the peasant was joyful because he did not have to lift his cow anymore.

The husband then returned home and solved his dilemma with the salt block. He and his wife lived happily ever after. Those experiences could have cured some of us too, if we had had an occasion to see another world.

I recalled all my pleasant and unpleasant memories as if I were going to another planet. I was living in a funeral procession, just as before I left Romania. I had to say good-bye to Europe. I had the feeling that I would not see this part of the world again, filled with my childhood memories of life in the countryside.

During summer, the people were in the fields, sowing, seeding, and reaping. The barns were full of animals, the sheds full of hay, the cellar full of provisions for winter. The roads were without asphalt and full of dust during the summer, or of mud on rainy days. There was no electricity, no newspapers, no radio, no television, no telephone, no computers. Everything was the same as it had been several hundred years ago: life in nature.

I went with the cattle into the field, along with children my age. We swam in the lake at Dragomirna Monastery. We enjoyed very much the little lambs that we kept in the house for a few days after birth, as well as the chicks.

When I was eleven years old, we moved from the countryside into Suceava. Life changed suddenly: sidewalks, electricity, *Zori Noi* newspaper, radio, provisions in the market, where we went to buy them almost daily. My father went to work every day.

After I finished fifth grade, I was the only pupil sent to a camp at the seaside, in Eforie Nord. I was the best in my school. What an honor! It was a new experience. I was appreciated, in spite of the fact that I was a repentant believer. The authorities probably hoped to convert me to atheism. It did not happen.

High school was the most important school. Life depended on what I accumulated during the four years of high school. There we shaped our life philosophy. I paid attention to what they taught us, but I only chose a profession.

Teachers had to follow the orders of the party and shape in us a spirit of duty and sacrifice that had to do only with life on this earth. They told us heaven and hell are here, and it depended on us what we chose in life.

I escaped unharmed by this materialistic and atheistic ideology. I had my own convictions about God that were much stronger. Life was and still is God's invention, and our destiny is to please Him. At the end, He will reward us according to our deeds and our beliefs.

When I finished school and military service, I realized the reality I was experiencing. The fight for life was exceeding human limitations. Corruption was everywhere. Life had become a fight for survival; the stronger wins. I made my calculations, and when I drew the line, only one thing was left: I had to solve by myself the problem of life.

I went to Constanţa harbor, hoping to become a mariner, something hard to do. I went then to work on a construction site. I stayed there for a year, preparing to go to the West. But because it was such hard work and difficult weather conditions, I decided to switch to cutting metals, a job that had better conditions and guaranteed work all year round.

It took me several days to make peace between my feelings and future possibilities. I cheered up and started packing my suitcase. I put the few clothes I had in. I was going to wear a suit and a tie. I did not need the heavy clothes; it was the middle of summer. I also put in some Bibles and song books in Romanian. In ten minutes, everything was ready.

I stopped by Prater's shop in Vienna. I bought an Atlantic watch for 350 schillings, and then walked on Maria Hilfe Street, saying good-bye to Vienna. I was ready for the flight.

VIOREL BILAUCA

Since the moment I found out I would leave, I had become like all the others who left before me: isolated. We were kind of graduates. I talked to my closest friends, Gheorghiță Gheorghe and Sandu Ardelean.

I went to work for several days, I gathered all my money and exchanged it into dollars. I hadn't talked to Enciu recently and I was becoming worried. I was supposed to get to him, but was I leaving on the guarantee of the church in Louisiana?

I received a letter from the Gherman family during those days. They informed me that they had moved to Detroit after an unpleasant experience with Americans. It was a letter that shone some light on the reality of an immigrant's life in America. Nobody else sent any word after getting to America, not even Vasile Tepei and Ghiță Costestu. I was expecting some news from them; I was convinced they would write to me. But I heard nothing.

Two weeks before leaving I bought a postcard and sent it to myself in America, congratulating myself for this success and wishing me all the best! Since I knew nobody and nobody knew me in America, I thought it would be a good idea to wish myself well. And it was a good idea.

The last days passed somehow, but the nights became longer and longer. I could not stop thinking of my children, wife, parents, brothers, and friends. I dreamed of the day when I would be waiting for my family at the airport in America. The children would be bigger. How would they look?

I prayed and asked God to keep me in health. Everything else could be replaced. There was no other miracle I wished for but to see my children and to see them healthy. I was morally prepared to see them in six years, the time people said reunion would take while I was still in Romania. Here in the camp, people said I might see them in less than two years. That was another victory I was dreaming of.

Thursday, July 12, at nine o'clock in the morning, I said good-bye to friends and acquaintances. I got on the bus that was to take me to the airport in Vienna. My suitcase was almost empty. With a briefcase in my hand, wearing my light-colored suit and tie, I was ready to meet America.

The plane took off without any problem on that rainy day. I could not see Vienna from on high, as I wished, but I saw Germany. We landed in Frankfurt in good weather. Our plane was about to fly over countries and seas. The two-hour stop gave us the opportunity to get off the plane and visit the airport. I walked through it with my mouth open, along with five other immigrants who had the same destination. We were only acquaintances. We promised we would not forget each other.

After two hours, the completely full plane took off toward the West, without any more stops until America. Those were historic moments in my life. For me, the Promised Land was being conquered.

After five months spent in the concentration camp, the desert in which I had anything I needed without work, I wasn't crossing the Red Sea, nor the Jordan, but the Atlantic Ocean. Some of the passengers did not feel well. I was excited to be flying above the clouds. I could not take my eyes off the clouds that looked like piles of snow. I tried to see myself arming for defeating the next giants and conquering the Promised Land.

# EPILOGUE

One year and six months after leaving my home in Romania, I met my wife and children again—in October 1980, at the Detroit airport. I embarked right away upon conquering the next heights. I was so happy.

I thank God that my mother, Aurelia; my father, Aurel; my brothers Ioan, George, and Cătălin; and my sisters Ileana, Silvia, Violeta, Lidia, and Doina, with their families, have also come to the United States. My brothers Constantin and Cornel, with their families, went to Canada. Only my sister Rodica is still in Romania. My friends Paulin and Teofil Martinuc, my brother-in-law Ioan Ciuriuc, and my friend and neighbor in the village, Vasile Bilauca, with their families, are also in the United States.

The victories I obtained through work, and all the different tests I went through, will be the subject of another book.

# ABOUT THE AUTHOR

Viorel Bilauca was not happy. Romania, under the dictator Ceaușescu, had for more than fifteen years closed its borders. Nobody could go out of the country, not even as a tourist. The regime cut all communication with the West. Life became very tough.

Viorel had no choice. Looking for a better standard of life and freedom, he was ready to do anything to save his large family from imminent disaster. He made the decision to escape.

Knowing that competition brought quality, he dreamed of getting on top of the world, so he headed to America. January 1979 became the turning point in his and his family's lives. He arrived, very happy to be an American, but not without paying the price.

Viorel lives in Scottsdale, Arizona.
author@bilauca.com

Printed in the United States
By Bookmasters